DAY HIKES ON THE
California
Central
Coast

120 COASTAL HIKES FROM SANTA CRUZ TO SANTA BARBARA

Robert Stone
2nd EDITION

Day Hike Books, Inc.
RED LODGE, MONTANA

Published by Day Hike Books, Inc.
P.O. Box 865
Red Lodge, Montana 59068
www.dayhikebooks.com

Distributed by The Globe Pequot Press
246 Goose Lane
P.O. Box 480
Guilford, CT 06437-0480
800-243-0495 (direct order) · 800-820-2329 (fax order)
www.globe-pequot.com

Photographs by Robert Stone
Design by Paula Doherty

The author has made every attempt to provide accurate information in this book. However, trail routes and features may change—please use common sense and forethought, and be mindful of your own capabilities. Let this book guide you, but be aware that each hiker assumes responsibility for their own safety. The author and publisher do not assume any responsibility for loss, damage, or injury caused through the use of this book.

Cover photo:
Sobranes Point, Hike 46

Back cover photo:
Cannery Point in Point Lobos State Reserve, Hike 41

ALSO BY ROBERT STONE

Day Hikes On the California Southern Coast

Day Hikes Around Sonoma County

Day Hikes Around Napa Valley

Day Hikes Around Big Sur

Day Hikes Around Monterey and Carmel

Day Hikes In San Luis Obispo County, California

Day Hikes Around Santa Barbara

Day Hikes Around Ventura County

Day Hikes Around Los Angeles

Day Hikes Around Orange County

Day Hikes In Sedona, Arizona

Day Hikes In Yosemite National Park

Day Hikes In Sequoia & Kings Canyon Nat'l. Parks

Day Hikes In Yellowstone National Park

Day Hikes In Grand Teton National Park

Day Hikes In the Beartooth Mountains

Day Hikes Around Bozeman, Montana

Day Hikes Around Missoula, Montana

Day Hikes On Oahu

Day Hikes On Maui

Day Hikes On Kauai

Day Hikes In Hawaii

Table of Contents

The Central California Coast 11

Map of the Hikes 12

THE HIKES

Santa Cruz County

Santa Cruz County 15

SANTA CRUZ COUNTY MAP (Hikes 1—20) 16

1. Atkinson Bluff Trail: Gazos Creek to Franklin Point and Cascade Beach
   Año Nuevo State Reserve 18

2. Point Año Nuevo and Cove Beach: Año Nuevo State Reserve 20

3. Skyline-to-the-Sea Trail: Waddell Beach to Berry Creek Falls
   Big Basin Redwoods State Park 24

4. Skyline-to-the-Sea Trail (one-way shuttle)
   Big Basin Redwoods State Park Headquarters to
   Waddell Beach 26

5. Greyhound Rock 30

6. Davenport Beach and Bluffs 31

7. Bonny Doon Beach and Bluffs 34

8. Laguna Creek Beach, Bluffs and Wetlands 36

9. Four Mile Beach to Three Mile Beach
   Wilder Ranch State Park 37

10. Old Cove Landing Trail to Fern Grotto
    Wilder Ranch State Park 39

11. Moore Creek Preserve 42

12. Natural Bridges State Beach 44

13. Lighthouse Trail · Point Santa Cruz
    Lighthouse Field State Beach to Natural Bridges State Beach 47

14. Pogonip Park 48

15. River Trail—Eagle Creek—Ridge Road Loop
    Henry Cowell Redwoods State Park 52

16. Top of the World: DeLaveaga Park 54

17. New Brighton State Beach 57

18. Seacliff State Beach from Rio del Mar Beach 59

19. Aptos Rancho Trail: The Forest of Nisene Marks State Park 60

20. Manresa State Beach 64

Monterey County

Monterey County 67

MONTEREY & CARMEL MAP (Hikes 21—40) 68

21. Zmudowski State Beach 70

22. Moss Landing State Beach 72

23. Moss Landing State Wildlife Area 74

24. Old Salinas River Road 76

25. Salinas River State Beach: Southern Access 77

26. Salinas River National Wildlife Refuge 80

27. Five Fingers—Long Valley Loop
    Elkhorn Slough National Estuarine Research Reserve 82

28. South Marsh Loop Trail
    Elkhorn Slough National Estuarine Research Reserve 83

29. Marina State Beach and Marina Dunes Open Space 86

MONTEREY PENINSULA MAP (Hikes 30—40) 88

30. Skyline Trail and Jacks Peak: Jacks Peak County Park 90

31. Monterey Bay Coastal Trail
    Monterey Bay Aquarium to Point Pinos 92

32. Asilomar State Beach and Coast Trail 94

33. The Links Nature Walk at Spanish Bay 96

34. The Bay Nature Walk at Spanish Bay 98

35. Point Joe to Bird Rock 100

36. Bird Rock to Indian Village 102

37. Carmel Beach 104

38. Scenic Bluff Pathway at Carmel Beach 104

39. Carmel River Lagoon and Wetlands Natural Preserve
    Carmel River State Beach 106

40. Carmel Meadows to Monastery Beach
    Carmel River State Beach 108

Big Sur Coastline

Big Sur 111

BIG SUR COASTLINE MAP (Hikes 41—72) 112

POINT LOBOS STATE RESERVE MAP (Hikes 41—45) 114

41. North Shore Trail: Point Lobos State Reserve 116

42. Cypress Grove Trail: Point Lobos State Reserve 118

43. Sea Lion Point Trail: Point Lobos State Reserve 120

44. South Shore Trail: Point Lobos State Reserve 123

45. Bird Island Trail: China Cove—Pelican Point—Gibson Beach
    Point Lobos State Reserve 125

46. Soberanes Point Trails: Garrapata State Park 126

47. Soberanes Canyon Trail: Garrapata State Park 128

48. Garrapata Beach and Bluff Trail: Garrapata State Park 132

49. Old Coast Road—Northern Access 134

50. Old Coast Road—Southern Access 135

51. Molera Point and Molera Beach: Andrew Molera State Park 138

52. Bluffs—Panorama—Ridge Loop: Andrew Molera State Park 140

53. River Trail—Hidden Trail—Ridge Trail Loop
    Andrew Molera State Park 144

54. Pfeiffer Falls—Valley View Loop: Pfeiffer Big Sur State Park 146

55. Mount Manuel Trail: Pfeiffer Big Sur State Park 148

56. Pine Ridge Trail to Terrace Creek
    Pfeiffer Big Sur State Park to Ventana Wilderness 152

57. Coast Ridge Road to Terrace Creek Trail 153

58. Pfeiffer Beach 156

JULIA PFEIFFER BURNS STATE PARK MAP (Hikes 59—63) 158

59. Partington Cove: Julia Pfeiffer Burns State Park 160

60. Tanbark Trail to Tin House: Julia Pfeiffer Burns State Park 162

61. Fire Road Trail to Tin House: Julia Pfeiffer Burns State Park 163

62. McWay Falls and Saddle Rock: Julia Pfeiffer Burns State Park 166

63. Ewoldsen Trail to Canyon Falls and Overlook
    Julia Pfeiffer Burns State Park 168

64. The Limekilns and Limekiln Falls: Limekiln State Park 170

65. Vicente Flat from Kirk Creek Campground 173

66. Vicente Flat from Cone Peak Road 174

67. Pacific Valley Flats 178

68. Sand Dollar Beach 180

SILVER PEAK WILDERNESS MAP (Hikes 69—72) 182

69. Cruickshank Trail to Cruickshank Camp
    Silver Peak Wilderness Area 184

70. Buckeye Trail to Buckeye Camp: Silver Peak Wilderness Area 185

71. Salmon Creek Falls from Salmon Creek Trail
    Silver Peak Wilderness Area 188

72. Salmon Creek Trail to Spruce Creek Camp and Estrella Camp
    Silver Peak Wilderness Area 190

San Luis Obispo County

San Luis Obispo County 193

SAN LUIS OBISPO COUNTY MAP (Hikes 73—98) 194

73. Ragged Point Inn: Cliffside and Nature Trails 196

74. Piedras Blancas Bluffs 198

75. San Simeon Point: William R. Hearst State Beach 200

76. San Simeon Trail: San Simeon Beach State Park 202

77. Moonstone Beach Trail 204

78. Fiscalini Bluff Trail: East West Ranch 206

79. Estero Bluffs State Park 208

MORRO BAY MAP (Hikes 80—85) 210

80. Cloisters Wetland to Morro Rock 212

81. White Point: from the museum to the heron rookery and marina
   Morro Bay State Park 214

82. Black Hill: Morro Bay State Park 218

83. Portola Point: Morro Bay State Park 220

84. Elfin Forest Natural Area 222

85. Sweet Springs Nature Preserve 224

MONTAÑA DE ORO STATE PARK MAP (Hikes 86—91) 226

86. Morro Bay Sand Spit: Morro Dunes Natural Preserve
   Montaña De Oro State Park 229

87. Hazard Canyon Road to East Boundary—Barranca Loop
   Montaña De Oro State Park 230

88. Hazard Peak—Islay Creek Canyon Loop
   Montaña De Oro State Park 234

89. Valencia Peak Trail: Montaña De Oro State Park 237

90. Bluff Trail: Montaña De Oro State Park 239

91. Coon Creek Trail: Montaña De Oro State Park 241

92. Point Buchon Trail 243

93. Pecho Coast Trail: Point San Luis 246

94. Bob Jones City to the Sea Bike Trail 248

95. Cave Landing and Pirate's Cove 250

96. Ontario Ridge: Shell Beach Bluffs Coastal Trail 251

97. Oceano Dunes Natural Preserve 254

98. Oso Flaco Lake Natural Area 256

Santa Barbara County

Santa Barbara County 259

SANTA BARBARA AREA MAP (Hikes 99—120) 260

99. Guadalupe—Nipomo Dunes Preserve to Mussel Rock 262

100. Ocean Beach County Park 264

101. Jalama Beach County Park 266

102. Gaviota Peak from Gaviota State Park 268

103. Tunnel View—Trespass Trail Loop: Gaviota State Park 269

104. Beach to Backcountry Trail: Gaviota State Park 272

105. El Capitan State Beach 274

106. Aniso Trail: El Capitan State Beach to Refugio State Beach 276

SANTA BARBARA—GOLETA MAP (Hikes 107—113) .278

107. Ellwood Bluffs: Santa Barbara Shores County Park
and Sperling Preserve at Ellwood Mesa 280

108. Coronado Butterfly Preserve and
Ellwood Main Monarch Grove 282

109. Coal Oil Point Reserve 284

110. Goleta Beach and the UCSB Lagoon 286

111. More Mesa 288

112. Douglas Family Preserve 290

113. Shoreline Park 292

MONTECITO—SUMMERLAND—CARPINTERIA MAP (Hikes 114—120) 294

114. Hammonds Meadow Trail 296

115. Summerland Beach from Lookout Park 298

116. Loon Point 300

117. Carpinteria Salt Marsh Nature Park 302

118. Tarpits Park: Carpinteria State Beach 304

119. Carpinteria Bluffs Nature Preserve and Seal Sanctuary 306

120. Rincon Point and Rincon Beach Park 308

Companion Guides 312

Index 315

The Central California Coast

The California coast has some of the most diverse and scenic geography in the state. These 120 day hikes are located in the four adjacent central coast counties of Santa Cruz, Monterey, San Luis Obispo, and Santa Barbara, lying between the major metropolitan areas of San Francisco and Los Angeles. The counties include 400 miles of Pacific coastline. Picturesque communities are linked together by Highway 1, the main access road to most of the hikes. The coast is backdropped by several mountain ranges that rise over 3,000 feet, separating the coastal zones from the rolling farmlands and agricultural valleys.

This guide is divided into the four counties plus the 80-mile Big Sur coast, which runs along the southern Monterey County coast to the northern San Luis Obispo County coast. The majority of these trails would be overlooked by simply driving along the coastline. The trails and descriptions include how and where to access the beaches from Highway 1; where to find tidepools, coves, and rock formations to explore; coastal bluffs and dunes; and wildlife observation sites. Several hikes lead to far-reaching panoramic overlooks of the coast. Trails parallel canyons and creeks that empty into the Pacific; waterfalls are often tucked in the canyons. The best trails in the state and county parks are featured, as well as city trails that are often overlooked. Large tracts of preserved land range from cool, undeveloped forests to open coastal scrub. Other highlights include lighthouses and historical sites. All of the hikes are on or adjacent to the scalloped coast, and all be completed during the day.

Use the hike summaries and statistics to choose a hike appropriate to your ability and intentions. An overall map on the next page identifies the general locations of the hikes and major roads. Each section begins with a more detailed map of the specific area.

Bring the basic necessities to help ensure an optimum outing. Wear supportive, comfortable hiking shoes and layered clothing. Take along hats, sunscreen, sunglasses, water, snacks, and appropriate outerwear. Be aware that ticks and poison oak may be present. Use good judgement about your capabilities, and allow extra time for exploration.

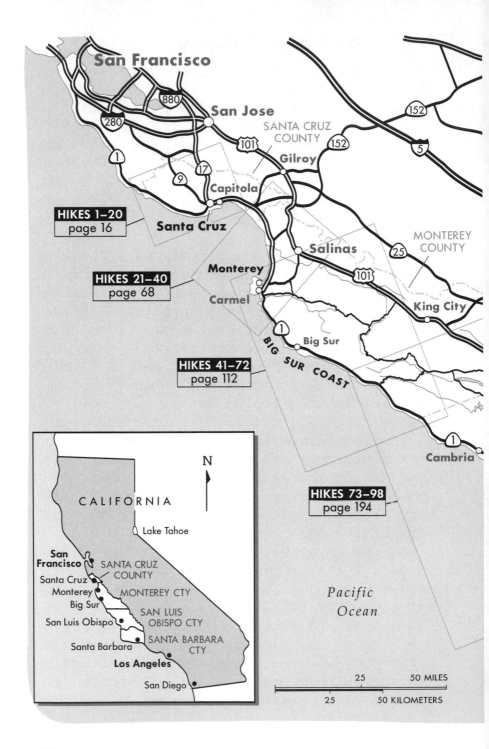

San Francisco

San Jose

880

280

SANTA CRUZ
COUNTY

152

152

5

101

Gilroy

1

17

9

Capitola

HIKES 1–20
page 16

Santa Cruz

Salinas

25

MONTEREY
COUNTY

Monterey

HIKES 21–40
page 68

Carmel

101

King City

1

Big Sur

HIKES 41–72
page 112

BIG SUR COAST

1

Cambria

N

HIKES 73–98
page 194

CALIFORNIA

Lake Tahoe

San
Francisco

SANTA CRUZ
COUNTY

Santa Cruz

Monterey

MONTEREY CTY

Big Sur

SAN LUIS
OBISPO CTY

San Luis Obispo

Santa Barbara

SANTA BARBARA
CTY

Los Angeles

San Diego

*Pacific
Ocean*

25   50 MILES

25   50 KILOMETERS

California Coastline

SANTA CRUZ to SANTA BARBARA

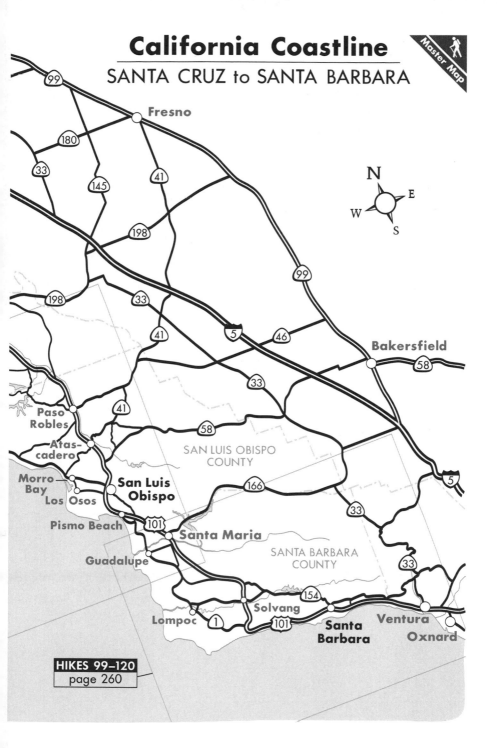

Master Map

Fresno

180

33

145

41

198

99

N
E
W
S

198

33

41

5

46

Bakersfield

58

33

Paso Robles

41

58

Atascadero

SAN LUIS OBISPO COUNTY

Morro Bay

Los Osos

San Luis Obispo

166

5

Pismo Beach

101

33

Santa Maria

SANTA BARBARA COUNTY

33

Guadalupe

154

Solvang

Lompoc

1

101

Santa Barbara

Ventura

Oxnard

HIKES 99–120
page 260

Santa Cruz County

Santa Cruz County stretches 42 miles along a stunning and varied coastline at the northern reaches of the Central California coastline. The rugged Santa Cruz Mountains merge into coastal terraces, verdant farmlands, and wide sandy beaches backed by sandstone bluffs. The coastal mountains are home to ancient redwood forests and a series of state parks, including Big Basin Redwoods State Park (California's oldest state park).

The city of Santa Cruz sits in the transitional coastal zone at the north tip of Monterey Bay. The city is a popular tourist destination with an oceanfront boardwalk and amusement park. The sandy beaches are popular areas for swimming, fishing, surfing, and sunbathing.

The trails explore a variety of landscapes around Santa Cruz, from long-stretching white sand beaches rimmed by oceanside cliffs to lush canyon basins with old-growth forests. Other highlights include lighthouses, intriguing tidepools, beach coves, blufftop trails for wildlife viewing, and wave-sculpted rock formations.

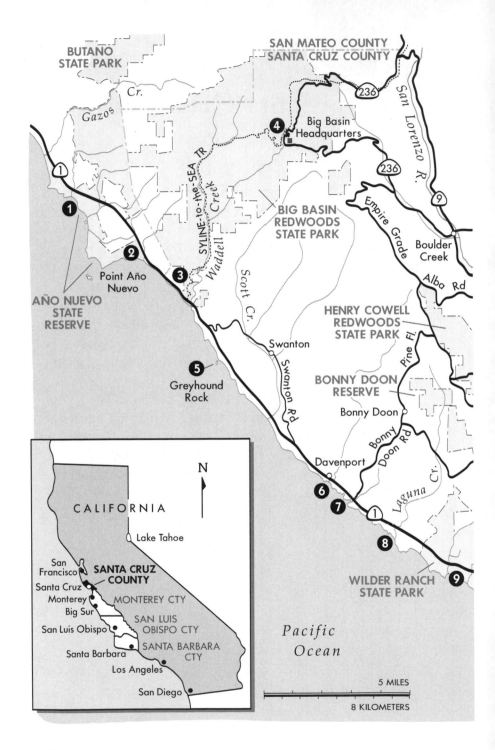

BUTANO
STATE PARK

SAN MATEO COUNTY
SANTA CRUZ COUNTY

236

Cr.

Gazos

San Lorenzo R.

4 Big Basin
Headquarters

236

9

BIG BASIN
REDWOODS
STATE PARK

Empire Grade

Boulder
Creek

1

SKYLINE-to-the-SEA TR

Waddell Creek

Alba Rd

2

3

Point Año
Nuevo

AÑO NUEVO
STATE
RESERVE

Scott Cr.

HENRY COWELL
REDWOODS
STATE PARK

Pine Fl.

Swanton

5

Greyhound
Rock

Swanton Rd

BONNY DOON
RESERVE

Bonny Doon

Bonny Doon Rd

Davenport

6

7

1

Laguna Cr.

8

9

N

CALIFORNIA

Lake Tahoe

San
Francisco

SANTA CRUZ
COUNTY

Santa Cruz

Monterey   MONTEREY CTY

Big Sur

San Luis Obispo   SAN LUIS
                  OBISPO CTY

Santa Barbara   SANTA BARBARA
                 CTY

Los Angeles

San Diego

WILDER RANCH
STATE PARK

Pacific
Ocean

5 MILES

8 KILOMETERS

Santa Cruz County

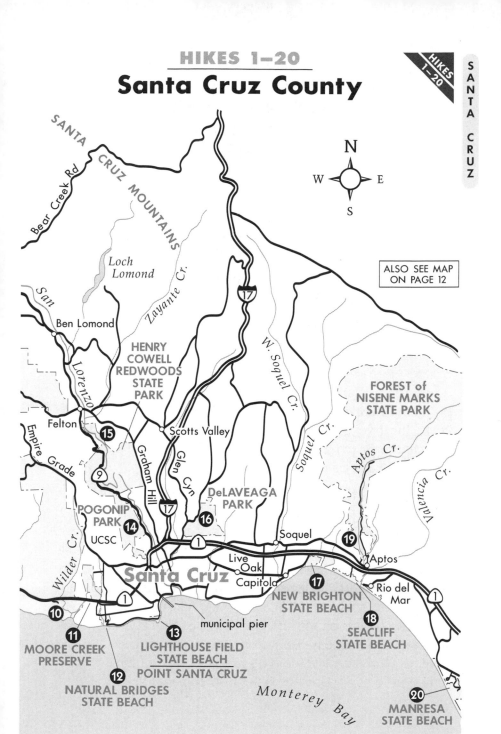

HIKES 1–20

SANTA CRUZ

N
W — E
S

SANTA CRUZ MOUNTAINS

Bear Creek Rd

Loch Lomond

ALSO SEE MAP
ON PAGE 12

Zayante Cr.

17

San

Ben Lomond

W. Soquel Cr.

HENRY
COWELL
REDWOODS
STATE
PARK

Lorenzo

FOREST of
NISENE MARKS
STATE PARK

Felton

15

Scotts Valley

Soquel Cr.

Aptos Cr.

Empire Grade

9

Graham Hill

Glen Cyn

DeLAVEAGA
PARK

Valencia Cr.

POGONIP
PARK

14

17

16

Soquel

19

UCSC

1

Wilder Cr.

Santa Cruz

Live
Oak

Capitola

Aptos

1

17

NEW BRIGHTON
STATE BEACH

Rio del
Mar

1

10

municipal pier

18

11

13

SEACLIFF
STATE BEACH

MOORE CREEK
PRESERVE

LIGHTHOUSE FIELD
STATE BEACH

12

POINT SANTA CRUZ

NATURAL BRIDGES
STATE BEACH

Monterey Bay

20

MANRESA
STATE BEACH

1. Atkinson Bluff Trail:
Gazos Creek to Franklin Point
and Cascade Beach
AÑO NUEVO STATE RESERVE

Hiking distance: 5.2 miles round trip

Hiking time: 3 hours

Elevation gain: 80 feet

map
page 23

Maps: U.S.G.S. Franklin Point

Location: 21 miles northwest of Santa Cruz off Highway 1
55 miles south of San Francisco

Summary of hike: Año Nuevo State Reserve is located just north of Santa Cruz County in San Mateo County. Año Nuevo, meaning *new year* in Spanish, was named by Spanish explorers to commemorate New Year's Day in 1603. The reserve encompasses 1,200 acres of pristine coastal bluffs along six miles of the ocean. The trail follows the coastal bluffs past sandy coves, dunes, rocky headlands, crashing waves, and offshore outcroppings, from Gazos Creek to Cascade Beach just north of Table Rock. The hike explores an overlook atop Franklin Point and Whitehouse Beach at the mouth of the creek. Pigeon Point Lighthouse can be seen to the north.

Driving directions: SANTA CRUZ. Año Nuevo State Reserve has five trailheads off of Highway 1 (the Cabrillo Highway). Follow the driving directions for Hike 2 to the main entrance turnoff. From the posted turnoff continue northbound on the Cabrillo Highway 2.2 miles to the Cascade Creek Trailhead, a dirt pullout on the left; 2.8 miles to the Whitehouse Creek Trailhead, a dirt pullout on the left; 3.5 miles to the Franklin Point Trailhead, also a dirt pullout on the left; and 4.4 miles to the Gazos Creek Trailhead, a paved day-use parking lot at the north end of the state reserve. A parking fee is only required at the main entrance. Parking pullouts are labeled on the map on pages 22—23.

Hiking directions: All four access trails from Highway 1 cross the coastal bluffs and join with the Atkinson Bluff Trail, connecting Franklin Point with Table Rock.

CASCADE CREEK TRAIL crosses the open expanse toward a distinct grove of cypress trees at the oceanfront bluffs. The trail joins the Atkinson Bluff Trail just south of the trees. Continuing south crosses Cascade Beach, a sandy pocket beach backed by the creek's low-lying wetlands, and leads to a flat offshore rock called Table Rock.

WHITEHOUSE CREEK TRAIL crosses the grassy plateau parallel to the creek, connecting with the Atkinson Bluff Trail. A short, steep path descends to a small pocket beach at the mouth of Whitehouse Creek. The main trail leads north and south atop the 40-foot bluffs to a series of overlooks with offshore rocks. To the north is Franklin Point and to the south is Cascade Creek and Table Rock.

FRANKLIN POINT TRAIL is the most direct and shortest route to Franklin Point. The trail crosses the marine terrace over grassy dunes, with views of the Pigeon Point Lighthouse in the distant north. The path ends at the beach and the Atkinson Bluff Trail, just north of Franklin Point. Continue exploring by heading south on the inland side of the dunes, then cross the dunes to Franklin Point. A boardwalk leads to a bench with awesome vistas up and down the crenulated coastline, including jagged sea stacks, tidal rocks, and tidepools.

GAZOS CREEK TRAIL begins at the day-use parking lot at the north boundary of the reserve. Descend to the creek, lagoon, and sandy beach, tucked between the vegetation-covered dunes and the ocean. The trail connects with the Atkinson Bluff Trail and all the previous routes to the south. From Gazos Creek, it is 1.25 miles to Franklin Point, 1.75 miles to Whitehouse Creek and 2.6 miles to Cascade Creek and Beach.■

2. Point Año Nuevo and Cove Beach
AÑO NUEVO STATE RESERVE

Hiking distance: 4 miles round trip
Hiking time: 2.5 hours
Elevation gain: 100 feet

map
next page

Maps: U.S.G.S. Point Año Nuevo
Location: 21 miles northwest of Santa Cruz off Highway 1
55 miles south of San Francisco

Summary of hike: Año Nuevo State Reserve is a major breeding, birthing, barking, and molting area for northern elephant seals. From mid-December through March, the area south of Cascade Creek is only open through guided tours with naturalists. During the rest of the year, a permit is required from the visitor center. The colony of blubbery pinnipeds, the largest seals in the world, can number up to 3,000. The males, with the large, droopy proboscis, reach up to 16 feet in length and weigh upwards of 5,000 pounds. The females reach up to 12 feet long and weigh up to 2,000 pounds.

Cove Beach sits at the mouth Año Nuevo Creek in a south-facing bay beneath steep bluffs. Offshore is 13-acre Año Nuevo Island, with an abandoned five-story lighthouse from 1890 and a large Victorian house built for the lighthouse keepers. The hike begins from the visitor center, a restored 1880s dairy barn. The trail crosses the marine terrace and dunes to Point Año Nuevo, where there are three observation points perched above the rocky cliffs of the elephant seal rookery. On the return, the hike explores Cove Beach.

Driving directions: SANTA CRUZ. From Highway 1 (Mission Street) in Santa Cruz, continue 21 miles northbound to the posted Año Nuevo State Reserve entrance on the left. The turnoff is in San Mateo County, 2.7 miles north of Waddell Beach and 1.2 miles north of the posted Santa Cruz County line. Turn left and drive 0.4 miles to the parking lot by the visitor center. A parking fee is required.

Hiking directions: Two trails lead from the parking lot. The trail to the visitor center is at the south end of the lot. Take the posted Año Nuevo Point Trail at the southwest corner of the parking lot. Wind through coastal scrub to a signed junction. The left fork returns to the visitor center on the New Years Creek Trail and continues to Cove Beach. Go to the right, staying on the Año Nuevo Point Trail. Continue 100 yards to a Y-fork by the remnants of Point Arena, an old steam schooner. The ship smashed against the coastal rocks in severe winter storms and was destroyed. The Pond Loop Trail veers left past a small marshy pond and connects with the main trail up ahead. Stay right, weaving across the marine terrace. Pass the second junction with the Pond Loop Trail to the seal staging area and exhibit building at one mile. Continue straight ahead, entering the wildlife protection area (permit required), walking parallel to the scalloped coastline. Cross a boardwalk and wind through the dune fields to a series of junctions with short paths leading to the seal overlooks. The spur trails on the left lead to three observation points—South Beach Overlook, Bight Beach Overlook, and North Beach Overlook.

Return to the visitor center, and take the New Years Creek Trail on a gentle downward slope. Descend wood steps to a trail fork. Straight ahead, the path leaves the state park on the original coastal road bridge over Año Nuevo (New Year's) Creek Canyon. The old roadbed leads past Monterey pines to Highway 1 in a half mile. To reach Cove Beach, bear right and descend the drainage to the mouth of the creek at the beach, tucked beneath the vertical sandstone cliffs.■

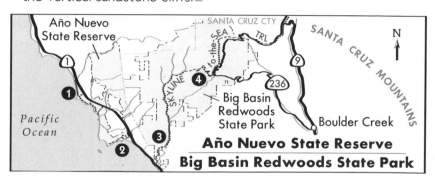

Año Nuevo State Reserve

Año Nuevo State Reserve
Big Basin Redwoods State Park

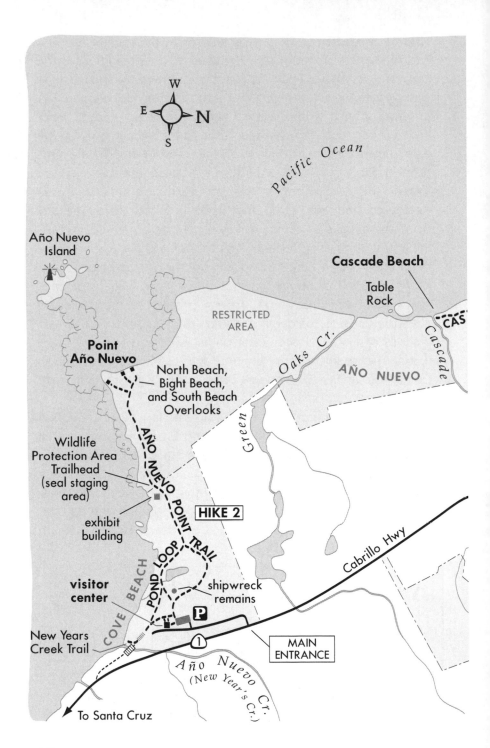

W

E · N

S

Pacific Ocean

Año Nuevo
Island

Cascade Beach

Table
Rock

RESTRICTED
AREA

CAS

Oaks Cr.

**Point
Año Nuevo**

North Beach,
Bight Beach,
and South Beach
Overlooks

AÑO NUEVO

Cascade

Wildlife
Protection Area
Trailhead
(seal staging
area)

Green Cr.

exhibit
building

AÑO NUEVO POINT TRAIL

HIKE 2

Cabrillo Hwy

POND LOOP TRAIL

BEACH

**visitor
center**

shipwreck
remains

COVE BEACH

P

New Years
Creek Trail

1

MAIN
ENTRANCE

*Año Nuevo Cr.
(New Year's Cr.)*

To Santa Cruz

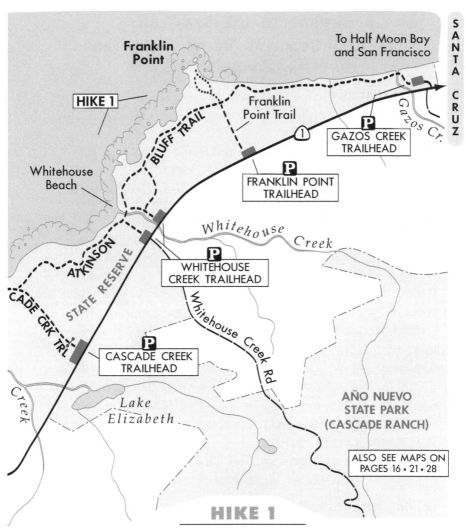

Franklin
Point

To Half Moon Bay
and San Francisco

SANTA CRUZ

HIKE 1

Franklin
Point Trail

BLUFF TRAIL

Gazos Cr.

P
GAZOS CREEK
TRAILHEAD

Whitehouse
Beach

P
FRANKLIN POINT
TRAILHEAD

Whitehouse Creek

ATKINSON

STATE RESERVE

P
WHITEHOUSE
CREEK TRAILHEAD

CADE CRK TRL

Whitehouse Creek Rd

P
CASCADE CREEK
TRAILHEAD

Creek

Lake
Elizabeth

AÑO NUEVO
STATE PARK
(CASCADE RANCH)

ALSO SEE MAPS ON
PAGES 16 • 21 • 28

HIKE 1

Gazo Creek to Franklin
Point and Cascade Beach

HIKE 2

Point Año Nuevo
and Cove Beach

AÑO NUEVO STATE RESERVE

3. Skyline-to-the-Sea Trail:
Waddell Beach to Berry Creek Falls
BIG BASIN REDWOODS STATE PARK

Hiking distance: 12 miles round trip
Hiking time: 6 hours
Elevation gain: 400 feet
Maps: U.S.G.S. Point Año Nuevo and Franklin Point
Big Basin Redwoods State Park map
Location: 18 miles northwest of Santa Cruz off Highway 1

map
page 28

Summary of hike: The white sand of Waddell Beach stretches for almost a mile at the southern tip of Big Basin Redwoods State Park by the Santa Cruz–San Mateo county line. Waddell Creek empties into the ocean at the beach after flowing six miles through the heart of the state park. The creek is fed by several tributary streams and winds through the extensive wetlands of Rancho del Oso near the trailhead. This hike follows the lower six miles of the Skyline-to-the-Sea Trail along Waddell Creek. The hike begins at Waddell Beach and leads to Berry Creek Falls, a gorgeous 65-foot cataract plunging over sandstone cliffs covered with moss and ferns. The waterfall flows through a lush canyon filled with towering redwoods and rich-smelling earth. The forested valley carved out by Waddell Creek supports a diverse mix of coastal redwood, Monterey pine, mixed evergreens, coastal scrub, and marshland vegetation.

Driving directions: SANTA CRUZ. From Highway 1 (Mission Street) in Santa Cruz, drive 18 miles northbound to the posted Waddell Beach and Big Basin Redwoods State Park. The beach is located 8 miles north of Davenport. Use the parking areas on either side of the highway.

Hiking directions: Pass the trailhead gate on the northwest side of Waddell Creek and the marshland. Walk up the paved road past the park map and interpretive panels. Wind along the edge of the huge marsh to the Rancho del Oso ranger office. Curve left at a quarter mile, past the Horse Trail Camp. Take the unpaved road 20 yards to the posted footpath and veer left on the Skyline-to-the-Sea Trail. Weave up the hillside through a mixed forest of coast live oaks, pines, firs, and alders, with views of Waddell Valley and the beach. Slowly descend into a lush, mossy area with ferns and redwoods. Pass the Clark Connection Trail on the left, which climbs 2 miles to the Westridge Trail. Drop down to Waddell Creek, and wade across or use the seasonal bridge on the left to a T-junction with a dirt road at 1.3 miles. The right fork leads 100 yards downstream to Alder Camp and returns to the trailhead. Bear left on the forested road, passing Twin Redwoods Camp on the left in a gorgeous creekside flat. Parallel the east side of the creek through a dense towering forest, passing Camp Herbert on the left in a grove of redwoods. The trail reaches a crossing of East Waddell Creek at 3 miles. Twenty yards shy of the crossing, hikers can veer right on the posted path to a high, arching metal bridge spanning the creek. After crossing, go to the right 80 yards to a junction with the McCrary Ridge Trail. (This is a good turn-around spot for an easy 6-mile hike.) Continue north while gently gaining elevation, parallel to West Waddell Creek. Pass the Henry Creek Trail on the left, and cross a vehicle bridge to the west side of the creek, reaching a map kiosk by another bridge. Cross the creek and steadily gain elevation, passing the Howard King Trail on the right, to an I-beam bridge at the confluence of Berry Creek and West Waddell Creek. Cross the bridge a short distance to a junction. The Skyline-to-the-Sea Trail bears right, across the bridge. For this hike continue straight, following the west bank of Berry Creek upstream to an observation deck overlooking Berry Creek Falls, a vertical sheet of water plunging over fern-covered cliffs into a small pool. This is our turn-around spot.

To extend the hike, zigzag up the hillside on two switchbacks to the brink of the falls. Upstream 0.7 miles, Silver Falls drops 50 feet over a rock face into a pool, and 0.1 mile farther, Golden Cascade tumbles over a sandstone slide.■

4. Skyline-to-the-Sea Trail
(one-way shuttle)
BIG BASIN REDWOODS STATE PARK HEADQUARTERS
to WADDELL BEACH and the PACIFIC OCEAN

Hiking distance: 10.5-mile one-way shuttle
Hiking time: 5 hours
Elevation gain: 1,000 feet loss

map next page

Maps: U.S.G.S. Big Basin, Franklin Point, and Point Año Nuevo
  Big Basin Redwoods State Park map
Location: 18 miles northwest of Santa Cruz off Highway 1

Summary of hike: Big Basin Redwoods State Park is the largest park in the Santa Cruz Mountains, spreading across the slopes facing the sea. The 18,000-acre park is also California's oldest state park, dating back to 1902. It is home to the largest continuous stand of ancient, old-growth redwoods south of San Francisco. Creeks, waterfalls, canyon basins, forested ridges, chaparral-covered slopes, a variety of wildlife, and more than 80 miles of hiking trails are found within the park. The Skyline-to-the-Sea Trail is a 38-mile trail that begins near Saratoga Gap at the crest of the Santa Cruz Mountains in Castle Rock State Park. This one-way shuttle hike follows the lower 10.5-mile section of the trail through the heart of Big Basin Redwoods State Park to Waddell Beach at the Pacific Ocean. The deep, forested route traverses the mountains through a lush canopy of towering 2,000-year-old redwoods along fern-lined creeks. The hike begins at the Nature Lodge Museum and park headquarters in Big Basin.

Driving directions: SANTA CRUZ. From Highway 1 and Highway 9 in Santa Cruz, drive 13 miles north on Highway 9 to the town of Boulder Creek. Turn left on Highway 236, and continue 9.3 miles to Big Basin Redwoods State Park headquarters and visitor center on the right side of the road. Park in the lot on the left, across from the headquarters. A parking fee is required.

Leave the shuttle car at Waddell Beach. Follow driving directions to Hike 3.

Hiking directions: Take the posted Redwood Trail directly across the road from the visitor center, and walk 30 yards to an intersection. Go straight ahead and cross the Opal Creek Bridge to a T-junction with the Skyline-to-the-Sea Trail. Bear left through a dense forest with a redwood grove to a junction with the Hihn Hammond Connector Trail on the left. Stay right towards Berry Creek Falls, 3.7 miles ahead. Wind through the deep, atmospheric forest. Cross a V-shaped bridge over a ravine to Middle Ridge Road atop the ridge at 0.8 miles. The road climbs right to Sunset Trail and left to Hihn Hammond Road (an old logging road) and the Mount McAbee Overlook. Continue straight, perched on the hillside, and traverse the redwood-filled canyon. Head down the canyon through redwood groves to the canyon floor, crossing a series of bridges over tributary streams of Kelly Creek. Cross a bridge over the headwaters of Kelly Creek and steadily descend, paralleling the creek to a junction with Timms Creek Trail. (En route, a short alternate loop follows the north side of Kelly Creek.) Stay straight along the banks of West Waddell Creek through majestic groves of redwoods, passing ferns and moss-covered boulders. Cross a bridge to the north bank of West Waddell Creek and an overlook of Berry Creek Falls with a bench. Descend to Berry Creek just above its confluence with West Waddell Creek. Cross the bridge to a T-junction at 4.2 miles. The Skyline-to-the-Sea Trail bears left. First, detour right and follow the west bank of Berry Creek upstream to a platform in front of the gorgeous Berry Creek Falls plunging 65 feet over sandstone cliffs into a pool. Return down the hill and head south where the two creeks merge. Cross an I-beam bridge, where the footpath widens to a dirt road. Pass the posted Howard King Trail on the left and stroll downhill, returning to the creek. Cross the creek on a bridge to a map kiosk and continue downstream. Head over a vehicle bridge to the east side of the creek, and pass the Henry Creek Trail on the right. Follow the main trail high above the creek, and gradually descend to the creek over the course of a mile. Pass the McCrary Ridge Trail on the left in a meadow and walk 70 yards, crossing an arching metal bridge over East Waddell

Creek. Continue past Camp Herbert, then Twin Redwoods Camp on the right, to a posted junction 80 yards ahead. Bear right on the hiking trail, and wade across the creek or use the seasonal bridge. Wind 1.3 miles through the forested hillside to the trail gate by Horse Trail Camp and the Rancho del Oso ranger office, where both routes merge. Wind down the paved road a quarter mile along the west edge of the protected marsh to the gate at Waddell Beach.■

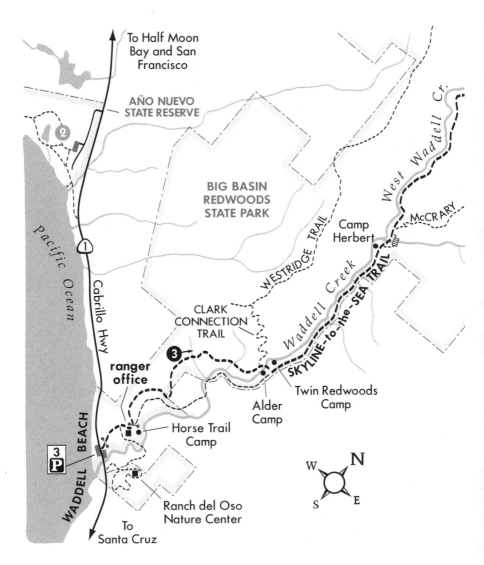

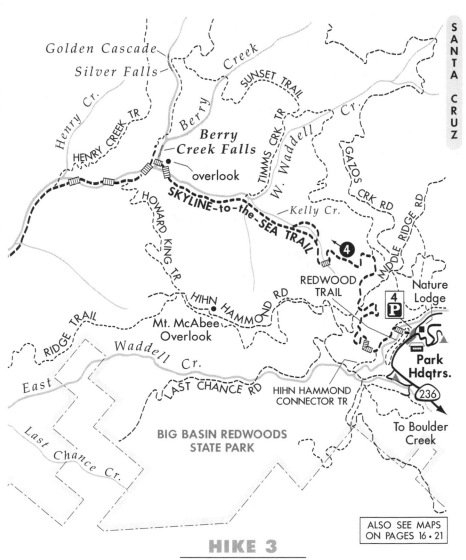

Golden Cascade

Silver Falls

Henry Cr.

Creek

SUNSET TRAIL

HENRY CREEK TR

Berry

Berry Creek Falls

overlook

TIMMS CRK TR

W. Waddell

GAZOS

CRK RD

MIDDLE RIDGE RD

SKYLINE-to-the-SEA TRAIL

Kelly Cr.

④

HOWARD KING TR

REDWOOD TRAIL

Nature Lodge

④ P

HIHN HAMMOND RD

Mt. McAbee Overlook

RIDGE TRAIL

Waddell Cr.

Park Hdqtrs.

236

East

LAST CHANCE RD

HIHN HAMMOND CONNECTOR TR

To Boulder Creek

Last Chance Cr.

BIG BASIN REDWOODS STATE PARK

ALSO SEE MAPS ON PAGES 16 • 21

SANTA CRUZ

HIKE 3

Waddell Beach to Berry Creek Falls

HIKE 4

Skyline-to-the-Sea Trail

BIG BASIN REDWOODS STATE PARK

5. Greyhound Rock

Hiking distance: 0.5 miles round trip
Hiking time: 30 minutes
Elevation gain: 160 feet
Maps: U.S.G.S. Point Año Nuevo
Location: 16.5 miles northwest of Santa Cruz off Highway 1

Summary of hike: Greyhound Rock is a gigantic gray sandstone boulder that sits a short distance offshore from Highway 1. During low tide, the shoreline extends to the rock, exposing a medley of intriguing tidepools. The prominent smooth sandstone formation rises 45 feet above the water and is a popular fishing spot. Sheer vertical cliffs drop from the grassy bluffs to the sea, bordering the beautiful triangular-shaped beach at the base of the cliffs. The 160-foot marine terrace is lined with mature cypress trees and picnic tables. A steep paved path, primarily used as a fishing access, descends the rugged, sculpted cliffs to the beach and tidepools.

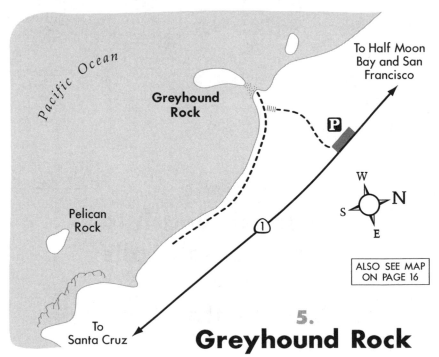

5.
Greyhound Rock

Driving directions: SANTA CRUZ · DAVENPORT. From Highway 1 (Mission Street) in Santa Cruz, drive 16.5 miles north to the posted "Coastal Access" on the left. Turn into the paved parking lot atop the bluffs. The turnoff is 6.5 miles north of Davenport and 1.3 miles south of Waddell Beach.

Hiking directions: Begin by savoring the aerial vistas of Greyhound Rock and the scalloped coastline from the ocean-front bluffs. Take the paved path on the south edge of the eroded draw. Descend down through the vegetation-covered sandstone cliffs between steep vertical walls. Near the bottom, steps lead to the sandy, crescent-shaped beach beneath the 160-foot cliffs. Just offshore, directly in front of the steps, is massive Greyhound Rock. To the north, a large offshore rock adjoins the beach. To the south, the sand ends where the steep cliffs meet the sea at Pelican Rock.■

6. Davenport Beach and Bluffs

Hiking distance: 2 miles round trip
Hiking time: 1 hour
Elevation gain: 100 feet

map
page 32

Maps: U.S.G.S. Davenport
Location: Davenport, 10 miles north of Santa Cruz off Hwy. 1

Summary of hike: Davenport, a historic whaling and shipping town, is now a small beach hamlet with about a dozen businesses along the coastal bluffs of Highway 1. Across the highway from town is a gorgeous, expansive beach nestled at the base of a 100-foot marine terrace. The crescent-shaped beach stretches just under a half mile and is rimmed by the massive wind-blown cliffs. Well-worn footpaths circle the sandstone bluffs and lead down to the sandy beach. On the north bluffs is Davenport Overlook, a promontory with mature cypress trees and grasses along the sheer eroding cliffs. Below are disintegrated pilings from a depression-era wharf. The skeletal remains provide nesting and roosting sites for cormorants. This hike explores the bluffs and beach.

Driving directions: SANTA CRUZ · DAVENPORT. From Highway 1 (Mission Street) in Santa Cruz, drive 10 miles northbound to the town of Davenport. Park in the large open area on the left, directly across from the Davenport post office and the prominent flashing yellow light at Ocean Street.

Hiking directions: Head south across the grassy bluff. Descend the natural rock steps by the old metal structure. Cross the railroad tracks to a fork. The left fork follows the railroad tracks on the bluffs overlooking Davenport Beach to the 100-foot terrace bordering the south end of the beach. Take the footpath straight ahead to a Y-fork. Bear left, descending the cliffs on a wide, sloping path to sandy Davenport Beach. The pocket beach has sea caves, tunnels, and tidepools on each end and a spire-shaped offshore rock. After exploring the crescent-shaped beach, return up the slope to the Y-fork. Curve around the perimeter of the dramatic promontory to the point, sur-

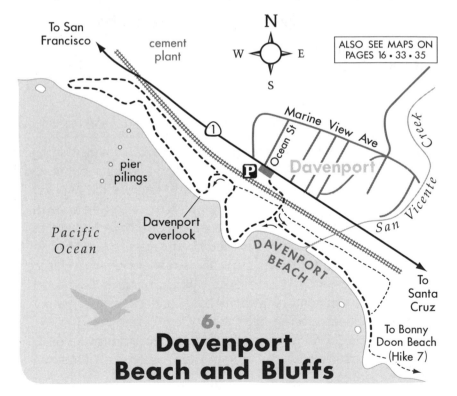

To San Francisco

cement plant

N
W ⬦ E
S

ALSO SEE MAPS ON
PAGES 16 · 33 · 35

Marine View Ave

Ocean St

San Vicente Creek

Davenport

①

P

pier pilings

Pacific Ocean

Davenport overlook

DAVENPORT BEACH

To Santa Cruz

6.
Davenport Beach and Bluffs

To Bonny Doon Beach
(Hike 7)

rounded by water on three sides. The sheer drop makes it physically difficult to stand close to the edge. Head north, crossing the head of a canyon parallel to the railroad tracks. Bear left to a Monterey cypress grove, and return to the edge of the bluffs. Continue northwest, passing the old pier pilings to a second point at the Davenport overlook above the crenulated coastline, caves, and sea stacks. Return by retracing your steps, or loop back on the path along the southwest side of the railroad tracks.■

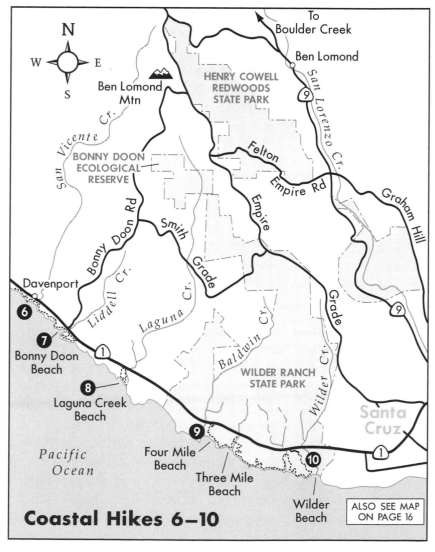

Coastal Hikes 6–10

7. Bonny Doon Beach and Bluffs

Hiking distance: 2 miles round trip
Hiking time: 1 hour
Elevation gain: 70 feet
Maps: U.S.G.S. Davenport and Santa Cruz
Location: 9 miles northw est of Santa Cruz off Highway 1

Summary of hike: Bonny Doon Beach is a sheltered cove beneath rugged cliffs accessed directly from Highway 1 northwest of Santa Cruz. The beach resembles a natural amphitheater. It is nearly enclosed by 70-foot sandstone walls and rock outcroppings, keeping the winds at bay. Liddell Creek flows out of the cliffs and drains into the sea through the sandy beach. To the south, a path follows the perimeter of the promontory, overlooking the beach from the ocean to the shoreline. The continually changing ocean views include large offshore rocks, arches, and tidepools. To the north, a path is perched along the marine terrace above a series of isolated pocket beaches, sea caves, and tunnels. This is a popular clothing–optional beach and surfing destination.

Driving directions: SANTA CRUZ. From Highway 1 (Mission Street) in Santa Cruz, drive 9 miles northbound to the long, paved parking area on the left, across from Bonny Doon Road. The parking lot is located one mile south of Davenport.

Hiking directions: From the north end of the parking lot, directly across from Bonny Doon Road, walk up the distinct trail. Cross the railroad tracks and descend into crescent-shaped Bonny Doon Beach. After exploring the sandy cove, return to the railroad tracks, and head south to the bluffs bordering the south end of the beach. Take the sandy path along the edge of the bluffs in an agricultural field. Follow the dirt road to the point, with a spectacular beach and shoreline view of the vertical cliffs, offshore rocks, sea caves, and tidepools. Curve left and head south to more coastal vistas with flat slab rocks, natural arches, and tidepools. It will be tempting to carefully inch to the edge of the cliffs to see the incredible formations below. As the bluffs narrow and the road/path nears the railroad tracks, return on the dirt road parallel to the tracks, forming a loop back to the trailhead.

Walk 30 yards north and take the footpath veering left. Follow the edge of the bluffs to the northwest point of Bonny Doon Beach, high above a series of isolated pocket beaches, sea caves, and tunnels. These beaches are backed by cliffs so steep that they can only be accessed at low tide. After rounding the point and leaving Bonny Doon Beach, the trail follows the scalloped cliffs 0.6 miles to Davenport Beach (Hike 6). Choose your own turn-around spot.■

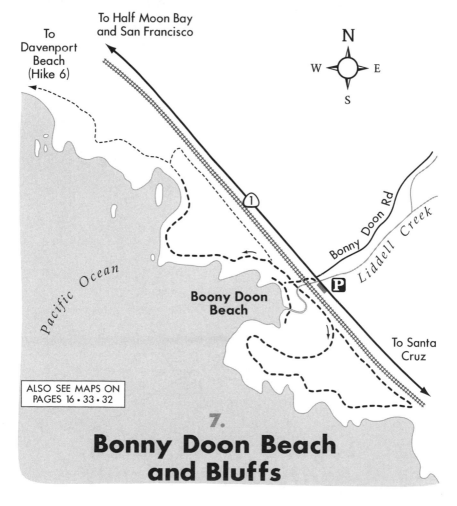

To Half Moon Bay
and San Francisco

To
Davenport
Beach
(Hike 6)

N
W ← → E
S

Bonny Doon Rd

Liddell Creek

Pacific Ocean

P

Boony Doon
Beach

To Santa
Cruz

ALSO SEE MAPS ON
PAGES 16 • 33 • 32

7.
Bonny Doon Beach
and Bluffs

8. Laguna Creek Beach, Bluffs and Wetlands

Hiking distance: 1 mile round trip
Hiking time: 30 minutes
Elevation gain: 75 feet
Maps: U.S.G.S. Santa Cruz
Location: 7.5 miles northwest of Santa Cruz off Highway 1

Summary of hike: Laguna Creek begins near the crest of Ben Lomond Mountain by Henry Cowell Redwoods State Park and Bonny Doon Ecological Reserve, then travels southward to the sea at Laguna Creek Beach. At the beach, the creek forms a huge wetland bordered on the south by Sand Hill Bluff. This hike loops

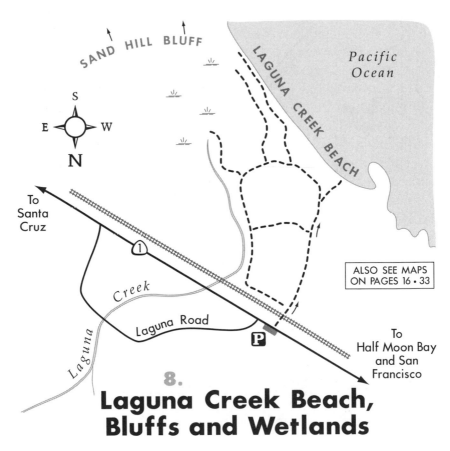

ALSO SEE MAPS
ON PAGES 16 • 33

8.
Laguna Creek Beach, Bluffs and Wetlands

around the grassy marine terrace and explores the isolated wetland. Several side paths connect to Laguna Creek Beach and the bluffs for further exploration.

Driving directions: SANTA CRUZ. From Highway 1 (Mission Street) in Santa Cruz, drive 7.5 miles northbound to Laguna Road on the right, just after crossing over Laguna Creek. Park in the large dirt pullout on the right, northwest of the creek and Laguna Road. The parking area is located 2.7 miles south of Davenport.

Hiking directions: From the north end of the parking area, cross the highway to the oak tree tucked between two hills. Take the distinct footpath and cross the railroad tracks. Follow the east edge of the lush draw and walk over a small rise. The grassy mesa leads to a coastal overlook and a Y-fork. Begin the loop to the right and descend to the lower plateau 20 feet above the sandy beach pocket on the right. A side path on the right drops down to the beach, bordered by 80-foot cliffs. On the main path, follow the rim of the marine terrace southeast above Laguna Creek Beach. Several side paths drop down to the sandy beach, Laguna Creek, and Sand Hill Bluff. Follow the terrace rim inland, overlooking the wetlands and estuary. More side paths lead down to the wetlands for bird observation and exploring. The main trail leads to a junction. The right fork follows the edge of the wetlands and ends at the railroad tracks southeast of the trailhead. The left fork crosses the north end of the grassy marine terrace, completing a smaller loop.■

9. Four Mile Beach to Three Mile Beach
WILDER RANCH STATE PARK

Hiking distance: 3—6 miles round trip
Hiking time: 1.5—3 hours
Elevation gain: 75 feet
Maps: U.S.G.S. Santa Cruz
Location: 3 miles north of Santa Cruz off Highway 1

map
page 41

Summary of hike: Wilder Ranch State Park sprawls over 7,000 acres to the west of Santa Cruz, adjacent to the university. The park, once a dairy farm dating back to the 1880s, covers miles of coastline and stretches across Highway 1 to the crest of Ben Lomond Mountain. Thirty-four miles of hiking, biking, and equestrian trails weave through various ecosystems, including coastal wave-cut terraces, stream-fed wooded valleys with redwoods, mixed evergreen and oak forests, open grasslands, and ocean-facing mountain slopes. Four Mile and Three Mile beaches, named for their respective distance from the city of Santa Cruz, are within Wilder Ranch State Park. Baldwin Creek, on the west edge of Four Mile Beach, forms a pond and freshwater marsh filled with birds. This hike follows the Ohlone Bluff Trail along a rugged stretch of coast with precipitous cliffs and isolated beaches. Throughout the hike are offshore rocks, sea stacks, natural mudstone arches, tidepools, and sandy beaches. Four Mile Beach is a surfing and clothing-optional getaway. To extend this hike, continue with Hike 10.

Driving directions: SANTA CRUZ. From Highway 1 (Mission Street) in Santa Cruz, drive 5 miles northbound to the parking pullouts along both sides of the highway by Baldwin Creek. The parking area is located 2 miles west of the main entrance into Wilder Ranch State Park.

Hiking directions: Pass through the trailhead gate on the south side of the highway. Follow the old paved path east a short distance, and curve right on the dirt path. Cross the railroad tracks and descend to Four Mile Beach on the east edge of the Baldwin Creek wetlands at 0.25 miles. Just before reaching the sandy beach, take the path on the left—the Ohlone Bluff Trail—and climb up the 60-foot bluffs between the lagoon and the ocean. Head east along the edge of the agricultural fields to an overlook at the east point of Four Mile Beach. Pass a pocket beach with a massive offshore sea stack. Follow the serpentine blufftop path to the west edge of Three Mile Beach, a wide sandy beach bordered by cliffs. Walk across the beach and climb back up the bluffs at the east end, or curve inland around the wetlands backing the beach, staying on the Ohlone Bluff Trail. Pass a couple of paths dropping down to the beach en route to the railroad tracks and a junction. A beach access path continues inland, parallel to the west edge of the arroyo, to parking pull-outs on Highway 1. The Ohlone Bluff Trail curves right and loops around the perimeter of the bluffs to the east end of Three Mile Beach. The trail continues to Needle Rock Point at 1.75 miles, the indented cove of Strawberry Beach, and Sand Plant Beach at 2.5 miles. Sand Plant Beach is at the junction with the Old Cove Landing Trail—Hike 10. Choose your own turn-around spot. ∎

10. Old Cove Landing Trail to Fern Grotto
WILDER RANCH STATE PARK

Hiking distance: 3 miles round trip
Hiking time: 1.5 hours
Elevation gain: 60 feet
Maps: U.S.G.S. Santa Cruz
Location: 3 miles northwest of Santa Cruz off Highway 1

map next page

Summary of hike: The Old Cove Landing Trail follows the pristine, wave-sculpted shoreline across the 50-foot coastal plateau of Wilder Ranch State Park. The trail starts from the Wilder Ranch Cultural Preserve, then explores the coastline along Wilder Beach, Old Cove Landing, Fern Grotto, and Sand Plant Beach. Wilder Beach is a natural, off-limits preserve with a wet-land and an observation deck. Old Cove Landing was used to load lumber onto coastal schooners from the 1850s to the 1890s. Offshore, huge flat rocks are covered with harbor seals. Fern Grotto is a shallow beach cave with ferns growing out of its walls and ceiling, fed by an underground spring. Crescent-shaped Sand Plant Beach is backed by a large wetland fed by Old Dairy Gulch. En route, the trail passes isolated pocket beaches and secluded caverns. The trail can be combined with Hike 9 for a 4-mile one-way hike to Four Mile Beach.

The Wilder Ranch Cultural Preserve is home to the original buildings from this historic dairy ranch. The complex includes an 1840 adobe, the 1897 Wilder Victorian home, workshops and bunkhouse from 1898, a stable, and a hand-hewn wood barn.

Driving directions: SANTA CRUZ. From Highway 1 (Mission Street) in Santa Cruz, drive 3 miles northbound to the posted Wilder Ranch State Park entrance on the left. (It is located 1.8 miles past the traffic light at Western Drive.) Turn left and continue a quarter mile to the parking lot on the right at the end of the road. A parking fee is required.

Hiking directions: Take the paved trail by the restrooms 30 yards to the Wilder Ranch Cultural Preserve boundary. Bear right on the footpath and cross the railroad tracks, weaving through the grassy terrace and farmland. Skirt the west edge of protected Wilder Beach (closed to the public) to a viewing platform at 0.6 miles. An estuary formed by Wilder Creek backs the sandy beach. Follow the seaward edge of the bluffs along the scalloped coastline. Pass Old Cove Landing, a small sandy beach surrounded by 60-foot vertical cliffs, and numerous sea caves. Continue along the jagged coastline with offshore rocks, flat rock terraces, tidepools, and caves. At signpost 8 is an overlook of Fern Grotto, a fern-filled cave at the back end of a deep sandy inlet. Curve around the cove and detour left on a footpath. Descend onto the beach for a close-up of the lush grotto and the perpetually dripping seepage from within the rock cliffs. Return to the Old Cove Landing Trail, and loop around the west side of Fern Grotto. Continue past another deep cove to Sand Plant Beach, where the Old Cove Landing Trail ends and the Ohlone Bluff Trail begins. The beach is backed by a privately owned lagoon and wetland that is closed to hikers. Return along the same route.

To extend the hike, the Ohlone Bluff Trail descends and crosses Sand Plant Beach en route to Strawberry Beach, Needle Rock Point at 2.3 miles, and Three Mile Beach at 3 miles (Hike 9). During high tide, take the trail to the right, looping around the lagoon. Choose your own turn-around spot.■

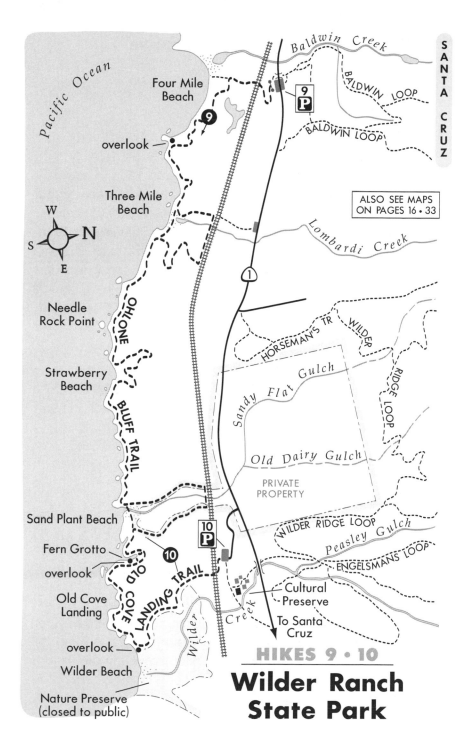

Pacific Ocean

Baldwin Creek

SANTA CRUZ

Four Mile
Beach

9

9 P

BALDWIN LOOP

BALDWIN LOOP

overlook

Three Mile
Beach

ALSO SEE MAPS
ON PAGES 16 • 33

Lombardi Creek

W N
S E

1

Needle
Rock Point

HORSEMAN'S TR

WILDER

Sandy Flat Gulch

OHLONE

RIDGE LOOP

Strawberry
Beach

Old Dairy Gulch

BLUFF TRAIL

PRIVATE
PROPERTY

Sand Plant Beach

WILDER RIDGE LOOP

Peasley Gulch

Fern Grotto

10

ENGELSMANS LOOP

overlook

OLD COVE LANDING TRAIL

Old Cove
Landing

10 P

Cultural
Preserve

Wilder Creek

overlook

To Santa
Cruz

Wilder Beach

HIKES 9 • 10

Nature Preserve
(closed to public)

Wilder Ranch
State Park

11. Moore Creek Preserve

Hiking distance: 2.5 miles round trip
Hiking time: 1.5 hours
Elevation gain: 200 feet
Maps: U.S.G.S. Santa Cruz
      Moore Creek Preserve map
Location: Santa Cruz

Summary of hike: Moore Creek Preserve is a 246-acre greenbelt in Santa Cruz that opened to the public in 2003. The undeveloped watershed has a variety of habitats, including wetlands, riparian forests, live oak groves, coastal terrace prairie, and spectacular views of the ocean. Seasonal Moore Creek meanders through the east side of the preserve en route to a seaside lagoon at Natural Bridges State Beach (Hike 12). The creek's headwaters begin just north in the lower foothills of the Santa Cruz Mountains.

Driving directions: SANTA CRUZ. From the west end of Santa Cruz, take Mission Street (Highway 1) to Western Drive. Drive one mile north on Western Drive to Meder Street. Turn left and park along the curb. Parking is not allowed past here.

At the lower (south) end of the preserve is a trailhead along Highway 1. The posted trailhead is located 0.3 miles west of Western Drive, directly across Highway 1 from Shaffer Road. Parking is available along the highway.

Hiking directions: Walk 0.4 miles west to the posted trailhead at the west end of Meder Street, a narrow, forested lane. Curve right on the East Meadow Trail to a signed junction at 0.1 miles. Bear left on the Moore Creek Trail, and drop into the oak-filled canyon. Traverse the east canyon slope along a rock wall with caves. Zigzag down two switchbacks to the canyon floor, and cross the bridge over seasonal Moore Creek. Ascend the west slope and pass through a trail gate. Leave the oak woodland to rolling grassy slopes and a T-junction. From here the views extend across Monterey Bay to Pacific Grove in Monterey County. The left fork descends 0.7 miles to the trailhead on

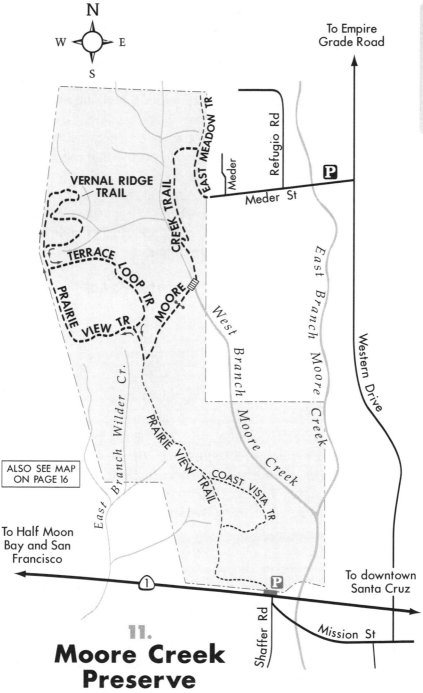

N
W E
S

To Empire
Grade Road

Refugio Rd

Meder

P

Meder St

EAST MEADOW TR

VERNAL RIDGE
TRAIL

CREEK TRAIL

TERRACE LOOP TR

PRAIRIE

VIEW TR

MOORE

East Branch Moore Creek

West Branch Moore Creek

Western Drive

ALSO SEE MAP
ON PAGE 16

East Branch Wilder Cr.

PRAIRIE VIEW TRAIL

COAST VISTA TR

To Half Moon
Bay and San
Francisco

1

P

To downtown
Santa Cruz

Shaffer Rd

Mission St

11.
Moore Creek
Preserve

Highway 1. Bear right on the Prairie View Trail, and cross the rolling terrain 100 yards to a fork. Begin the loop to the left, staying on the Prairie View Trail to the fenceline bordering a private ranch. Go to the right, skirting the edge of the preserve, parallel to the fence. Climb the sloping meadow to the ridge and a trail split. The Terrace Loop Trail, our return route, is on the right. For now, go straight ahead on the Vernal Ridge Trail along the preserve boundary. Curve right along the edge of a thick oak woodland draped with lace lichen. Meander on the B-shaped loop through the wooded draw, returning to the ridge overlooking the bay. Go to the left on the Terrace Loop Trail, following the 400-foot ridge east. Curve right, completing the second loop. Veer left 100 yards, returning to the Moore Creek Trail junction. Bear left, back to the trailhead on the same route.■

12. Natural Bridges State Beach

Hiking distance: 1-mile loop
Hiking time: 45 minutes
Elevation gain: 50 feet
Maps: U.S.G.S. Santa Cruz
　　　　Natural Bridges State Beach map
Location: Santa Cruz

Summary of hike: Natural Bridges State Beach overlooks the ocean on the west edge of Santa Cruz. The 54-acre park was named for three picturesque offshore rock formations with water-carved arches. The last of the three natural stone bridges collapsed after the devastating 1989 earthquake, but the gorgeous rock sculptures still remain. Along the shore is a sandy, half-moon beach backed by a large lagoon fed by Moore Creek. At the west end of the beach are rock terraces filled with tidepools in shallow depressions. Near the center of the park is a eucalyptus grove, which attracts an annual monarch butterfly migration. The renowned site is home to one of the largest populations of wintering monarch butterflies in the United States (September through February). This hike loops around the state park on an interpretive trail through the diverse habitats.

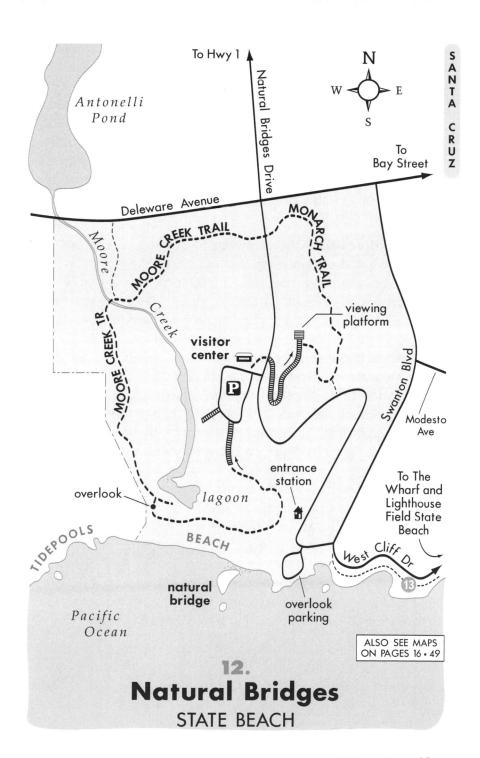

To Hwy 1

Natural Bridges Drive

N
W E
S

SANTA CRUZ

Antonelli Pond

To Bay Street

Deleware Avenue

Moore

MOORE CREEK TRAIL

MONARCH TRAIL

MOORE CREEK TR.

Creek

viewing platform

visitor center

P

Swanton Blvd

Modesto Ave

overlook

lagoon

entrance station

To The Wharf and Lighthouse Field State Beach

TIDEPOOLS

BEACH

West Cliff Dr

13

natural bridge

Pacific Ocean

overlook parking

ALSO SEE MAPS
ON PAGES 16 • 49

12.
Natural Bridges
STATE BEACH

Driving directions: SANTA CRUZ. From the junction of Beach Street and West Cliff Drive by the wharf (Municipal Pier) in downtown Santa Cruz, head south on West Cliff Drive. Drive 2.7 miles along the oceanfront cliffs, passing the Point Santa Cruz Lighthouse, to the state beach entrance at Swanton Boulevard. Drive straight ahead into the parkland. To the left is the coastal overlook parking lot. Stay to the right and continue 0.4 miles to the parking lot at the visitor center. An entrance fee is required.

The park can also be accessed from the north via Natural Bridges Drive.

Hiking directions: You may wish to pick up an interpretive brochure at the visitor center. The walk starts on the right (west) side of the visitor center at the posted Monarch Trail. Follow the boardwalk path through eucalyptus groves, descending to the floor of the ravine and a junction. The left fork leads 50 yards to the Monarch Resting Area viewing platform. Return to the junction and continue down-canyon on the dirt path. Curve left and climb natural rock steps out of the ravine. Follow the ridge north through Monterey pines and eucalyptus groves. Cross the upper end of the park road near Delaware Avenue, and continue on the Moore Creek Trail. Curve south to a junction by seasonal Moore Creek. The right fork leads to Delaware Avenue. Veer left and cross through the riparian corridor on a boardwalk, curving toward the beach. After the boardwalk ends, the trail crosses a series of short bridges through groves of blackberries to the west banks of the Moore Creek estuary. Scramble up the short rocky terrace on the right to a coastal overlook. Descend the hill to the beach between the lagoon and the ocean. Walk 200 yards along the sandy beach to the base of the cliffs, viewing the offshore natural bridge outcroppings. Loop around the lagoon to the wide trail at the back of the beach. Return 30 yards to the parking lot.■

13. Lighthouse Trail • Point Santa Cruz

LIGHTHOUSE FIELD STATE BEACH to
NATURAL BRIDGES STATE BEACH

Hiking distance: 4.5 miles round trip
Hiking time: 2.5 hours
Elevation gain: Level
Maps: U.S.G.S. Santa Cruz
Location: Santa Cruz

map
page 49

Summary of hike: Lighthouse Field State Beach covers 40 acres atop Point Santa Cruz (also called Lighthouse Point) near downtown Santa Cruz. The point, with a stone lighthouse and surfing museum, defines the northern tip of Monterey Bay. A large, grassy open space with cypress trees lines the coastal terrace, interspersed with picnic areas and informal paths. The dog-friendly park acts as a buffer between the residential area and the oceanfront bluffs. Hugging the 40-foot eroding cliffs is undulating West Cliff Drive. A popular two-mile walking path, known as the Lighthouse Trail, hugs the cliffs parallel to West Cliff Drive. The path links Lighthouse Field State Beach with Natural Bridges State Beach (Hike 12). Along this stretch, the pounding surf has created caves, sculpted rock formations, natural bridges, indented cliffs, sheltered coves, and tidepools. The trail passes scenic overlooks with benches and a series of small pocket beaches with stairways accessing the shoreline.

Driving directions: SANTA CRUZ. From the junction of Beach Street and West Cliff Drive by the wharf (Municipal Pier) in downtown Santa Cruz, head south on West Cliff Drive. Drive 0.4 miles on the oceanfront cliffs towards the lighthouse to the first parking lot on the left (ocean side). Parking pullouts are spaced along the road on both sides.

Hiking directions: Take the paved blufftop path south, overlooking Monterey Bay from Point Santa Cruz at the lighthouse to Soquel Point and Pacific Grove. At 0.4 miles, steps lead down to a landing above a beach with large boulders. Across West Cliff Drive is a natural off-leash dog area. The state parkland has open meadows with native grasses, pockets of trees, and a network of meandering paths. At a half mile is the lighthouse at Point Santa Cruz. Off the point is Seal Rock and other outcroppings. Fingers of land extend seaward with natural arches and small sandy coves. The park ends at 0.8 miles, but the coastal trail continues, passing a series of flat rock ledges and off-shore formations. At just over one mile, cross a seasonal stream drainage. An unpaved path follows the drainage 0.4 miles inland through a narrow greenbelt park, connecting West Cliff Drive with Delaware Avenue. Continue on the coastal path to Sunset Ave, where a stairway leads down to the beach by large rock outcroppings. At 1.7 miles, by John Street, short dirt paths on the left meander through ice plants to the edge of the cliffs. Below are fingers of land and water-carved rock shelves with tidepools. At just over 2 miles is an enclosed U-shaped sandy beach with a shallow cave. The path ends at Swanton Boulevard by the entrance to Natural Bridges State Beach (Hike 12).■

14. Pogonip Park

Hiking distance: 3.5-mile loop
Hiking time: 2 hours
Elevation gain: 300 feet
Maps: U.S.G.S. Santa Cruz and Felton
      Pogonip Park map
Location: Santa Cruz

map
page 51

Summary of hike: Pogonip Park is a 640-acre expanse in the coastal hills at the north end of Santa Cruz. The park lies between Highway 9, the University of California, and Henry Cowell Redwoods State Park. The dog-friendly park has several diverse habitats that include shady glens with oaks; sycamore, willow, and madrone groves; second-growth stands of redwoods; riparian creekside vegetation along Pogonip Creek and Redwood

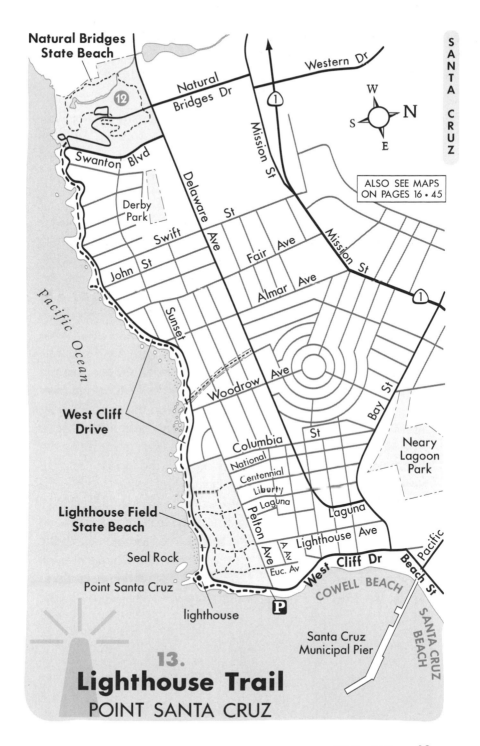

Natural Bridges
State Beach

12

SANTA CRUZ

Western Dr

Natural
Bridges Dr

Mission St

W
N
S
E

ALSO SEE MAPS
ON PAGES 16 • 45

Swanton Blvd

Delaware

Derby
Park

St

Swift

Ave

Fair Ave

Mission St

1

John St

Almar Ave

Pacific Ocean

Sunset

Woodrow Ave

Bay St

West Cliff
Drive

Columbia St

Neary
Lagoon
Park

National

Centennial

Liberty

Laguna

Lighthouse Field
State Beach

Pelton

Laguna

Lighthouse Ave

Seal Rock

Ave

A Av

Lighthouse Ave

Pacific

Point Santa Cruz

Euc. Av

West Cliff Dr

Beach St

lighthouse

P

COWELL BEACH

SANTA CRUZ BEACH

13.
Lighthouse Trail
POINT SANTA CRUZ

Santa Cruz
Municipal Pier

Creek; and open grassland meadows. A nine-mile network of trails crosses Pogonip Park. This hike explores cool, shady forests and mountain meadows to great views of Monterey Bay and the city of Santa Cruz.

Driving directions: SANTA CRUZ. From River Street (Highway 9) and Highway 1 in Santa Cruz, drive 0.4 miles north on River Street to Golf Club Drive on the left. Turn left and continue 0.1 miles. Park along the road, just before crossing under the train trestle.

Hiking directions: Walk a quarter mile up the narrow, paved road past agricultural gardens to the park entrance. Stroll through rolling grassy meadows with coast live oaks and ocean views, staying on the road. Pass the Pogonip Creek Trail to the historic Pogonip Clubhouse from 1911. Curve left around the structure to the ranger cabins; the Prairie Trail will be on the left. Continue on the road as it narrows to a footpath, entering an oak canopy on the Brayshaw Trail. At the posted junction with the Fern Trail, bear right and walk 100 yards to a Y-fork. Begin the loop to the right, staying on the Fern Trail. Cross a wooden footbridge over Redwood Creek in a redwood grove. Wind up the shady hillside, crossing through a sloping meadow. Steadily climb to the top in a shaded, lush forest. Cross the hilltop on a level grade along the north end of a meadow to a junction with the Rincon Trail, 0.8 miles from the ranger cabins. The Rincon Trail leads 0.4 miles to Highway 9 and connects to Henry Cowell Redwoods State Park (Hike 15). Bear left on the Spring Trail, and stroll through oaks and redwoods, with glimpses through the trees of Santa Cruz and the sea. Pass the Spring Box Trail on the right to the Ohlone Trail on the left. Bear left and descend through meadows and oaks, completing the 1.5-mile loop. Return by retracing your steps to the right.■

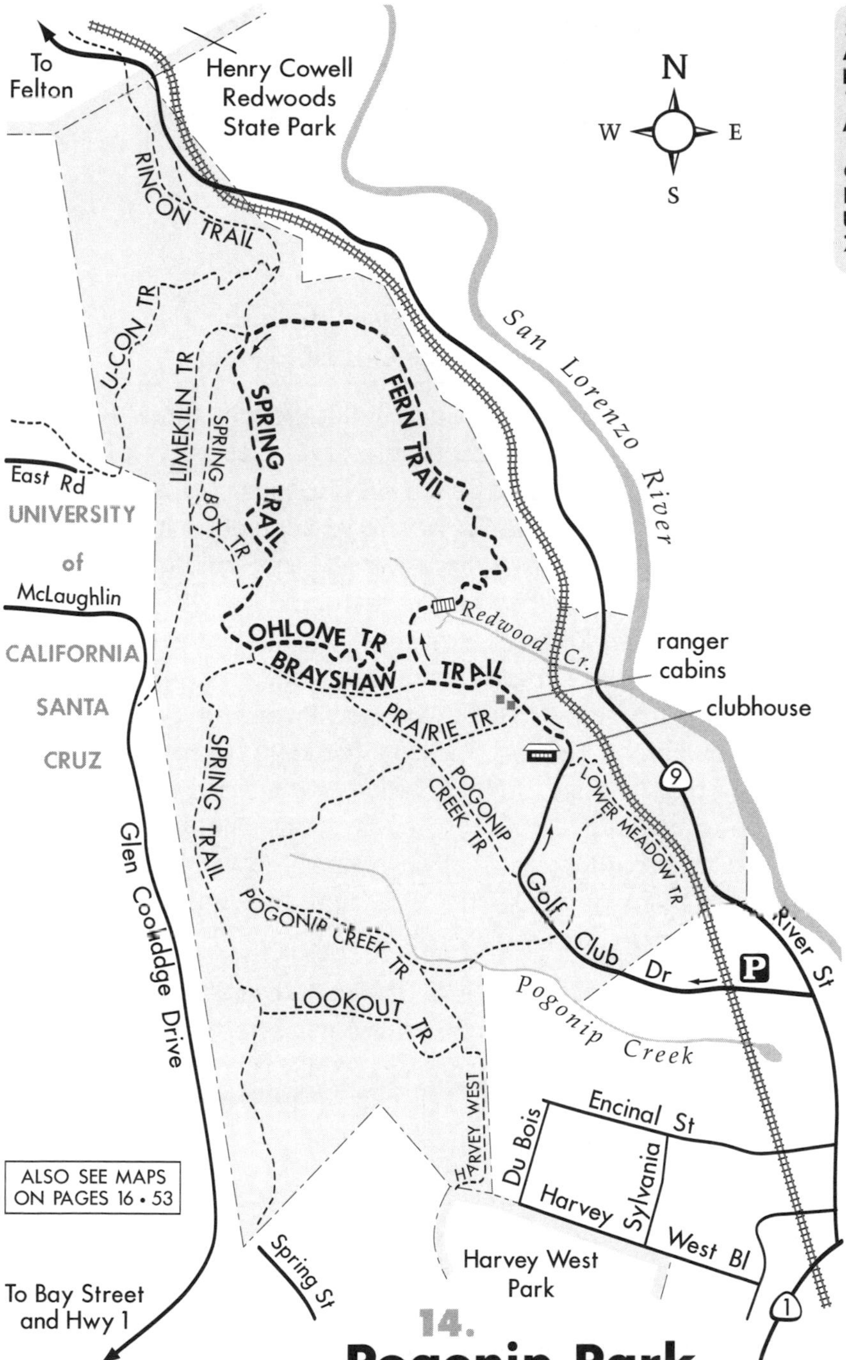

To Felton

Henry Cowell Redwoods State Park

N
W E
S

RINCON TRAIL

U-CON TR

LIMEKILN TR

SPRING BOX TR

SPRING TRAIL

FERN TRAIL

San Lorenzo River

East Rd

UNIVERSITY

of

McLaughlin

CALIFORNIA

SANTA

CRUZ

Glen Coolidge Drive

SPRING TRAIL

OHLONE TR

BRAYSHAW TRAIL

PRAIRIE TR

Redwood Cr.

ranger cabins

clubhouse

POGONIP CREEK TR

LOWER MEADOW TR

9

Golf Club Dr

River St

P

POGONIP CREEK TR

LOOKOUT TR

Pogonip Creek

ALSO SEE MAPS ON PAGES 16 • 53

HARVEY WEST

Encinal St

Du Bois

Sylvania

Harvey

West Bl

To Bay Street and Hwy 1

Spring St

Harvey West Park

1

14.
Pogonip Park

15. River Trail—Eagle Creek—
Ridge Road Loop
HENRY COWELL REDWOODS STATE PARK

Hiking distance: 4.6-mile loop
Hiking time: 2.5 hours
Elevation gain: 500 feet
Maps: U.S.G.S. Felton
Henry Cowell Redwoods State Park map
Location: 6 miles north of Santa Cruz of Highway 9

Summary of hike: Henry Cowell Redwoods State Park is tucked into the coastal mountains a few miles north of Santa Cruz. The huge 4,000-acre park is divided into two disconnected units. This hike is located in the smaller southern unit, just south of Felton and adjacent to the university and Pogonip Park. The lower 1,800-acre park includes majestic old-growth redwoods up to 1,800 years old; oak, pine and sycamore forests; stream-fed canyons; open grassland meadows; dry chaparral-covered ridges; and the serpentine San Lorenzo River with riparian river gorges and sandy beaches. The dog-friendly park has a network of more than 15 miles of hiking, biking, and equestrian trails. This loop hike explores all of these ecosystems. The route follows the San Lorenzo River, strolls through moist redwood groves, and climbs to an observation deck at 800 feet, with views of the surrounding mountains and Monterey Bay.

Driving directions: SANTA CRUZ. From River Street (Highway 9) and Highway 1 in Santa Cruz, drive 6 miles north on Highway 9 to the posted state park entrance on the right. Turn right and continue 0.6 miles to the parking lot on the right by the nature store. A parking fee is required.

Hiking directions: The River Trail can be accessed behind the nature store or just west of the visitor center. Take the paved Pipeline Road to the posted River Trail located between the two buildings. Follow the dirt path 20 yards to an elevated overlook of the San Lorenzo River. Bear left and head downstream. The

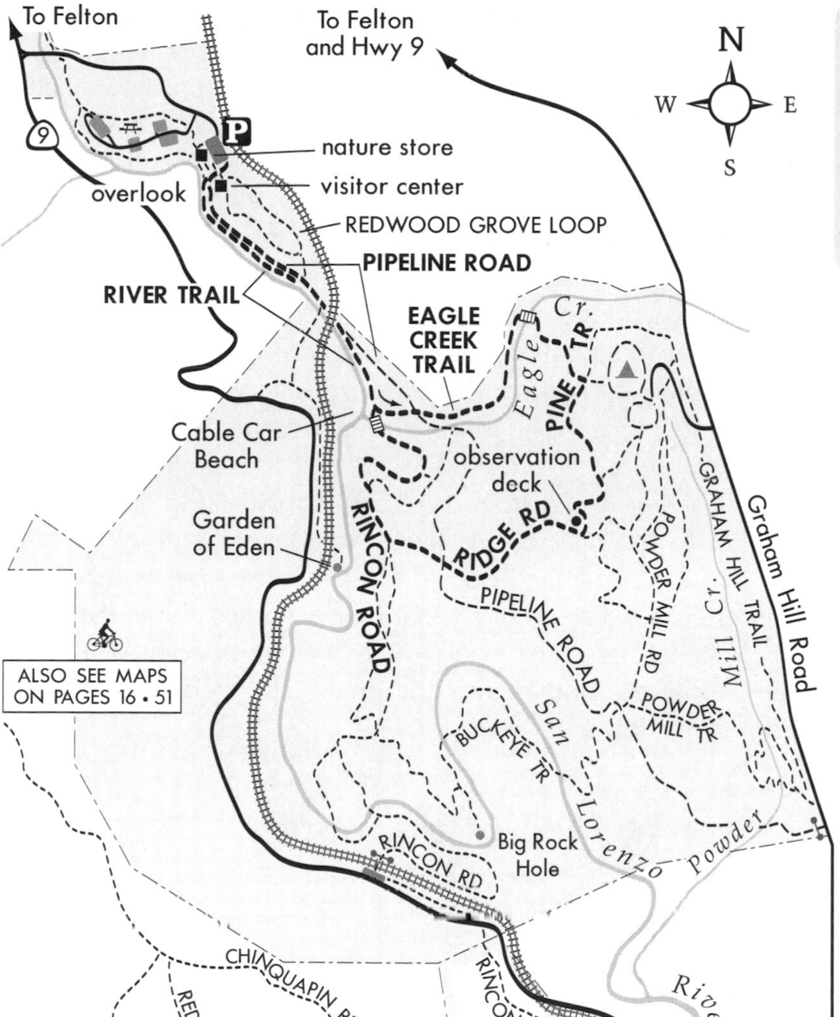

To Felton

To Felton
and Hwy 9

N
W ⬦ E
S

SANTA CRUZ

nature store

visitor center

REDWOOD GROVE LOOP

PIPELINE ROAD

RIVER TRAIL

**EAGLE
CREEK
TRAIL**

Eagle Cr.

PINE TR.

overlook

P

Cable Car
Beach

observation
deck

Garden
of Eden

RINCON ROAD

RIDGE RD

GRAHAM HILL TRAIL

POWDER MILL RD

Graham Hill Road

Mill Cr.

PIPELINE ROAD

POWDER
MILL TR

ALSO SEE MAPS
ON PAGES 16 • 51

BUCKEYE TR

San Lorenzo

Powder

RINCON RD

Big Rock
Hole

River

CHINQUAPIN RD

RED HILL RD

WEST RD

RINCON RD

To
Santa
Cruz

FERN TR

9

UNIVERSITY of CALIFORNIA
SANTA CRUZ

Chinquapin-East

McLaughlin

Dr

SPRING TR

14

**Pogonip
Park**

**15.
Henry Cowell Redwoods
STATE PARK**

forested Pipeline Road and the bluff-edge River Trail run close together and parallel. The road route allows bikes and dogs. Meander through a forest of maple and redwood groves a half mile to the train trestle, where the two paths merge. Cross under the trestle 100 yards and curve right on the River Trail. Descend to a trail fork. The River Trail crosses Eagle Creek on a bridge, our return route. Begin the loop to the left on the Eagle Creek Trail. Curve through the shaded forest on the undulating path, and cross a wood bridge over Eagle Creek. Curve right and leave the creek. Climb to a posted junction with the Pine Trail just before reaching the campground. Go right through an oak, pine, and madrone forest, steadily gaining elevation to the 800-foot summit and observation deck atop a knoll at 2.6 miles. The platform has 360-degree vistas from the ocean to the inland mountains. Continue to the right on the Ridge Road, and descend to the west into the dense redwood forest. Cross the Pipeline Road to a T-junction with Rincon Road. Bear right and wind down the hillside. Veer left onto the River Trail to the south edge of Eagle Creek. Cross the bridge over the creek, completing the loop. Return to the left.■

16. Top of the World
DeLAVEAGA PARK

Hiking distance: 3-mile loop
Hiking time: 1.5 hours
Elevation gain: 350 feet
Maps: U.S.G.S. Santa Cruz, Soquel, Felton and Laurel
Location: Santa Cruz

map
page 56

Summary of hike: DeLaveaga Park encompasses 565 acres on the northeast side of Santa Cruz. Jose Vicente DeLaveaga, a San Francisco businessman, owned the land in the late 1800s and willed it to the city in 1894 for recreational use. The dog-friendly park includes a golf course, disc golf course, athletic fields, picnic areas, and hiking/biking trails. Branciforte Creek, a tributary of the San Lorenzo River, flows through the west edge of the park. An unsigned trail system of old dirt roads and single-track footpaths weaves through the wooded hills. This hike begins at the creek and climbs through the shaded forest to the 456-foot La Corona Lookout, locally known as Top of the World. From the summit are sweeping vistas of Santa Cruz and Monterey Bay.

Driving directions: SANTA CRUZ. From the intersection of Market Street (just east of Ocean Street) and Water Street in Santa Cruz, drive 1.7 miles north on Market Street, crossing under Highway 1, to the posted park entrance on the right. (En route, Market Street becomes Branciforte Drive.) Turn right into DeLaveaga Park, and continue 0.15 miles to the parking lot by the soccer field.

A lower trailhead is located 1.1 miles from the Market Street and Water Street junction (0.6 miles before reaching the main park entrance). Park in the long dirt pullout on the right by the gated dirt road (Sand Pit Road) veering uphill.

Hiking directions: Climb the steps on the southeast side of the park road by the restrooms to a T-junction. Begin the loop and bear left on the footpath, entering the forest. Traverse the hillside, gaining elevation, then descend to the far end of the grassy parkland and baseball field. Follow the Creek Trail to the right along the east side of Branciforte Creek. Climb the hillside and follow the watercourse upstream, weaving through the dense forest with redwood groves. Curve right and zigzag up the hill on the unsigned Adak Trail to a meadow surrounded with coast live oaks, pines, and bay laurel. At the top of the meadow is a junction. The Adak Trail continues to the left and La Corona Trail, our return route, veers to the right. Go left and follow the contours of the hill to a trail split on the exposed ridge over-looking the forested canyon and Branciforte Creek Valley. Bear right and loop back to a dirt road on the summit. Go to the right 60 yards to a bench at the Top of the World summit, overlook-ing the disc golfing course, Santa Cruz, and the ocean. Return back down the hill to the junction with La Corona Trail. Take La Corona Trail (the left fork) along the hillside. Loop through a side canyon, crossing a couple of footbridges. The baseball diamonds come into view far below. The trail merges with Sand Pit Road—the fire road that parallels Branciforte Drive 0.6 miles to the lower trailhead. Thirty yards shy of this trail merge, bear right and descend to the parking lot, completing the loop.■

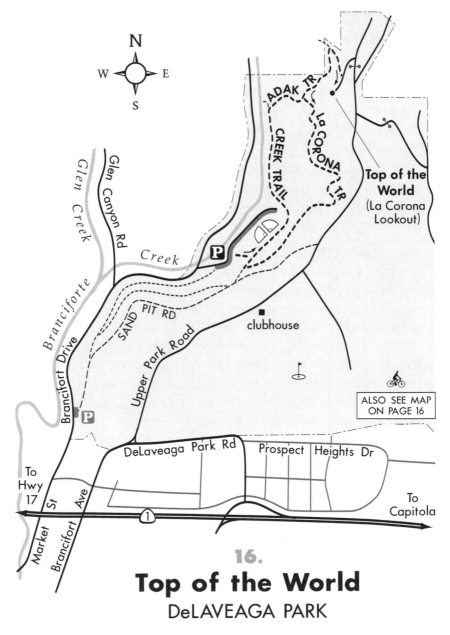

16.
Top of the World
DeLAVEAGA PARK

17. New Brighton State Beach

Hiking distance: 1-mile loop
Hiking time: 45 minutes
Elevation gain: 75 feet

map
page 58

Maps: U.S.G.S. Soquel
New Brighton State Beach map
Location: Capitola

Summary of hike: New Brighton State Beach stretches for a half mile along the coastline in Capitola just east of Santa Cruz. The beach encompasses 68 acres and is spread out along a forested 75-foot coastal terrace overlooking Soquel Cove. The west end of the beach, formerly known as China Beach, was named for a village of Chinese fisherman who lived there in the 1870s and 1880s. A campground atop the grassy bluffs is nestled among towering cypress, Monterey pines, and eucalyptus groves, a wintering site for migrating monarch butterflies. Trails weave through the shady glens and down the cliffs to the soft sand beach. The wide beach connects with Seacliff State Beach (Hike 18) in one mile and continues uninterrupted for 15 miles to the town of Moss Landing farther south.

Driving directions: CAPITOLA. From Highway 1 in Capitola, exit on Park Avenue. Drive 0.1 mile south to Kennedy Drive and turn left. Continue 0.15 miles to the posted state beach entrance and turn right. Drive 0.3 miles, staying to the right, to the day use parking lot. An entrance fee is required.

Hiking directions: From the far south end of the parking lot, descend on wood stairs from the China Cove trailhead to the beach. To the west (right) the beach ends in 200 yards where the cliffs jut out into the sea. Go left and follow the wide path above the sandy beach. At 0.2 miles (just past the restrooms), stairs and a sloping walkway lead up the 100-foot cliffs to the forested campground. To the right, a path leads to the amphitheater. Continue straight ahead and cross the campground road. Take the Oak Trail, and head north through the oak and pine forest. Pass the ranger station on the left, and descend into a lush forest to the railroad tracks. Walk over the tracks and head downhill, crossing a wooden footbridge over Tannery Gulch to the park entrance station. Return to the railroad tracks and continue 100 yards to wood steps on the right. Climb the steps to the park road, just west of the ranger station. Bear left to the Oak Trail by the ranger station. Retrace your steps to the right, returning to the beach.

To extend the hike, stroll along the beach for just over a mile to Seacliff State Beach and the pier (Hike 18). The remains of the Palo Alto extend from the pier's end (see next hike). ■

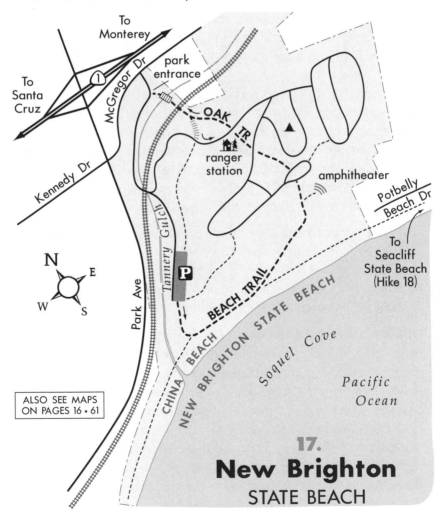

17.
New Brighton
STATE BEACH

18. Seacliff State Beach
from RIO del MAR BEACH

Hiking distance: 1.6 miles round trip
Hiking time: 1 hour
Elevation gain: 100 feet
Maps: U.S.G.S. Soquel
     Seacliff State Beach map
Location: Aptos

map
page 61

Summary of hike: Seacliff State Beach is a long oceanfront park in Aptos. The two-mile stretch of ocean frontage in Soquel Cove is backed by steep, 100-foot sandstone cliffs. For thousands of years it was the village site of the Ohlone Indians. In the heart of the state beach is Seacliff Pier, a 500-foot-long wooden pier. Attached to the end of the pier are the remains of the Palo Alto, an old supply ship from World War 1. The historic ship was towed to Seacliff in 1930 and now extends seaward from the end of the pier. For a few years during the early 1930s, the 435-foot ship housed a swimming pool, dance floor, and casino. Since the late 1930s, the converted tanker acts as a popular fishing pier. At the southernmost section of Seacliff State Beach is Rio del Mar Beach, where Aptos Creek empties into the ocean. A beachfront esplanade begins at the beach, crosses Aptos Creek, and strolls along the beachfront walkway to the pier and beyond. Side paths climb the cliffs to coastal overlooks.

Driving directions: APTOS. From Highway 1 in Aptos, exit on Rio del Mar Boulevard. Drive 1.3 miles southwest to the beachfront parking lot at the end of the road.

Hiking directions: Walk west on the paved esplanade toward the cliffs. Cross the bridge over Aptos Creek by the lagoon at the mouth of the creek. At the base of the cliffs is a short detour. Follow the west bank of the creek a short distance to the cul-de-sac on Creek Drive. Just before the cul-de-sac, a dirt path on the left climbs wood steps to the upper terrace on Seacliff Drive. One hundred yards to the left is a coastal overlook on the

100-foot cliffs. The views extend across Monterey Bay from Soquel Point to Moss Landing and Pacific Grove. Return to the paved esplanade, elevated above the sandy beach, and continue west between the 100-foot cliffs and the wide stretch of sand. Just before reaching the old wood pier, a long flight of wood steps climbs the eroded sandstone cliffs to the parking lot near the main entrance of Seacliff State Beach. Continue past the pier and the park visitor center. A dirt path climbs up the sedimentary cliffs under a canopy of cypress to a beach access on Beachgate Way. Continue northwest on the beachfront path to the end of the trail at a tree-lined rock wall.

To extend the hike, follow the beach strand north to New Brighton State Beach (Hike 17). ■

19. Aptos Rancho Trail
THE FOREST of NISENE MARKS STATE PARK

Hiking distance: 4 miles round trip
Hiking time: 2 hours
Elevation gain: 100 feet
Maps: U.S.G.S. Soquel and Laurel
The Forest of Nisene Marks State Park map
Location: Aptos

map
page 63

Summary of hike: The Forest of Nisene Marks State Park in Aptos encompasses 10,000 acres on the southern range of the Santa Cruz Mountains. The undeveloped park rises from sea level to more than 2,600 feet at Rosalia Ridge. Aptos Creek, a perennial coastal stream, runs through the heart of the park from Rosalia Ridge to the sea at Rio del Mar Beach. The park has rugged, rolling countryside and is covered with dense forests, including second-growth redwood forests, riparian woodlands, and oak groves. The vast dog-friendly refuge has more than 40 miles of hiking and biking trails. This hike follows the lower park trails from the south boundary to George's Picnic Area. The Aptos Rancho Trail weaves through the creek canyon, following the riparian

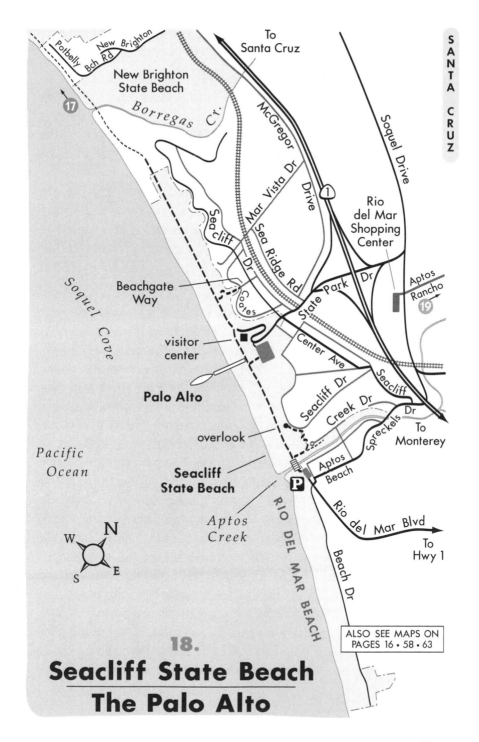

To
Santa Cruz

Potbelly Bch Rd

New Brighton

New Brighton
State Beach

Borregas Cr.

17

McGregor

Drive

Mar Vista Dr

Sea Ridge Rd

Seacliff

Dr

1

Rio
del Mar
Shopping
Center

Soquel Drive

Aptos
Rancho

19

Beachgate
Way

Coates

State Park

Dr

Soquel Cove

visitor
center

Center Ave

Palo Alto

Seacliff Dr

Seacliff

overlook

Creek Dr

Dr

Speckels

To
Monterey

*Pacific
Ocean*

**Seacliff
State Beach**

P

Aptos
Beach

*Aptos
Creek*

RIO DEL MAR BEACH

Rio del Mar Blvd

To
Hwy 1

W

N

E

S

Beach Dr

ALSO SEE MAPS ON
PAGES 16 • 58 • 63

18.

Seacliff State Beach
The Palo Alto

corridor amid gorgeous redwoods. The preserve was at the epi-
center of the devastating 1989 Loma Prieta earthquake.

Driving directions: APTOS. From Highway 1 in Aptos, exit on
State Park Drive. Drive 0.3 miles north to Soquel Drive at the first
light. Turn right and continue 0.1 miles to the light signal at the first
street—Aptos Rancho Road. The trailhead is one block to the
left, but parking is restricted to residents. Turn right into the
Rancho del Mar shopping center and park.

Additional trailheads can be accessed from Aptos Creek
Road, the main park entrance: From State Park Drive and Soquel
Drive, go 0.4 miles east on Soquel Drive to Aptos Creek Road on
the left. Turn left and drive 0.8 miles to the park entrance station
or 1.9 miles to George's Picnic Area. A parking fee is required at
these trailheads.

Hiking directions: Cross Soquel Drive at the signal. Walk 0.1
miles down Aptos Rancho Road to the posted trailhead at road's
end. Drop into a dense, mixed forest of redwood, oak, maple,
pine, fir, and willow. Wind through the lush riparian habitat on the
west slope of Aptos Creek Canyon. At 0.4 miles, rock hop over
Aptos Creek beneath a 100-foot vertical wall covered with moss
and ferns. Follow the creek upstream, passing the entrance station on Aptos Creek Road and the Old Growth Loop at 0.6 miles.
Continue north, parallel to Aptos Creek Road. Drop back into the
canyon, and descend to a posted junction with the Terrace Trail
by Aptos Creek at 1.1 miles. Stay on the Aptos Rancho Trail, following the creek. Merge briefly with the lower end of the Vienna
Woods Trail. Climb a short distance to the Tillman Memorial
Grove, a gorgeous redwood grove. Head up the east canyon
slope overlooking the creek (passing the north junction with the
Terrace Trail) to Aptos Creek Road at 2 miles. Across the road is
George's Picnic Area. Pick up the Buggy Trail, and weave through
the forest on the hillside parallel to the road. Traverse the hill a
half mile, dropping down to the road. Cross the road and head
downhill to the Aptos Rancho Trail. Retrace your steps to the
left.■

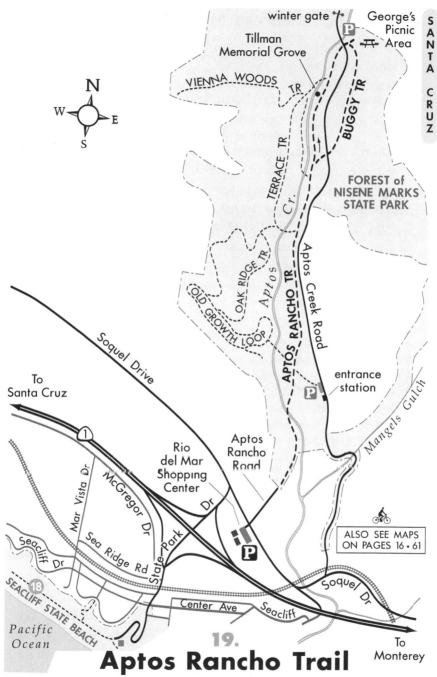

winter gate

George's Picnic Area

SANTA CRUZ

Tillman Memorial Grove

P

VIENNA WOODS

TR

BUGGY TR

N
W E
S

TERRACE TR

Cr.

FOREST of NISENE MARKS STATE PARK

OAK RIDGE TR

OLD GROWTH LOOP

Aptos

Aptos

APTOS RANCHO TR

Aptos Creek Road

Soquel Drive

To Santa Cruz

entrance station

P

Mangels Gulch

1

Rio del Mar Shopping Center

Aptos Rancho Road

Mar Vista Dr

McGregor Dr

Dr

State Park

Seacliff Dr

Sea Ridge Rd

Center Ave

Seacliff

Soquel Dr

18

SEACLIFF STATE BEACH

Pacific Ocean

P

ALSO SEE MAPS ON PAGES 16 • 61

To Monterey

19.

Aptos Rancho Trail
FOREST of NISENE MARKS STATE PARK

20. Manresa State Beach

Hiking distance: 1-mile loop
Hiking time: 45 minutes
Elevation gain: 100 feet
Maps: U.S.G.S. Watsonville West
Location: 4 miles southeast of Aptos

Summary of hike: Located just south of Aptos, Manresa State Beach is a long stretch of clean white sand backed by steep sandstone cliffs and bordered by blufftop homes. The state beach has two separate access points and feels like two separate parks. The main (northern) section is a narrow two-mile-long beach strand popular with surfers. This hike begins from the Manresa Uplands, the southern portion of the park by the campground. The campground sits atop a 100-foot coastal terrace with grasslands, tree groves, and sweeping vistas of Monterey Bay. This hike forms a loop from the bluffs to the sandy beach. A steep wooden stairway atop the bluffs leads 170 steps down the cliffs to the beach.

Driving directions: SEASCAPE. From Highway 1 in Seascape (south of Aptos), exit on San Andreas Road. Drive 3 miles south to Sand Dollar Drive and turn right. Continue a quarter mile to Manresa Beach Road and turn left. Drive 0.3 miles to the Uplands Campground entrance station. Just beyond the entrance, bear right to the beach parking area 200 yards ahead. An entrance fee is required.

HIGHWAY 1. From the Mar Monte Avenue exit off of Highway 1, turn left on Mar Monte Avenue and drive 0.8 miles to San Andreas Road. Turn left and continue 1.5 miles to Sand Dollar Drive. Turn right and follow the directions above.

Hiking directions: Head south through the picnic area on the posted trail. Follow the blufftop 100 yards to a stairway. The steep staircase descends 100 feet to the sandy beach, our return route. Begin the loop on the bluffs along the perimeter of the campground. Stroll through a dense eucalyptus grove, passing campground connector paths on the left and an amphitheater on the right. Curve right to a paved beach access road on the right. Cross the road and continue on the dirt path. Loop around the forested campground through oaks, pines and cypress, returning to the paved road. Bear left toward the sea, and follow the road downhill through the draw to the ocean. The hike can be extended along the beach for miles in both directions. For this hike, go to the right to the north end of the uplands and the long set of wooden stairs. En route the views extend across Monterey Bay from Santa Cruz Point to the stacks at Moss Landing and Pacific Grove. Climb the 170-step stairway, returning to the blufftop.■

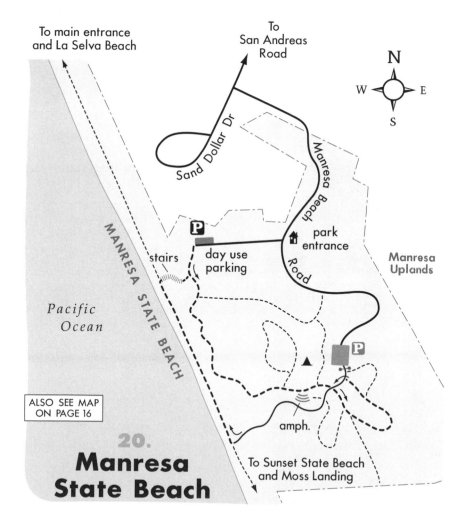

20.
Manresa State Beach

Monterey County

Monterey County, along the Central California coast, encompasses some of the most beautiful and diverse scenery in the world. A hundred miles of coastline stretches from Monterey Bay to the rugged Big Sur oceanfront. Mountains run parallel to the coast, separating the coastline from the rich agricultural land. Picturesque communities dot a landscape abundant with green valleys, beaches, woodlands, parks, natural preserves, and calm bays along the scalloped coastline.

At the north end of Monterey County, near the small fishing village of Moss Landing, are a series of state beaches and wildlife and wetland preserves stretching along Monterey Bay.

The oceanfront communities of Monterey, Pacific Grove, Pebble Beach, and Carmel are located on the Monterey Peninsula at the south end of the crescent-shaped Monterey Bay. The peninsula is a beautiful meeting of land and sea. It is at the heart of the Monterey Bay National Marine Sanctuary, the largest marine sanctuary in the nation. In addition to its communities and world-class golf courses, the peninsula is also known for migrating monarch butterflies; groves of gnarled cypress; Monterey pines; and a jagged shoreline that overlooks tidepools, beaches, and rock formations. Birds, sea lions, harbor seals, whales, and other wildlife may be spotted along the shore.

The south end of the Monterey Peninsula borders Carmel, a quaint European-style village with an array of galleries, restaurants, boutiques, gardens, and courtyards tucked within the tree-lined meandering streets.

Monterey • Carmel
MONTEREY BAY and PENINSULA

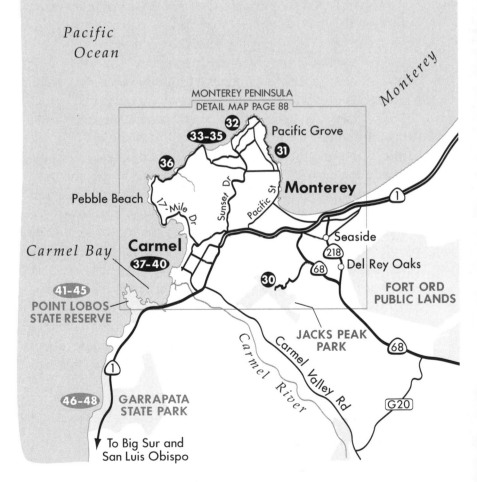

Pacific Ocean

MONTEREY PENINSULA
DETAIL MAP PAGE 88

32

33-35

Pacific Grove

31

36

Monterey

Pebble Beach

17-Mile Dr

Sunset Dr

Pacific St

Monterey

①

Seaside

Carmel Bay

Carmel

37-40

218

Del Rey Oaks

68

30

41-45
POINT LOBOS
STATE RESERVE

FORT ORD
PUBLIC LANDS

JACKS PEAK
PARK

68

①

46-48 GARRAPATA
STATE PARK

Carmel River

Carmel Valley Rd

G20

▼ To Big Sur and
San Luis Obispo

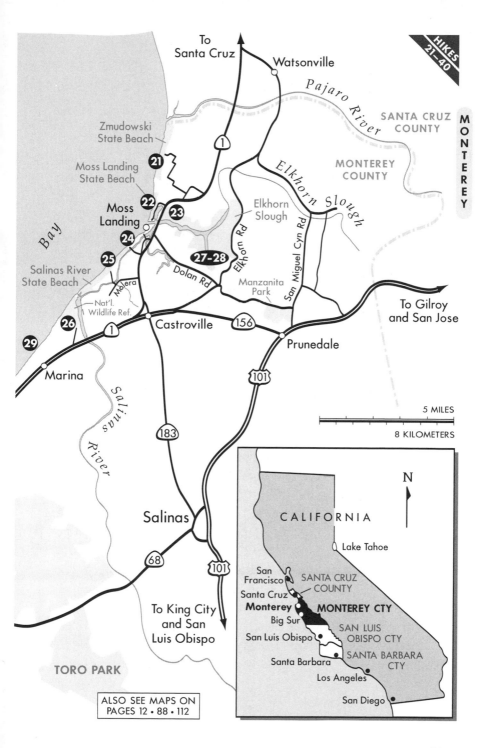

To
Santa Cruz

Watsonville

Pajaro River

SANTA CRUZ
COUNTY

**M
O
N
T
E
R
E
Y**

Zmudowski
State Beach

Moss Landing
State Beach

21

MONTEREY
COUNTY

Elkhorn Slough

Moss
Landing

22

23

Elkhorn
Slough

24

Elkhorn Rd

San Miguel Cyn Rd

27-28

Salinas River
State Beach

25

Molera

Dolan Rd

Manzanita
Park

To Gilroy
and San Jose

Nat'l.
Wildlife Ref.

26

1

Castroville

156

29

Marina

Prunedale

101

Salinas

183

River

5 MILES

8 KILOMETERS

Salinas

N

CALIFORNIA

Lake Tahoe

68

101

San
Francisco

SANTA CRUZ
COUNTY

Santa Cruz

Monterey

MONTEREY CTY

Big Sur

SAN LUIS
OBISPO CTY

To King City
and San
Luis Obispo

San Luis Obispo

SANTA BARBARA
CTY

Santa Barbara

Los Angeles

TORO PARK

San Diego

ALSO SEE MAPS ON
PAGES 12 • 88 • 112

21. Zmudowski State Beach

Hiking distance: 3.2 miles round trip
Hiking time: 1.5 hours
Elevation gain: Level
Maps: U.S.G.S. Moss Landing
Location: 20 miles north of Monterey off Highway 1

Summary of hike: Zmudowski State Beach, the northernmost beach in Monterey County, is a long, sandy beach stretching across 177 acres. The wide, isolated beach on the eastern shore of Monterey Bay is backed by sand dunes and expansive agricultural fields. The Pajaro River forms the boundary between Monterey County and Santa Cruz County, flowing into Monterey Bay at Zmudowski State Beach. To the south, the state beach ends near Moss Landing State Beach (Hike 22).

Driving directions: MONTEREY. Drive 17 miles north of Monterey on Highway 1 to Moss Landing. Drive 1.3 miles north of the Elkhorn Slough Bridge to Struve Road and turn left. Continue a quarter mile to Giberson Road and turn left. Wind through the agricultural fields and past McClusky Slough for 2 miles to the state beach parking area.

Hiking directions: Take the signed path adjacent to the information board. Walk up and over the dune, dropping onto the hard-packed sand at the oceanfront. Follow the shoreline north (right), parallel to the vegetation-covered dunes. At a half mile, as the dunes flatten out, views open up to the vast agricultural fields with scattered Monterey cypress. At just under one mile, the beach ends at the mouth of the Pajaro River at the county line. The homes across the river are in Santa Cruz County. Return south to the parking area access. Continue 0.7 miles to the Zmudowski State Beach boundary. The beach continues an additional 1.3 miles to the channel at Elkhorn Slough in Moss Landing State Beach (Hike 22).■

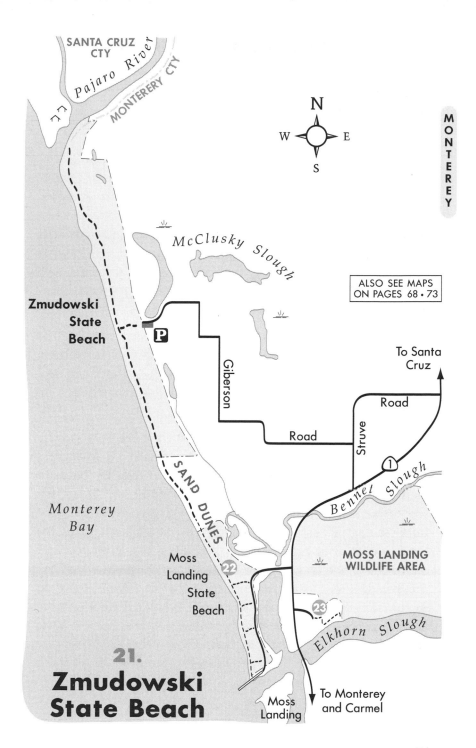

SANTA CRUZ
CTY

Pajaro River

MONTEREY CTY

N
W ⬥ E
S

MONTEREY

McClusky Slough

ALSO SEE MAPS
ON PAGES 68 • 73

Zmudowski
State
Beach

P

Giberson

To Santa
Cruz

Road

Struve

Road

1

Bennet Slough

Monterey
Bay

SAND DUNES

MOSS LANDING
WILDLIFE AREA

Moss
Landing
State
Beach

22

23

Elkhorn Slough

21.
Zmudowski
State Beach

Moss
Landing

To Monterey
and Carmel

22. Moss Landing State Beach

Hiking distance: 2.6 miles round trip
Hiking time: 1.5 hours
Elevation gain: Level
Maps: U.S.G.S. Moss Landing
Location: 18 miles north of Monterey off Highway 1

Summary of hike: Moss Landing State Beach (also known as Jetty Beach) is at the north end of Moss Landing, a small fishing community north of Monterey. The beach is bordered on the east by Bennett Slough and on the south by the rock jetty of Moss Landing Harbor. The beach extends north towards Zmudowski State Beach (Hike 21) and is backed by dunes restored with native vegetation. It is a popular beach for surfing, fishing, clamming, viewing birds, and riding horses.

Driving directions: MONTEREY. Drive 17 miles north of Monterey on Highway 1 to Moss Landing. Turn left on Jetty Road, located 0.6 miles north of the Elkhorn Slough Bridge. Drive past the entrance kiosk 0.6 miles to the parking area on the left. An entrance fee is required.

Hiking directions: Within the short half-mile span along Jetty Road are four posted beach accesses. The first and third accesses have slat-board walkways that cross up and over the dunes to the beachfront. This hike begins from the fourth access at the southern end. From the parking area, which is across the road from the third access, follow the paved road south (left) to the Moss Landing Channel at the mouth of Elkhorn Slough. (If you walk out to sea on the rock jetty, be cautious and use careful footing.) The views extend across Monterey Bay from Pacific Grove to Santa Cruz. Follow the hard-packed sand north between the dunes and the ocean, passing the other beach accesses. Moss Landing State Beach officially ends at 0.8 miles, but the sandy beachfront continues toward Zmudowski State Beach (Hike 21) at 1.3 miles. Choose your own turn-around spot. ■

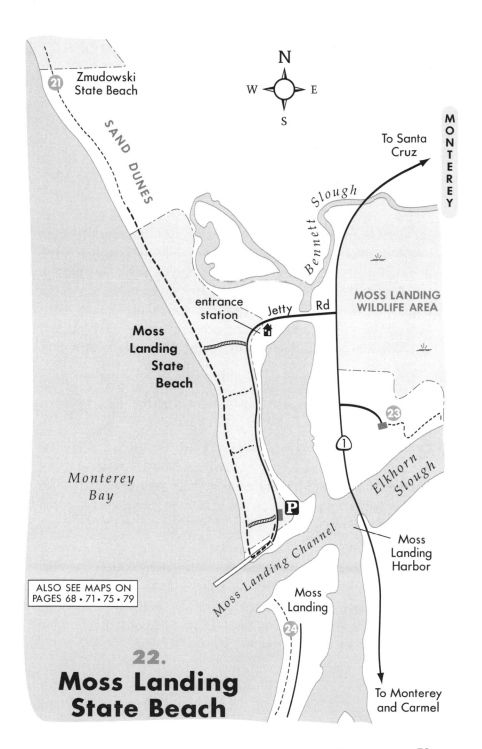

N
W ◆ E
S

Zmudowski
State Beach

SAND DUNES

To Santa
Cruz

MONTEREY

Bennett Slough

entrance
station

Jetty Rd

MOSS LANDING
WILDLIFE AREA

Moss
Landing
State
Beach

Monterey
Bay

P

Elkhorn Slough

Moss
Landing
Harbor

Moss Landing Channel

ALSO SEE MAPS ON
PAGES 68 • 71 • 75 • 79

Moss
Landing

22.
Moss Landing
State Beach

To Monterey
and Carmel

23. Moss Landing State Wildlife Area

Hiking distance: 0.8 miles round trip
Hiking time: 30 minutes
Elevation gain: Level
Maps: U.S.G.S. Moss Landing
Location: 17.5 miles north of Monterey off Highway 1

Summary of hike: The Moss Landing Wildlife Area is an 800-acre wetland on the north bank of Elkhorn Slough at Moss Landing. The coastal wetlands and marshes provide protection for wildlife and an area for scientific study. It is the north-south migration route for coastal birds and a nesting area for the Snowy Plovers. During April and May, harbor seals give birth in the Elkhorn Slough channel. This short trail enters the Moss Landing State Wildlife Area from the southwest corner along Elkhorn Slough. The path meanders across dikes (levees) and past salt harvesting ponds dating back to the 1800s. Notice the tidal fluctuations in the creeks flowing through the mud flats.

The extensive trail system at the northern entrance of the wildlife area has been permanently closed by the Department of Fish, Wildlife and Game due to public abuse.

Driving directions: MONTEREY. Drive 17.5 miles north of Monterey on Highway 1 to the Elkhorn Slough Bridge at Moss Landing, just beyond the towering smokestacks. Continue across the bridge and turn right on the dirt road. Drive past the old buildings, following the signs to the wildlife trail and parking area 0.2 miles ahead.

Hiking directions: Walk to the left (east) and cross the wooden bridge. Bear right to the edge of Elkhorn Slough. Follow the levees along the north bank of the slough to an observation platform. The levee is closed beyond the lookout to protect the nesting area for the endangered Snowy Plover.■

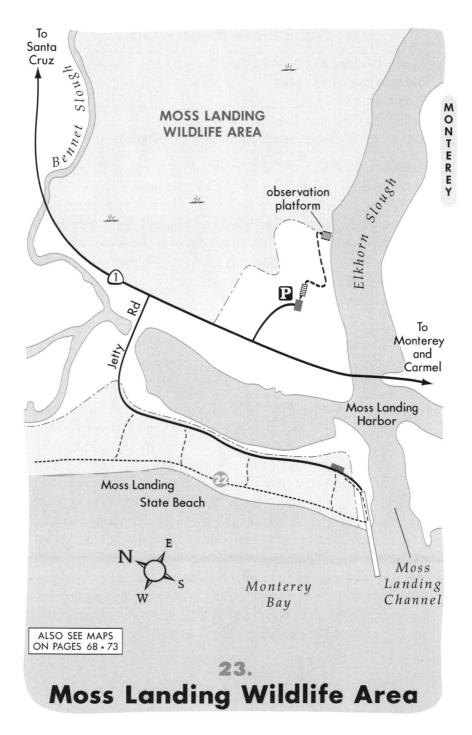

To
Santa
Cruz

Bennet Slough

**MOSS LANDING
WILDLIFE AREA**

M O N T E R E Y

observation
platform

Elkhorn Slough

1

Jetty Rd

P

To
Monterey
and
Carmel

Moss Landing
Harbor

22

Moss Landing
State Beach

N
E
S
W

*Monterey
Bay*

*Moss
Landing
Channel*

ALSO SEE MAPS
ON PAGES 68 • 73

23.
Moss Landing Wildlife Area

24. Old Salinas River Road

Hiking distance: 1.5-mile loop
Hiking time: 45 minutes
Elevation gain: Level
Maps: U.S.G.S. Moss Landing
Location: 17 miles north of Monterey off Highway 1

map
page 79

Summary of hike: The Old Salinas River Road is an unpaved walking road (closed to vehicles) that parallels the wide, slow-rolling slough. The slough, formerly part of the Salinas River, runs between the community of Moss Landing and the Salinas River Wildlife Area (Hike 26). The trail begins in Moss Landing and follows dunes to the northern boundary of Salinas River State Beach (Hike 25).

Driving directions: MONTEREY. Drive 17 miles north of Monterey on Highway 1 to Moss Landing. Turn left on Sandholdt Road, located a quarter mile south of the towering smokestacks. Cross Sandholdt Bridge over the Old Salinas River, and turn left into the Salinas River State Beach parking lot.

Hiking directions: From the south end of the parking lot, take the unpaved gravel road between the Old Salinas River channel on the east and the dunes on the west. At 0.7 miles the road exits at the parking area at the west end of Potrero Road at the Salinas River State Beach boundary. Straight ahead is the Dunes Trail that crosses the state beach to the access off of Molera Road (Hike 25). For this hike, take the trail to the right, crossing over the scrub-covered dunes to the hard-packed sand at the beachfront. Follow the shoreline north, returning to the beach access. Cross over the dunes and back to the trailhead parking lot.

To extend the hike, continue north along the oceanfront for 0.3 miles to the southern end of the Moss Landing Channel at the mouth of Elkhorn Slough.■

25. Salinas River State Beach
SOUTHERN ACCESS

Hiking distance: 2.2 miles round trip
Hiking time: 1.5 hours
Elevation gain: Near level
Maps: U.S.G.S. Moss Landing
Location: 16 miles north of Monterey off Highway 1

map
next page

Summary of hike: Salinas River State Beach, just north of Marina, stretches along the coast between the ocean and the Old Salinas River channel. Driftwood is often scattered across the beach, backed by fragile, vegetation-covered sand dunes. A hiking and equestrian trail leads through the rolling dunes.

Driving directions: MONTEREY. Drive 15.5 miles north of Monterey on Highway 1 towards Moss Landing. Turn left on Molera Road, located 0.9 miles past the turnoff to Highway 183 South/Castroville. Drive 0.8 miles on Molera Road to Monterey Dunes Way. Turn right and continue 0.5 miles to the parking lot at the end of the road.

Hiking directions: Take the signed boardwalk trail 30 yards west to a trail split. The left fork leads over the dune to the beachfront. Begin the loop to the right, leaving the boardwalk. A short distance ahead is another trail split. Again, the left fork leads to the beach. Stay to the right on the Dunes Trail, and cross the rolling dunes. The views look inland over the wetlands and agricultural fields, with occasional glimpses of the ocean and the bay. The sandy path meanders through the dunes for a mile and gradually descends to the Potrero Road parking lot at the north end of the state park. Straight ahead is the Old Salinas River Road (Hike 24), a dirt road that parallels the Old Salinas River to Moss Landing. Bear left and cross over the dunes to the hard-packed sand at the oceanfront. Follow the shoreline to the left, parallel to the dunes that were just crossed. Watch for the access trail that crosses the dunes to the parking lot. If you reach the Monterey Dunes Colony, you have passed the beach access trail by 100 yards. ■

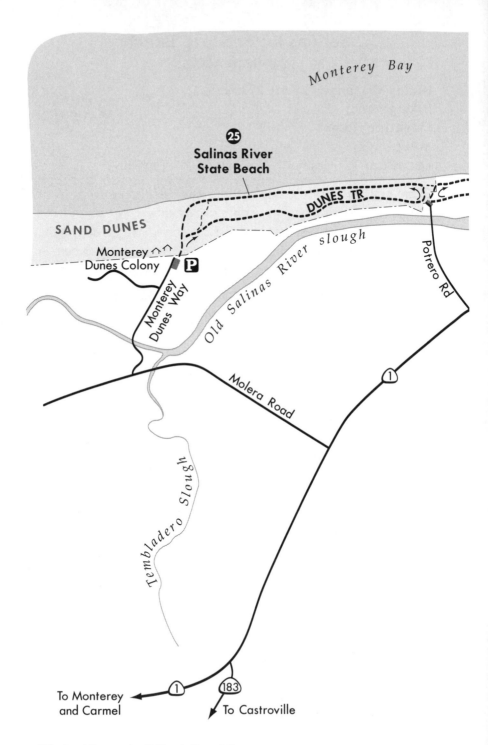

Monterey Bay

㉕
**Salinas River
State Beach**

DUNES TR

SAND DUNES

Monterey
Dunes Colony

Old Salinas River slough

Potrero Rd

Monterey
Dunes Way

Molera Road

①

Tembladero Slough

To Monterey
and Carmel ① 183
To Castroville

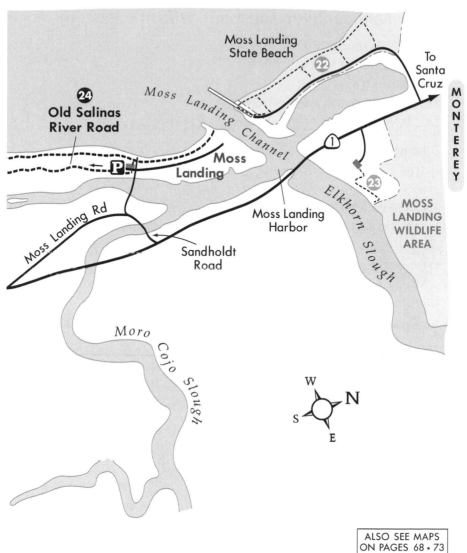

ALSO SEE MAPS
ON PAGES 68 • 73

HIKE 24
Old Salinas River Road
HIKE 25
Salinas River State Beach

26. Salinas River National Wildlife Refuge

Hiking distance: 4 miles round trip
Hiking time: 2 hour
Elevation gain: Level
Maps: U.S.G.S. Marina and Moss Landing
Location: 13 miles north of Monterey off Highway 1

Summary of hike: The 518-acre Salinas River National Wildlife Refuge is a sanctuary for nesting and migrating birds. It is a great area for wildlife observation, photography, fishing, and hiking. The trail through the preserve crosses grassland meadows to the bird-filled South Marsh, a brackish lagoon and estuary. A ridge of dunes separates South Marsh from the ocean. The hike continues past undisturbed, vegetation-covered dunes to the isolated, sandy oceanfront. From the trailhead, another path leads to the banks of the wide Salinas River.

Driving directions: MONTEREY. Drive 13 miles north of Monterey on Highway 1 to the Del Monte Boulevard exit, located between the Reservation Road and Nashua-Molera Road exits. Turn left and drive straight ahead 0.6 miles to the end of the dirt road at the signed trailhead and parking area.

Hiking directions: Walk past the metal gate to a trail junction. The right fork is a short side trip on a two-track path to the banks of the Salinas River. The Beach Trail to the left heads west across the flat grassy meadows to the edge of South Marsh, a lagoon and estuary. Bear left towards the coastal dunes. Cross the north edge of the scrub-covered dunes along the south side of the lagoon, reaching the sandy beach at 0.8 miles. At the oceanfront, follow the sandy shoreline for a little more than a mile to the lagoon at the mouth of the Salinas River, adjacent to Salinas River State Beach. The river attracts brown pelicans, ducks, and gulls. Return along the same route. ■

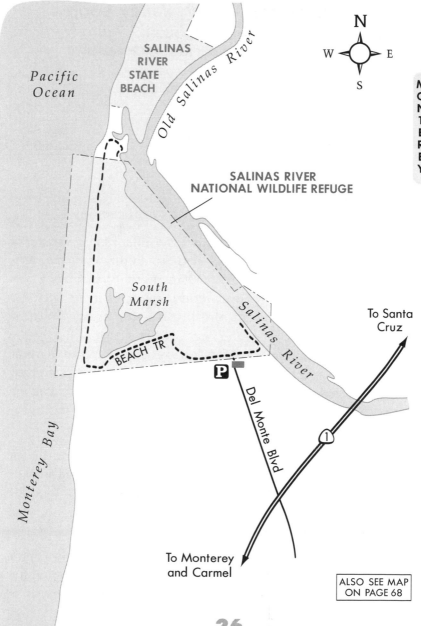

N
W E
S

Pacific
Ocean

SALINAS
RIVER
STATE
BEACH

Old Salinas River

Salinas River

SALINAS RIVER
NATIONAL WILDLIFE REFUGE

South
Marsh

Salinas River

To Santa
Cruz

BEACH TR

P

Del Monte Blvd

1

Monterey Bay

To Monterey
and Carmel

ALSO SEE MAP
ON PAGE 68

26.
Salinas River
National Wildlife Refuge

27. Five Fingers—Long Valley Loop
ELKHORN SLOUGH
NATIONAL ESTUARINE RESEARCH RESERVE
1700 Elkhorn Road · Watsonville
Open Wednesday—Sunday · 9 a.m.—5 p.m.

Hiking distance: 2.3 miles round trip
Hiking time: 1.5 hours
Elevation gain: Near level
Maps: U.S.G.S. Prunedale
      Elkhorn Slough Trail Map
Location: 22.5 miles north of Monterey off Highway 1

map
page 85

Summary of hike: Elkhorn Slough is a tidal inlet in Monterey Bay midway between Monterey and Santa Cruz. The main channel extends seven miles across 3,000 acres of marshland and tidal flats from Moss Landing. The wetland supports more than 250 species of birds, 80 species of fish, and 400 species of invertebrates. This hike begins in the heart of the slough at the 1,400-acre Elkhorn Slough National Estuarine Research Reserve. The trail leads to the five fingers of Parson's Slough (a smaller side channel), an overlook, and a wildlife blind. The path winds through coastal marshland, meadows, native oak woodlands, and eucalyptus groves.

Driving directions: MONTEREY. Drive 17 miles north of Monterey on Highway 1 to Dolan Road (at the towering smokestacks). Turn right and drive 3.6 miles to Elkhorn Road. Turn left and go 2 miles to the visitor center and parking lot on the left. An entrance fee is required.

Hiking directions: Take the paved path past the visitor center 100 yards to the signed Long Valley Loop Trail. Bear left on the wide grassy path. Cross the meadow and descend through an oak grove to Parson's Slough. Follow the north edge of the slough under an oak canopy. A boardwalk pier on the left extends out into the slough. Loop back to the north, and gently climb up the hillside to a posted junction. Bear left on the Five Fingers Loop

Trail, and gradually descend to a junction. Detour to the left and walk 0.3 miles to the fenced Parson's Slough Overlook. Return to the junction and continue 100 yards to another trail fork. Take the left fork 130 yards to a long set of stairs. Descend to the wildlife blind on the edge of the slough. Return to the main trail again, and bear left through a eucalyptus grove to a 4-way junction with the South Marsh Loop Trail (Hike 28). Bear right and complete the loop back at the visitor center. ■

28. South Marsh Loop Trail
ELKHORN SLOUGH
NATIONAL ESTUARINE RESEARCH RESERVE

Hiking distance: 3.3 miles round trip
Hiking time: 1.5 hours
Elevation gain: Near level
Maps: U.S.G.S. Prunedale
        Elkhorn Slough Trail Map
Location: 22.5 miles north of Monterey off Highway 1

map
page 85

Summary of hike: Elkhorn Slough is an undisturbed 3,000-acre wetland. The marshlands and tidal flats are a resting, nesting, and feeding ground for tens of thousands of migratory birds. This hike begins at the Elkhorn Slough National Estuarine Research Reserve. The trail passes through native oak woodlands and grasslands to overlooks of the marsh and slough, old dairy barns, a heron rookery pond, and an "art in nature" project on the banks of Elkhorn Slough.

Driving directions: Same as Hike 27.

Hiking directions: From the visitor center, take the paved path west. Pass the Long Valley Loop Trail and the Five Fingers Loop Trail on the left (Hike 27) to the Elkhorn Slough Overlook. Descend on the wide, unpaved trail to a 4-way junction near the old abandoned Elkhorn dairy barn. Begin the loop on the left fork of the South Marsh Loop Trail, walking toward the barn. Skirt around the south side of the barn, and pass a wooden boardwalk extending out to the marsh on the left. Cross a footbridge over a channel of South Marsh, and follow the raised path across the wetland to a T-junction. Take a detour on the left fork, pass Fadley Dock, and continue towards Hummingbird Island. Walk through a trail gate and cross the railroad tracks, reaching the main channel of Elkhorn Slough in a eucalyptus grove. Bear left along the slough past a row of eucalyptus trees to a small pond and arch at the "art in nature" project. Complete the small loop at the railroad tracks, and return to the South Marsh Loop Trail. Pass a posted junction to the North Marsh Overlook on the left. Cross a wooden boardwalk along the rookery pond. Curve south through an oak grove while overlooking South Marsh, reaching Cattail Swale at an unsigned trail split. Stay to the right and complete the loop back at the barn.■

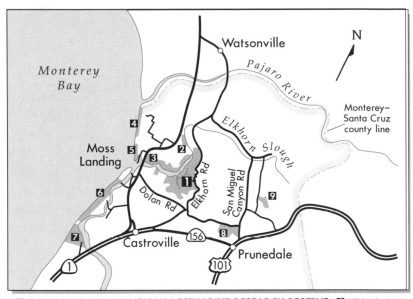

1 ELKHORN SLOUGH NATIONAL ESTUARINE RESEARCH RESERVE **2** KIRBY PARK
3 MOSS LANDING WILDLIFE AREA   **4** ZMUDOWSKI STATE BEACH   **5** MOSS LANDING
STATE BEACH   **6** SALINAS RIVER STATE BEACH   **7** SALINAS RIVER NATIONAL
WILDLIFE REFUGE   **8** MANZANITA PARK   **9** ROYAL OAKS PARK

HIKES 27 • 28
Elkhorn Slough
NATIONAL ESTUARINE RESEARCH RESERVE

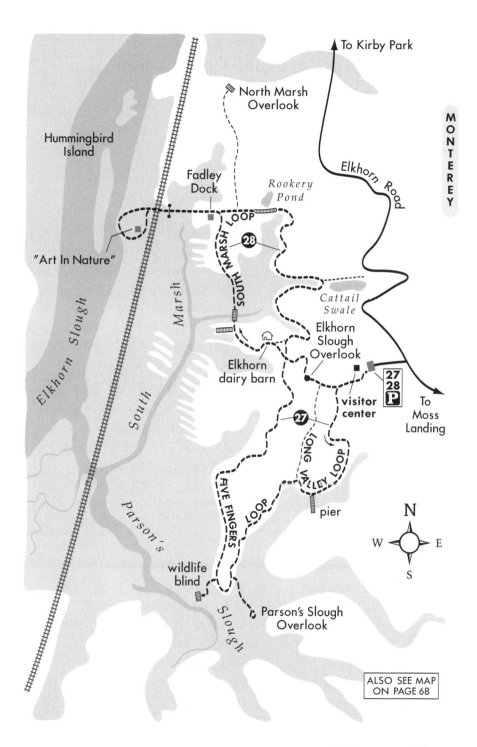

To Kirby Park

North Marsh
Overlook

Hummingbird
Island

Elkhorn Road

Fadley
Dock

Rookery
Pond

"Art In Nature"

SOUTH MARSH LOOP

28

Elkhorn Slough

Cattail
Swale

South Marsh

Elkhorn
Slough
Overlook

Elkhorn
dairy barn

27
28
P

visitor
center

To
Moss
Landing

27

LONG VALLEY LOOP

FIVE FINGERS LOOP

Parson's

pier

N

W ◇ E

S

wildlife
blind

Slough

Parson's Slough
Overlook

ALSO SEE MAP
ON PAGE 68

120 Great Hikes - **85**

29. Marina State Beach and Marina Dunes Open Space

Hiking distance: 2 miles round trip
Hiking time: 1 hour
Elevation gain: 100 feet
Maps: U.S.G.S. Marina
Location: 8 miles north of Monterey at the town of Marina

Summary of hike: The 170-acre Marina State Beach is home to huge dunes and sandy cliffs overlooking the Pacific along Monterey Bay. The Dunes Trail at the beach crosses rolling 80-foot living sand dunes stabilized by thick mats of low-growing vegetation. An interpretive nature trail follows a 2,000-foot-long boardwalk through the dune restoration area. The trail leads to the beach and an observation platform that overlooks Monterey Bay. Interpretive displays describe the rare and endangered vegetation, invasive plants, and creatures living in the dunes. Several trails cross the dunes and cliffs for continued exploration. The state park is also a popular hang gliding launch site.

Driving directions: MONTEREY. Access 1: Drive 8 miles north of Monterey on Highway 1 to Marina, and take the Reservation Road exit. Turn left and drive 0.3 miles into the Marina State Beach parking lot, just past Dunes Drive.

Access 2: Marina Dunes Open Space: Head north on Dunes Drive a half mile to the signed trailhead at the end of the road.

Access 3: The southern access to Marina State Beach is off of Del Monte Boulevard at the intersection of Lake Drive and Lake Court.

Hiking directions: Access 1: The Marina State Beach parking lot—at the west end of Reservation Road—is perched above the ocean with unobstructed views of the bay. After enjoying the views, walk to the signed trailhead by the entrance road. The path winds south through the dunes on a wooden boardwalk. Numerous benches and interpretive displays line the trail. The dune path exits on the sandy beachfront at just under a half mile. Return via the beach or retrace your steps.

Access 2: The Marina Dunes Open Space trail—at the north end of Dunes Drive—is a 0.7-mile round trip hike. The wide, hard-packed sand path begins at the display panels and heads west to the crest of the huge dune. Gradually descend towards the ocean in the softer sand to the interpretive displays on the low bluffs overlooking the bay. The rolling dunes can be explored on a variety of distinct paths.

Access 3: From the southern access to Marina State Beach—off Lake Drive—walk past the trailhead display. Climb up the steep scrub-covered dune on a wide sand path to the ridge. Sharply descend to the edge of the sandy cliffs overlooking the isolated oceanfront. Towering 150-foot wind-sculpted sand cliffs, the tallest along Monterey Bay, back the remote beach.■

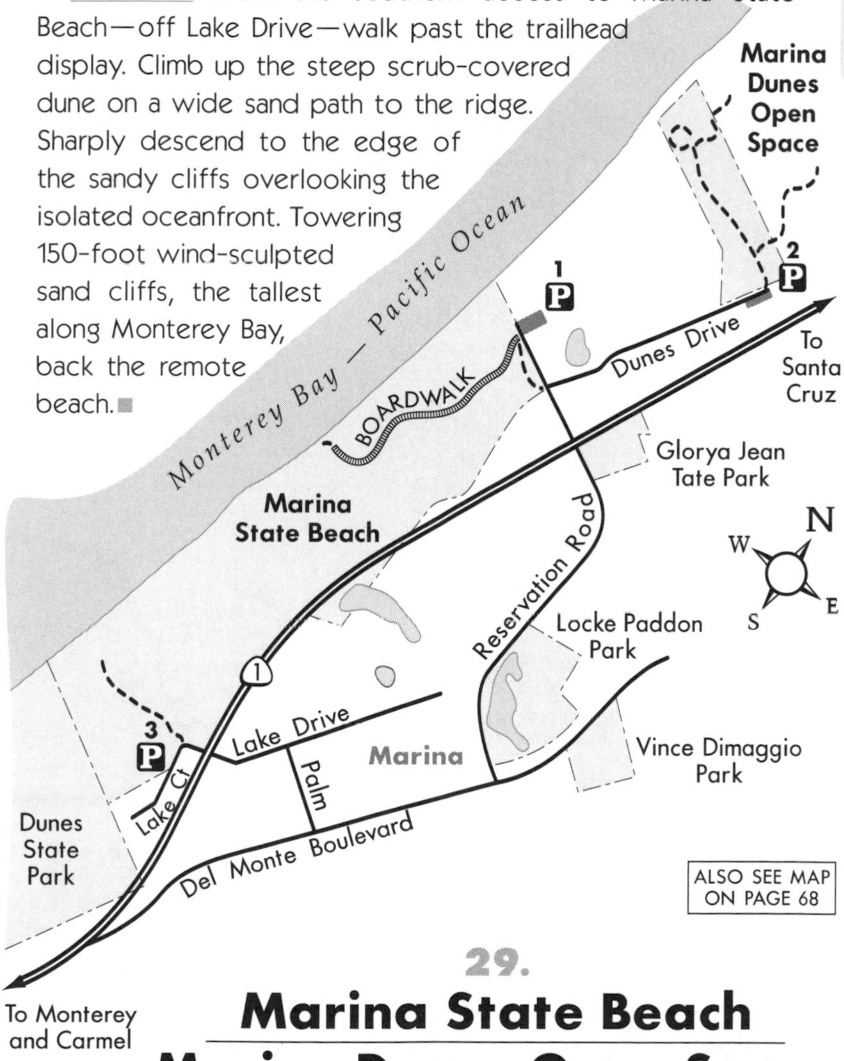

Marina
Dunes
Open
Space

Monterey Bay — Pacific Ocean

1 P

2 P

Dunes Drive

BOARDWALK

To
Santa
Cruz

Glorya Jean
Tate Park

Marina
State Beach

Reservation Road

N
W   E
S

Locke Paddon
Park

1

Lake Drive

Marina

Palm

Vince Dimaggio
Park

3 P

Lake Ct

Dunes
State
Park

Del Monte Boulevard

ALSO SEE MAP
ON PAGE 68

29.
Marina State Beach
Marine Dunes Open Space

To Monterey
and Carmel

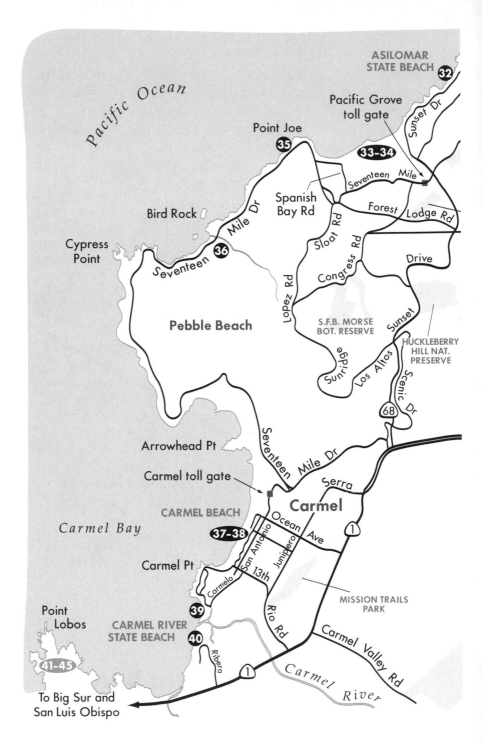

Pacific Ocean

ASILOMAR
STATE BEACH **32**

Pacific Grove
toll gate

Sunset Dr

Point Joe
35

33-34

Seventeen Mile

Spanish
Bay Rd

Forest Lodge Rd

Bird Rock

Seventeen Mile Dr

Sloat Rd

Congress Rd

Drive

Cypress
Point

36

Lopez Rd

S.F.B. MORSE
BOT. RESERVE

Sunset

HUCKLEBERRY
HILL NAT.
PRESERVE

Pebble Beach

Sunridge

Los Altos

Scenic Dr

68

Arrowhead Pt

Seventeen Mile Dr

Serra

Carmel toll gate

Carmel

CARMEL BEACH

Ocean Ave

1

Carmel Bay

37-38

San Antonio

Juniper

Carmel Pt

Carmelo

13th

MISSION TRAILS
PARK

Point
Lobos

39

CARMEL RIVER
STATE BEACH

40

Rio Rd

Carmel Valley Rd

41-45

Ribera

1

Carmel River

To Big Sur and
San Luis Obispo

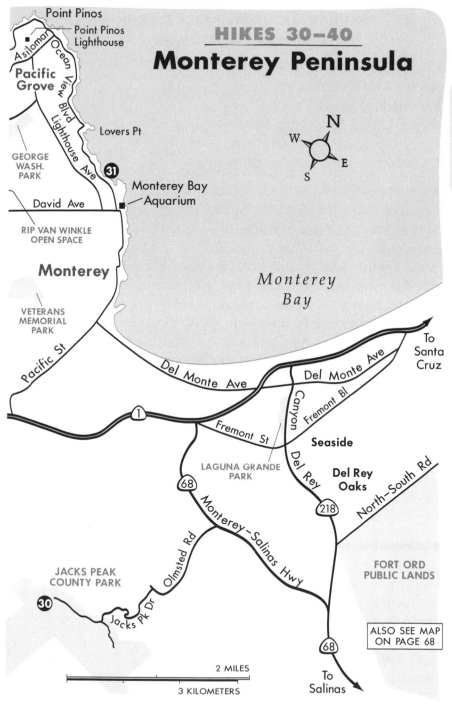

Point Pinos

Point Pinos
Lighthouse

Asilomar

Ocean View Blvd

Lighthouse Ave

**Pacific
Grove**

Lovers Pt

GEORGE
WASH.
PARK

David Ave

RIP VAN WINKLE
OPEN SPACE

Monterey

VETERANS
MEMORIAL
PARK

③①

Monterey Bay
Aquarium

N
W   E
S

*Monterey
Bay*

To
Santa
Cruz

Pacific St

Del Monte Ave

Del Monte Ave

Canyon

Fremont Bl

Fremont St

①

Seaside

LAGUNA GRANDE
PARK

Del Rey

**Del Rey
Oaks**

North–South Rd

⑥⑧

②①⑧

FORT ORD
PUBLIC LANDS

JACKS PEAK
COUNTY PARK

Olmsted Rd

Jacks Pk Dr

Monterey – Salinas Hwy

③⓪

ALSO SEE MAP
ON PAGE 68

2 MILES

3 KILOMETERS

⑥⑧

To
Salinas

30. Skyline Trail and Jacks Peak
JACKS PEAK COUNTY PARK

Hiking distance: 1.2-mile loop
Hiking time: 40 minutes
Elevation gain: 200 feet
Maps: U.S.G.S. Seaside and Monterey
       Jacks Peak County Park map
Location: 2 miles southeast of Monterey

Summary of hike: Jacks Peak County Park sits on a wooded ridge separating the Monterey Peninsula from Carmel Valley. The Skyline Trail, a self-guided nature trail set amid native Monterey pines, traverses Jacks Peak to the 1,068-foot summit. Jacks Peak is the highest point on the Monterey Peninsula in this 525-acre ridgetop preserve. From the peak are picturesque bird's-eye views of Carmel Valley, the Santa Lucia Mountains, Carmel, Point Lobos, the Monterey Peninsula, and the Pacific. Interpretive pamphlets highlight the geology, forest ecology, plants, and birds. Several other trails crisscross through the park. For continued hiking, consult the park map, available at the entrance station.

Driving directions: MONTEREY. From Highway 1 in Monterey, take the Highway 68 East/Salinas exit, and drive 1.6 miles to the signed turnoff for Jacks Peak Park at Olmsted Road. Turn right and continue 1 mile to Jacks Peak Drive. Turn left and drive 1.2 miles to the entrance station and road split. Turn right and follow the park road 0.6 miles to the Jacks Peak parking area at the end of the road. An entrance fee is required.

Hiking directions: Take the signed Skyline Trail at the far southwest end of the parking area. Head gently uphill through the Monterey pine forest on the soft needle-covered path. Traverse the hillside to a scenic vista with a map highlighting landmarks in Monterey Bay. A short distance ahead, cross the Coffeeberry Trail, and pass a wall of aguajito shale on the left, a whitish rock with marine fossils. Continue to a junction with the Jacks Peak Trail. Detour left about 60 yards to the bench on a round grassy knoll at Jacks Peak. From the peak, the Jacks Peak Trail returns directly to the parking area. For this hike, return to the Skyline Trail and continue south, walking down steps. Bear left and traverse the southern slope overlooking Carmel Valley. Switchbacks descend through the forest. Curve left, leaving the upper slopes of Carmel Valley to a T-junction with the Iris Trail. Take the left fork, passing the Rhus Trail on the right. Complete the loop on the south side of the parking area.■

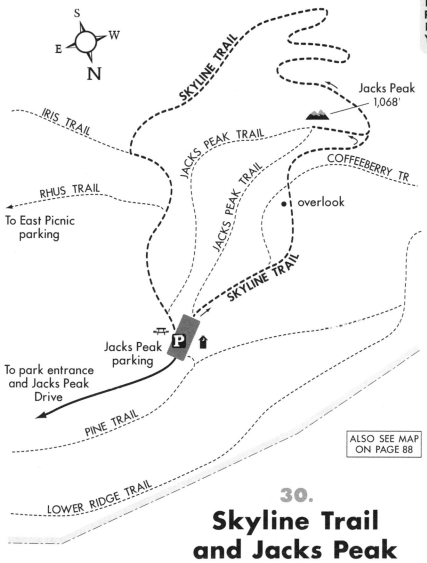

ALSO SEE MAP
ON PAGE 88

30.
Skyline Trail
and Jacks Peak

31. Monterey Bay Coastal Trail
MONTEREY BAY AQUARIUM to POINT PINOS

Hiking distance: 4.6 miles round trip
Hiking time: 2 hours
Elevation gain: Level
Maps: U.S.G.S. Monterey
Location: Monterey · Pacific Grove

Summary of hike: The Monterey Bay Coastal Trail follows the beautiful rocky coastline along the blufftop in Pacific Grove on the Monterey Peninsula. Beginning at the Monterey Bay Aquarium, the trail threads through several parks en route to the northern tip of Pacific Grove at Point Pinos. Parklands surround the entire peninsula on the coastal side of Ocean View Boulevard. The coastal route passes dramatic rock formations, tidepools, small beach coves, and overlooks. The waters surrounding the peninsula are part of the Pacific Grove Marine Gardens Fish Refuge, a national marine sanctuary.

Driving directions: MONTEREY. The hike begins by the Monterey Bay Aquarium in Monterey, at the intersection of Ocean View Boulevard and David Avenue. From Highway 1, take the Monterey exit and follow the signs to the aquarium.

Hiking directions: From the aquarium, take the paved path northwest, parallel to Ocean View Boulevard. Follow the coastline past beautiful rock formations and small pocket beaches. Stay to the right of the paved bike path. Continue past Victorian homes and benches along the trail. At Berwick Park, a side path meanders to the right, rejoining the main trail a short distance ahead. At one mile, Ocean View Boulevard and the trail turn right at Lovers Point. Explore the rocky granite headland jutting out into the ocean. Stairways descend from the grassy picnic area to the sandy beaches of Otter Cove, Lovers Point Beach, and Pacific Grove Beach. For a 2-mile round-trip hike, turn around here.

To continue, follow the cliffside trail past the promontory. Weave through Perkins Park, a landscaped park with stairways, to small beach pockets. The trail overlooks the marine refuge past continuous rocky coves and tidepools to Point Pinos at the north tip of Pacific Grove. Return by retracing your steps.■

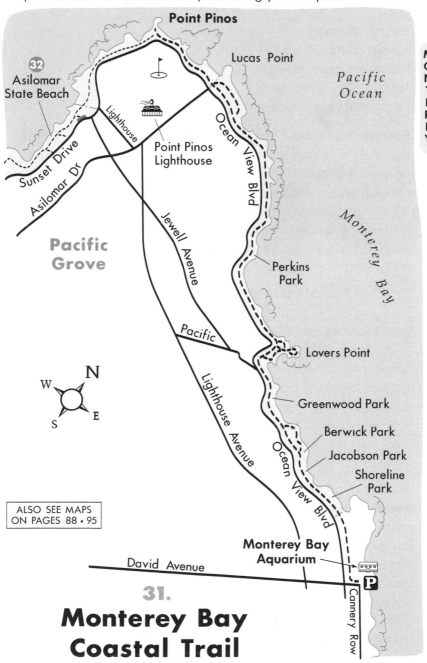

Point Pinos

Lucas Point

Pacific Ocean

32

Asilomar State Beach

Lighthouse

Point Pinos Lighthouse

Ocean View Blvd

Sunset Drive

Asilomar Dr

Monterey Bay

Pacific Grove

Jewell Avenue

Perkins Park

Pacific

Lovers Point

N
W   E
S

Lighthouse Avenue

Ocean View Blvd

Greenwood Park

Berwick Park

Jacobson Park

Shoreline Park

ALSO SEE MAPS ON PAGES 88 • 95

Monterey Bay Aquarium

P

David Avenue

Cannery Row

31.
Monterey Bay Coastal Trail

32. Asilomar State Beach and Coast Trail
PACIFIC GROVE • MONTEREY PENINSULA

Hiking distance: 2.4 miles round trip
Hiking time: 1.5 hours
Elevation gain: Level
Maps: U.S.G.S. Monterey
Location: Pacific Grove

Summary of hike: Asilomar State Beach (meaning "refuge by the sea") encompasses 107 acres at the windswept, southwest corner of Pacific Grove on the Monterey Peninsula. The state park has an exposed rocky headland with spectacular views of the Pacific Ocean. The coastal park has tidepools, dunes, cove beaches, a wind-sculpted Monterey pine and cypress forest, sheltered overlooks, and boardwalk paths. The park includes the Asilomar Conference Grounds, a national historic landmark.

Driving directions: PACIFIC GROVE: HIGHWAY 1. Asilomar State Park is on the western coastline in Pacific Grove. From Highway 1, take Highway 68 West (which becomes Sunset Drive) to the ocean. Park in the pullouts on the left along the ocean side of Sunset Drive, south of Jewell Avenue.

PACIFIC GROVE: DOWNTOWN. From downtown Pacific Grove, follow Ocean View Boulevard around the northern tip of Monterey Bay. After rounding the tip, Ocean View Boulevard becomes Sunset Drive. Park in the pullouts south of Jewell Avenue.

Hiking directions: Take the signed trailhead on the gravel paths leading toward the shoreline. To the right is a covered overlook. Follow the meandering trail left (south) above the rocky coves and tidepools, crossing boardwalks and bridges. Numerous connector trails along Sunset Drive join the main path. The trail connects with the Links Nature Walk (Hike 33) at the south end of the state park by the sandy shoreline adjacent to Asilomar Beach (also known as North Moss Beach) in Spanish Bay. Across Sunset Drive, a boardwalk crosses the dunes and weaves through a forest of Monterey pines to the Asilomar Conference Grounds. Return along the same route. ■

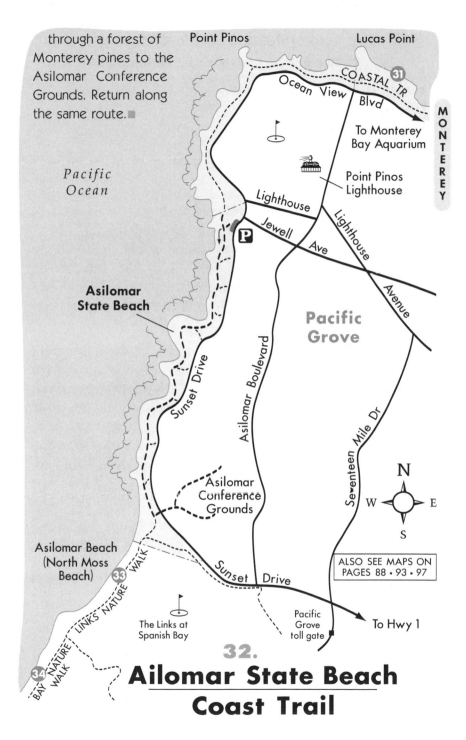

Point Pinos

Lucas Point

COASTAL TR

31

Ocean View Blvd

To Monterey Bay Aquarium

Point Pinos Lighthouse

MONTEREY

Pacific Ocean

Lighthouse

Jewell Ave

Lighthouse Avenue

P

Asilomar State Beach

Pacific Grove

Asilomar Boulevard

Sunset Drive

Seventeen Mile Dr

Asilomar Conference Grounds

N
W   E
S

Asilomar Beach (North Moss Beach)

33

BAY NATURE LINKS NATURE WALK

34

Sunset Drive

The Links at Spanish Bay

Pacific Grove toll gate

To Hwy 1

ALSO SEE MAPS ON PAGES 88 • 93 • 97

32.

Ailomar State Beach
Coast Trail

33. The Links Nature Walk at Spanish Bay
PEBBLE BEACH • MONTEREY PENINSULA

Hiking distance: 1.3-mile loop
Hiking time: 1 hour
Elevation gain: 150 feet
Maps: U.S.G.S. Monterey
Pebble Beach Nature Trails booklet
Location: Pebble Beach

Summary of hike: The Links Nature Walk is a boardwalk trail that crosses the windswept dunes between the Del Monte Forest and the broad, sandy North Moss Beach on the Monterey Peninsula. The trail begins at The Inn at Spanish Bay and follows the coastline around the perimeter of The Links at Spanish Bay Golf Course, returning through a forest of Monterey pines and coastal live oaks.

Driving directions: PEBBLE BEACH. Access to the trail is from the scenic Seventeen Mile Drive, a toll road in Pebble Beach. From the Pacific Grove toll gate off of Sunset Drive, drive 0.3 miles on Seventeen Mile Drive to the turnoff on the right for The Inn at Spanish Bay. Park in the lot near the entrance to the lodge.

CARMEL. From the Carmel toll gate off of Ocean Avenue in downtown Carmel, drive 0.2 miles to Seventeen Mile Drive. Turn left and continue 9 miles to the turnoff on the left for The Inn at Spanish Bay. Park in the lot near the entrance to the lodge.

Hiking directions: The trail begins on the ocean side of the lodge. Take the paved path right to the signed boardwalk trail on the left. Head towards the ocean, weaving through the golf course to a boardwalk on the right. Bear right, crossing the dunes to the oceanfront at a T-junction. The left fork is the Bay Nature Walk (Hike 34). Take the right fork on the Links Nature Walk, following the boardwalk north along the coastline. Pass rock outcroppings, tidepools, and a beach access on the left at the south border of Asilomar Beach. Continue north for a short distance along Asilomar Beach. Curve inland, crossing over scrub-covered dunes, bordered by the golf course on the right and Sunset Drive to the left. Cross a wooden footbridge over a stream, parallel to Sunset Drive. Pick up the signed trail on the right and head southeast, away from the road. Wind through a Monterey pine forest to Seventeen Mile Road. Parallel the road on the forested path, crossing the entrance road to The Inn at Spanish Bay. Continue to a junction with the Bay Nature Walk. Bear right past a picnic area, completing the loop at the inn.

To extend the hike by one mile, continue with Hike 34.■

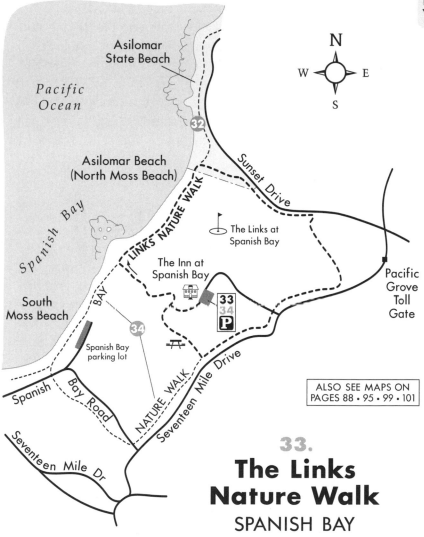

Asilomar State Beach

Pacific Ocean

N

W ← → E

S

Asilomar Beach (North Moss Beach)

Sunset Drive

Spanish Bay

LINKS NATURE WALK

The Links at Spanish Bay

The Inn at Spanish Bay

BAY

South Moss Beach

33
34
P

Pacific Grove Toll Gate

Spanish Bay parking lot

Spanish Bay Road

NATURE WALK

Seventeen Mile Drive

Seventeen Mile Dr

ALSO SEE MAPS ON
PAGES 88 • 95 • 99 • 101

33.
The Links
Nature Walk
SPANISH BAY

34. The Bay Nature Walk at Spanish Bay
PEBBLE BEACH • MONTEREY PENINSULA

Hiking distance: 1-mile loop
Hiking time: 30 minutes
Elevation gain: 120 feet
Maps: U.S.G.S. Monterey
        Pebble Beach Nature Trails booklet
Location: Pebble Beach

Summary of hike: The Bay Nature Walk and the Links Nature Walk (Hike 33) are two short trails at Spanish Bay in Pebble Beach. This hike along the Bay Nature Walk begins at The Inn at Spanish Bay between the Del Monte Forest and North Moss Beach, a broad white sand beach. The trail crosses the windswept dunes along a boardwalk to the Spanish Bay shoreline. The path returns through the dunes and weaves through a forest of Monterey pines and coastal live oaks.

Driving directions: Same as Hike 33.

Hiking directions: The trail begins on the ocean (west) side of the lodge. Take the paved path right to the signed boardwalk trail on the left. Head towards the ocean, weaving through the golf course to a boardwalk on the right. Follow the boardwalk, crossing the dunes to the oceanfront at a T-junction. The right fork is the Links Nature Walk (Hike 33). Take the left fork on the Bay Nature Walk, following the boardwalk south past rock formations and tidepools along Spanish Bay. Stay to the right along the shoreline, skirting the Spanish Bay parking lot. A short distance past the parking lot, cross Spanish Bay Road to a wooden footbridge on the inland side of the road. The sandy path crosses the dunes parallel to Spanish Bay Road. Curve left at the restrooms, and cross the road again just before Seventeen Mile Drive. The forested path follows the west side of Seventeen Mile Drive through groves of Monterey pines to a junction near the lodge. Bear left past a picnic area, completing the loop at the inn. ■

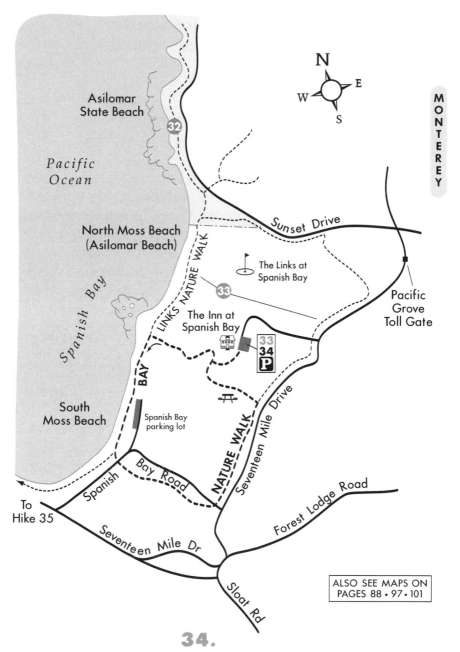

Asilomar
State Beach

32

*Pacific
Ocean*

North Moss Beach
(Asilomar Beach)

The Links at
Spanish Bay

33

The Inn at
Spanish Bay

33
34
P

Spanish Bay

South
Moss Beach

Spanish Bay
parking lot

Sunset Drive

Pacific
Grove
Toll Gate

M
O
N
T
E
R
E
Y

N
W · E
S

LINKS NATURE WALK

BAY

NATURE WALK

Seventeen Mile Drive

Spanish Bay Road

To
Hike 35

Seventeen Mile Dr

Forest Lodge Road

Sloat Rd

ALSO SEE MAPS ON
PAGES 88 · 97 · 101

34.
The Bay Nature Walk
SPANISH BAY

35. Point Joe to Bird Rock
PEBBLE BEACH · MONTEREY PENINSULA

Hiking distance: 3.4 miles round trip
Hiking time: 2 hours
Elevation gain: Level
Maps: U.S.G.S. Monterey
Location: Pebble Beach

Summary of hike: This hike follows the coastal terrace from Point Joe, at the southern end of Spanish Bay, to Bird Rock and Seal Rock, large granite outcroppings carved by waves and wind. The trail includes scenic vistas, promontories, and beach coves along the Monterey Peninsula. This stretch of coastline is an excellent whale watching location from December through March, when gray whales make their way from Baja California to Alaska. Interpretive displays are at Point Joe and Bird Rock.

Driving directions: PEBBLE BEACH. Access to the trail is from the scenic Seventeen Mile Drive, a toll road in Pebble Beach. From the Pacific Grove toll gate, located off of Sunset Drive, drive 1.7 miles on Seventeen Mile Drive to the Point Joe parking lot on the right, at the south end of Moss Beach.

CARMEL. From the Carmel entrance gate, off of Ocean Avenue in downtown Carmel, drive 0.2 miles to Seventeen Mile Drive. Turn left and continue 7.6 miles to the Point Joe parking lot on the left.

Hiking directions: From the bluffs at Point Joe, savor the views north, overlooking South Moss Beach, Spanish Bay, and the jagged coastline. Head south along the granite rock point, parallel to Seventeen Mile Drive and the ocean cliffs. The meandering path passes sculpted granite outcroppings and tidepools. As you pass a sandy pocket beach surrounded by boulders, Bird Rock (the destination) can be seen offshore. The path reaches Bird Rock at 1.9 miles. To the south are views of Fan Shell Beach and Cypress Point. To the north are views back to Point Joe and Spanish Bay. Continue to an overlook of Seal Rock, where sea otters, sea lions, and harbor seals can be observed. Return along the same trail.

To extend the hike by one mile, the trail to Indian Village—Hike 36—begins here.■

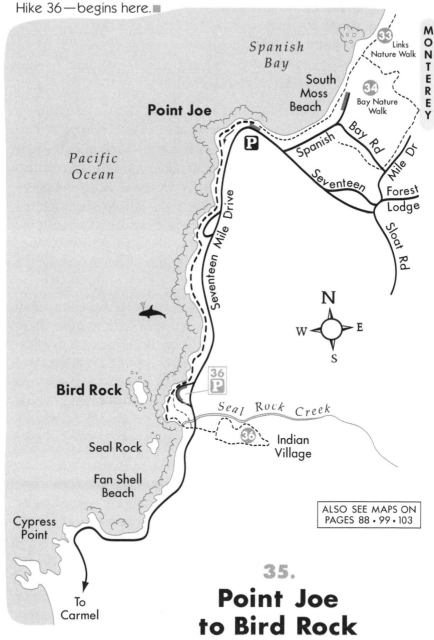

Spanish Bay

South Moss Beach

Point Joe

Pacific Ocean

Links Nature Walk

Bay Nature Walk

Spanish

Bay Rd

Seventeen

Mile Dr

Forest Lodge

Sloat Rd

Seventeen Mile Drive

Bird Rock

Seal Rock Creek

Indian Village

Seal Rock

Fan Shell Beach

Cypress Point

To Carmel

N
W E
S

ALSO SEE MAPS ON
PAGES 88 • 99 • 103

35.
Point Joe
to Bird Rock

36. Bird Rock to Indian Village
PEBBLE BEACH • MONTEREY PENINSULA

Hiking distance: 1-mile loop
Hiking time: 30 minutes
Elevation gain: 50 feet
Maps: U.S.G.S. Monterey
　　　　Pebble Beach Nature Trails booklet
Location: Pebble Beach

Summary of hike: The hike to Indian Village begins at Bird Rock, a large offshore rock that is home to numerous shoreline birds, sea lions, and harbor seals. A self-guided nature trail follows the coastline towards Seal Rock before crossing the dunes into the Del Monte Forest. The path winds through Monterey pines to Indian Village, a site thought to be used by the Costanoan Indians as a spa before the Spanish missionaries arrived in the 1700s. It is now a large, grassy picnic area with a log cabin.

Driving directions: PEBBLE BEACH. Access to the trail is from the scenic Seventeen Mile Drive, a toll road in Pebble Beach. From the Pacific Grove toll gate off of Sunset Drive, drive 3 miles on Seventeen Mile Drive to the signed Bird and Seal Rock Picnic Area on the right.

CARMEL. From the Carmel entrance gate, off of Ocean Avenue in downtown Carmel, drive 0.2 miles to Seventeen Mile Drive. Turn left and continue 6.2 miles to the Bird and Seal Rock Picnic Area on the left.

Hiking directions: After marveling at Bird Rock and the coastline, walk south (left) to the signed trail. Continue following the coastline towards Seal Rock. Cross Seventeen Mile Drive and pick up the trail, heading inland. A boardwalk leads through the fragile dunes. Climb the stairs at the east end of the dunes, and enter the shady forest to an unsigned junction. Bear left, following the south banks of Seal Rock Creek. Pass a natural spring on the right, reaching Indian Village in a meadow and picnic area. For the return loop, bear right on the gravel road. Just before reaching the "Gingerbread House" on the right, watch for the trail on the right . Bear right to the junction, completing the loop. Recross the dunes back to the trailhead. ■

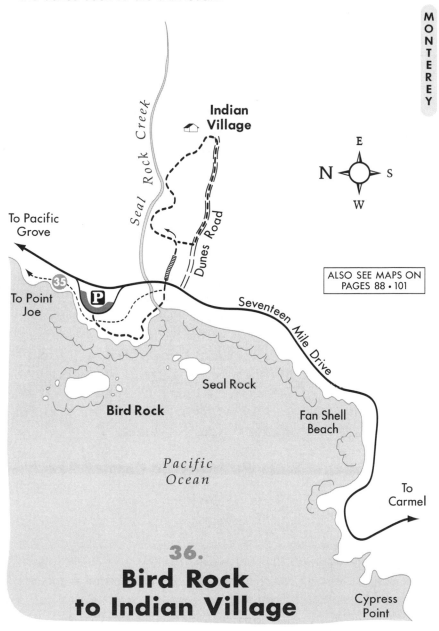

Indian
Village

Seal Rock Creek

To Pacific
Grove

Dunes Road

E
N ✛ S
W

ALSO SEE MAPS ON
PAGES 88 • 101

To Point
Joe

35

P

Seventeen Mile Drive

Seal Rock

Bird Rock

Fan Shell
Beach

*Pacific
Ocean*

To
Carmel

36.
Bird Rock
to Indian Village

Cypress
Point

37. Carmel Beach

Hiking distance: 2.4 miles round trip
Hiking time: 1.5 hours
Elevation gain: Level
Maps: U.S.G.S. Monterey
Location: Carmel

Summary of hike: Fronting the heart of downtown Carmel lies Carmel Beach, an arc of white sand between Pebble Beach and Carmel Point. The crescent-shaped beach is backed by twisted wind-swept Monterey cypress perched on a large sand dune. Behind the dune are erosion-sculpted bluffs (Hike 38). Numerous stairways access the blufftop. Granite rock outcroppings and tidepools lie at the north end of the beach.

Driving directions: CARMEL. From downtown Carmel, take Ocean Avenue west to the end of the road at the beachfront.

Hiking directions: The west end of Ocean Avenue opens up to the wide sandy beach. Walk down the steep sand dune to the shoreline. Heading north, the beach extends 0.4 miles, passing several pocket coves to the craggy cliffs and tidepools near Arrowhead Point. Heading south, the white sand beach extends 0.7 miles. Along the way, numerous stairways lead up the rocky bluffs to the Scenic Bluff Pathway along Scenic Road (Hike 38). At the south end of Carmel Beach, as the bluffs curve west to Carmel Point, the beach strand ends. A stairway leads up the rocky bluffs to the residential area near the point. ■

38. Scenic Bluff Pathway at Carmel Beach

Hiking distance: 1.6 miles round trip
Hiking time: 45 minutes
Location: Carmel

Summary of hike: The Scenic Bluff Pathway is a well maintained gravel pathway that parallels Scenic Road on the bluffs above Carmel Beach. Eight stairways access the white sand beach below (Hike 37). The trail meanders through the shade of

Monterey cypress and landscaped gardens to Carmel Point. Throughout the hike are panoramic views of the jagged coastline from Pebble Beach to Point Lobos. This easy stroll is especially enjoyable for watching sunsets over the Pacific Ocean.

Driving directions: CARMEL. From downtown Carmel, take Ocean Avenue west to Scenic Road, located a block east of the oceanfront. Turn left on Scenic Road, and drive 2 blocks to the parking spaces on the right.

Hiking directions: Take the gravel path south above the sandy beach strand. The path meanders through the shade of Monterey cypress. Every block has a stairway leading down the rocky cliffs to the beach below. At 0.8 miles, the trail jogs a few times, then ends near Ocean View Avenue as the bay curves west towards Carmel Point. To return, take the same path back, or descend on a stairway and follow the sandy beach strand back.■

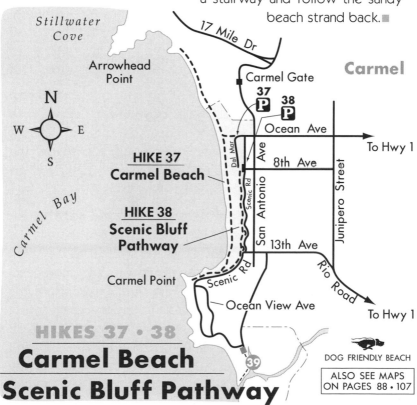

HIKES 37 • 38

Carmel Beach
Scenic Bluff Pathway

DOG FRIENDLY BEACH

ALSO SEE MAPS
ON PAGES 88 • 107

39. Carmel River Lagoon and Wetlands Natural Preserve

CARMEL RIVER STATE BEACH

Hiking distance: 1 mile round trip
Hiking time: 30 minutes
Elevation gain: 50 feet
Maps: U.S.G.S. Monterey
Location: Carmel

Summary of hike: The Carmel River Lagoon and Wetlands is a protected sanctuary for migrating birds and shorebirds within Carmel River State Beach. The brackish lagoon sits at the mouth of the Carmel River. A sandbar interrupts the river's flow to the sea, filling the lagoon and forming a marshy wetland area. The sandbar breaks away during rainstorms, emptying the lagoon into the ocean. The sanctuary is fringed with eucalyptus and Monterey cypress groves. This hike begins on the north bank of the Carmel River, then climbs a hillside to scenic views. The path continues to the Portola-Crespi Cross, the historic site where a cross was erected in 1769 to signal passing ships.

Driving directions: CARMEL. From downtown Carmel, take Ocean Avenue west to Scenic Road, located a block east of the oceanfront. Turn left (south) on Scenic Road, and follow the winding blufftop road 1.4 miles to Carmelo Street. Turn right into the signed Carmel River State Beach parking lot.

Hiking directions: Head left (eastward) to the edge of the lagoon and past the interpretive displays. Follow the shoreline to the sandbar near the oceanfront. Cross the sandbar to the south shore of the Carmel River. If the river is flowing into the ocean, wade across. Climb a few steps to a T-junction. The right fork follows the lower ocean terrace to Middle Beach. Take the left fork and follow the river upstream on the terraced ledge. Gradually gain elevation, overlooking the wetland preserve. Views extend inland up Carmel Valley. The path ends on the hilltop at the Portola Cross. Scenic views stretch across Carmel Bay to Point Lobos and the surrounding mountains.

To continue walking, descend the hill to the south, and take the cliffside footpath to Middle Beach and Monastery Beach (Hike 31). ■

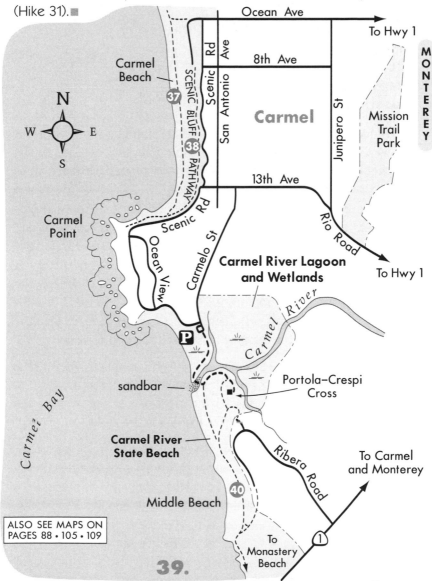

39.
Carmel River Lagoon and Wetlands Natural Preserve
CARMEL RIVER STATE BEACH

40. Carmel Meadows to Monastery Beach
CARMEL RIVER STATE BEACH

Hiking distance: 2.2 miles round trip
Hiking time: 1.5 hours
Elevation gain: 150 feet
Maps: U.S.G.S. Monterey
Location: Carmel

Summary of hike: This hike combines beach and bluff trails along Carmel River State Beach at the south end of Carmel. The Carmel River flows through the north end of this 106-acre state beach, forming a lagoon and bird sanctuary (Hike 39). The beach is bordered on the south by Point Lobos State Reserve (Hikes 41—45). The hike connects Carmel Meadows in the grassland bluffs to San Jose Creek Beach, known locally as Monastery Beach (named after the Carmelite Monastery in the hills above). A short side trip leads to Portola Cross, the site where the Portola-Crespi Expedition erected a cross to signal passing ships in 1769. From the cross are panoramic views of Carmel Bay, the bird sanctuary, the surrounding mountains, and Point Lobos.

Driving directions: CARMEL. From Highway 1 and Rio Road in Carmel, drive 0.9 miles south on Highway 1 to Ribera Road. Turn right and continue 0.7 miles to the trailhead at the end of the road.

Hiking directions: Take the hilltop trail past rock outcroppings through grasslands and brush. Follow the blufftop path 0.2 miles to a junction. The right fork descends down steps to a lower path (the return route). Continue along the top above Middle Beach. The path descends to the lower trail and down to the tidepools and rock formations at the beachfront. Follow the beach south, reaching San Jose Creek, which pools into a small lagoon near Monastery Beach. The serrated cliffs of Point Lobos extend west out into the ocean. (Point Lobos State Reserve can be accessed by crossing San Jose Creek.) Return back to the tidepools, and take the lower trail, passing below a few cliffside homes to a junction at the base of a hill. The right fork is the return route. First, bear left up the hill for a short detour to Portola Cross and a scenic vista point. Return to the junction at the base of the hill, and head up the paved path to Calle La Cruz. Walk one block to Ribera Road. Go right a quarter mile to the trailhead at the end of the road.■

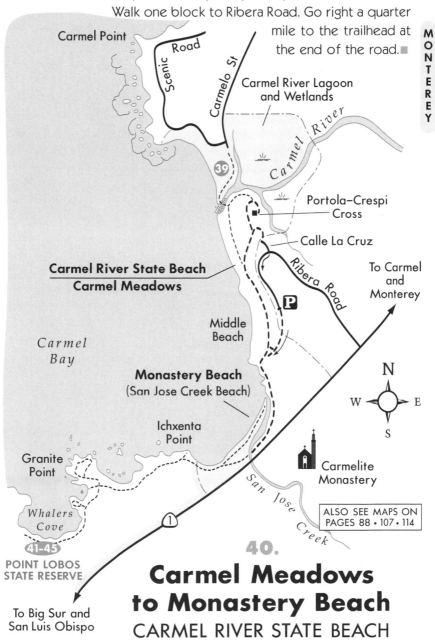

Carmel Point

Scenic Road

Carmelo St

Carmel River Lagoon and Wetlands

Carmel River

39

Portola–Crespi Cross

Calle La Cruz

Carmel River State Beach
Carmel Meadows

To Carmel and Monterey

Ribera Road

P

Middle Beach

Carmel Bay

Monastery Beach
(San Jose Creek Beach)

N
W — E
S

Ichxenta Point

Granite Point

Carmelite Monastery

Whalers Cove

1

San Jose Creek

ALSO SEE MAPS ON
PAGES 88 • 107 • 114

41-45

POINT LOBOS
STATE RESERVE

To Big Sur and San Luis Obispo

40.

Carmel Meadows
to Monastery Beach
CARMEL RIVER STATE BEACH

Big Sur

Big Sur is an awesome stretch of spectacular coastline where the Santa Lucia Mountains rise over 5,000 feet from the ocean. This magnificent landscape begins near Carmel at Point Lobos State Reserve and extends 75 miles south to Ragged Point in San Luis Obispo County, just south of the Monterey County line. The steep coastal mountain range and rugged shoreline isolate the Big Sur country, which maintains an unspoiled, rustic charm and a relaxed, leisurely pace.

Point Lobos State Reserve, encompassing 1,276 acres, is the crown jewel among California's state parks. The incredible reserve has bold headlands, ragged cliffs, sculpted coves, eroded inlets with tidepools, isolated beaches, craggy islets, marine terraces, large stands of Monterey cypress, rolling meadows, and miles of hiking trails.

Highway 1 snakes along the rugged Big Sur coast. The road hugs the edge of the precipitous cliffs and winds its way along the steep headlands. There are endless views of the scalloped coastline and the deep blue Pacific. Stunning bridges span numerous creeks and deep canyons. Other sections of the road cross flat, grassy marine terraces that gently slope to the eroded shoreline. Wave-worn rock pillars rise offshore.

Undoubtedly, these hikes include some of the best scenery along the California coast.

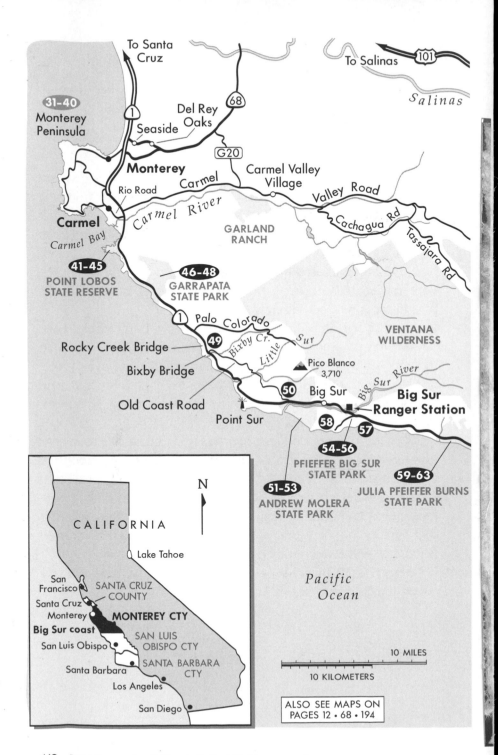

To Santa Cruz

To Salinas

US 101

Salinas

31-40
Monterey
Peninsula

1

68

Del Rey
Oaks

Seaside

G20

Monterey

Rio Road

Carmel

Carmel Valley
Village

Valley Road

Cachagua Rd

Tassajara Rd

Carmel River

Carmel

Carmel Bay

GARLAND
RANCH

41-45
POINT LOBOS
STATE RESERVE

46-48
GARRAPATA
STATE PARK

1

Palo Colorado

Bixby Cr.

Sur

Little

VENTANA
WILDERNESS

Rocky Creek Bridge

49

Pico Blanco
3,710'

Bixby Bridge

50

Big Sur

Big Sur River

**Big Sur
Ranger Station**

Old Coast Road

Point Sur

58

57

54-56
PFIEFFER BIG SUR
STATE PARK

59-63
JULIA PFEIFFER BURNS
STATE PARK

51-53
ANDREW MOLERA
STATE PARK

N

CALIFORNIA

Lake Tahoe

San
Francisco

SANTA CRUZ
COUNTY

Santa Cruz

Monterey

MONTEREY CTY

Big Sur coast

San Luis Obispo

SAN LUIS
OBISPO CTY

SANTA BARBARA
CTY

Santa Barbara

Los Angeles

San Diego

*Pacific
Ocean*

10 MILES

10 KILOMETERS

ALSO SEE MAPS ON
PAGES 12 • 68 • 194

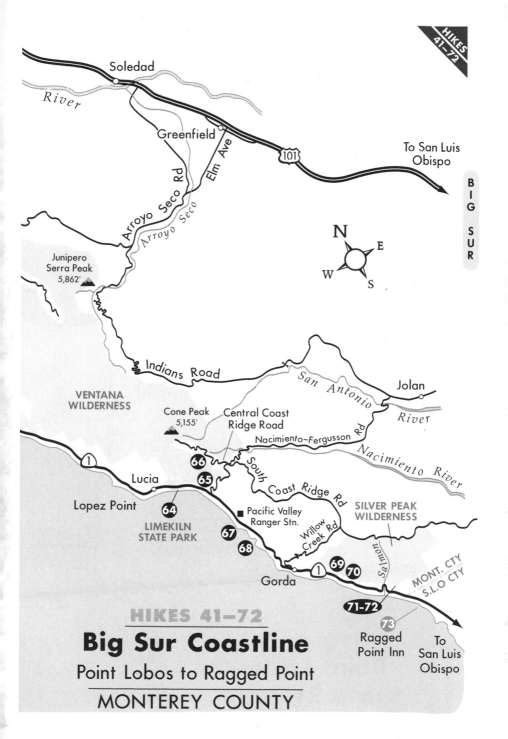

Soledad

River

Greenfield

101

To San Luis
Obispo

Arroyo Seco Rd

Elm Ave

Arroyo Seco

Junipero
Serra Peak
5,862'

N

E

W

S

BIG SUR

Indians Road

San Antonio

Jolan

River

VENTANA
WILDERNESS

Cone Peak
5,155'

Central Coast
Ridge Road

Nacimiento-Fergusson Rd

Nacimiento River

1

66

65

South Coast Ridge Rd

Lucia

SILVER PEAK
WILDERNESS

Lopez Point

64

Pacific Valley
Ranger Stn.

LIMEKILN
STATE PARK

67

68

Willow
Creek Rd

Salmon

69

70

1

MONT. CTY
S.LO CTY

Gorda

71-72

73

HIKES 41–72
Big Sur Coastline
Point Lobos to Ragged Point
MONTEREY COUNTY

Ragged
Point Inn

To
San Luis
Obispo

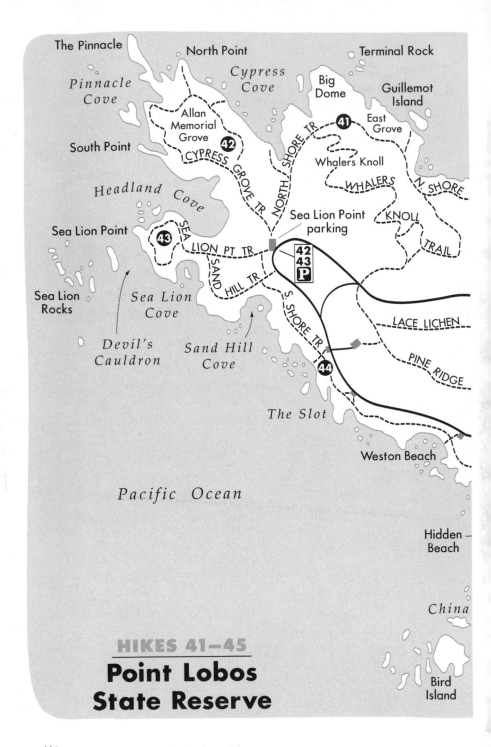

The Pinnacle

North Point

Terminal Rock

Pinnacle
Cove

*Cypress
Cove*

Big
Dome

Guillemot
Island

Allan
Memorial
Grove

East
Grove

South Point

42

CYPRESS GROVE TR

41

NORTH SHORE TR

Whalers Knoll

WHALERS

N. SHORE

Headland Cove

SEA

Sea Lion Point

KNOLL

Sea Lion Point

43

LION PT. TR

parking

TRAIL

SAND

HILL TR

S. SHORE TR

42 43 P

Sea Lion
Rocks

*Sea Lion
Cove*

LACE LICHEN

*Devil's
Cauldron*

*Sand Hill
Cove*

PINE RIDGE

44

The Slot

Weston Beach

Pacific Ocean

Hidden –
Beach

China

HIKES 41–45

Point Lobos
State Reserve

Bird
Island

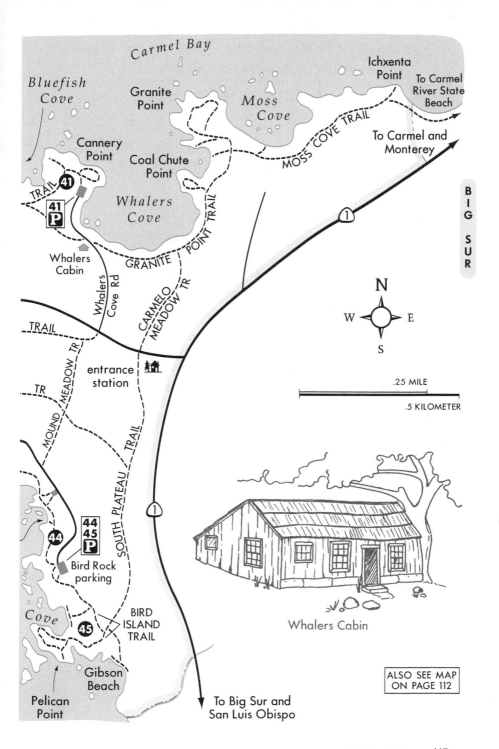

Carmel Bay

Bluefish Cove

Granite Point

Moss Cove

Ichxenta Point

To Carmel River State Beach

Cannery Point

Coal Chute Point

MOSS COVE TRAIL

To Carmel and Monterey

TRAIL

41

41 P

Whalers Cove

GRANITE POINT TRAIL

Whalers Cabin

Whalers Cove Rd

CARMELO MEADOW TR

1

B I G

S U R

TRAIL

entrance station

N

W E

S

.25 MILE

.5 KILOMETER

TR

MOUND MEADOW TR

SOUTH PLATEAU TRAIL

1

44 45 P

44

Bird Rock parking

Cove

45

BIRD ISLAND TRAIL

Whalers Cabin

Gibson Beach

Pelican Point

To Big Sur and San Luis Obispo

ALSO SEE MAP ON PAGE 112

41. North Shore Trail

POINT LOBOS STATE RESERVE

Hiking distance: 2.8—3.2 miles round trip
Hiking time: 1.5—2 hours
Elevation gain: 250 feet
Maps: U.S.G.S. Monterey
Point Lobos State Reserve map
Location: 2.5 miles south of Carmel

Summary of hike: Point Lobos State Reserve is the crown jewel among California's state parks. It is located along the north end of the Big Sur coastline just south of Monterey and Carmel. The incredible 1,276-acre reserve has bold headlands, ragged cliffs, sculpted coves, eroded inlets with tidepools, isolated beaches, craggy islets, marine terraces, large stands of Monterey cypress, rolling meadows, and many miles of hiking trails (back cover photo). The area is a great area to view oceanside wildlife.

The North Shore Trail in Point Lobos State Reserve follows the exposed and rugged northern headlands past sheer granite cliffs and coves. A spur trail leads to an overlook of Guillemot Island, a rocky offshore nesting site for seabirds. A second spur trail leads to Cypress Cove and Old Veteran, a windswept, gnarled Monterey cypress clinging to the cliffs of the cove. The main trail winds through a canopy of Monterey pines and cypress draped with veils of lichen.

Additional side trips lead to vistas atop Whalers Knoll and to Whalers Cabin, an old cabin that now houses a museum.

Driving directions: CARMEL. From Highway 1 and Rio Road in Carmel, drive 2.2 miles south on Highway 1 to the signed Point Lobos State Reserve entrance. Turn right (west) to the entrance station. Continue 0.1 mile to the Whalers Cove turnoff. Turn right and drive 0.3 miles to the parking area at the end of the road. An entrance fee is required.

BIG SUR RANGER STATION. From the ranger station, located 27 miles south of Carmel, drive 24 miles north to the state park entrance and turn left.

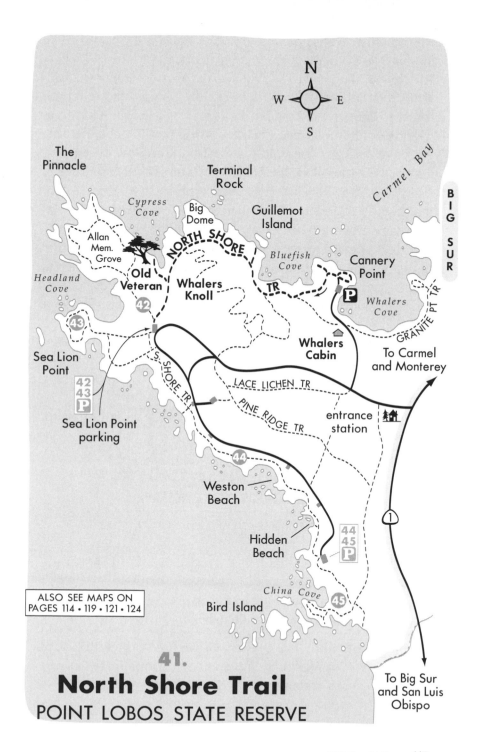

N
W E
S

The Pinnacle

Terminal Rock

Carmel Bay

Cypress Cove

Big Dome

Guillemot Island

BIG SUR

NORTH SHORE

Allan Mem. Grove

Bluefish Cove

Cannery Point

Old Veteran

Headland Cove

Whalers Knoll

TR

P

Whalers Cove

42

43

GRANITE PT TR

Whalers Cabin

Sea Lion Point

To Carmel and Monterey

42
43
P

S. SHORE TR

LACE LICHEN TR

Sea Lion Point parking

PINE RIDGE TR

entrance station

44

Weston Beach

1

Hidden Beach

44
45
P

China Cove

45

ALSO SEE MAPS ON
PAGES 114 • 119 • 121 • 124

Bird Island

To Big Sur and San Luis Obispo

41.
North Shore Trail
POINT LOBOS STATE RESERVE

Hiking directions: Walk up the rock steps at the north end of the parking lot to a junction. The right fork loops around Cannery Point at the west end of Whalers Cove (back cover photo). Back at the first junction, ascend a long set of steps, and enter the forest to another junction. The short fork on the right leads to an overlook of Bluefish Cove. On the North Shore Trail, curve around the cove to a junction with the Whalers Knoll Trail on the left. Continue weaving along the coastal cliffs around Bluefish Cove to a short spur trail leading to the Guillemot Island overlook. Back on the main trail, continue northwest past a native grove of Monterey cypress in East Grove. Cross a saddle past Big Dome to a second junction with the Whalers Knoll Trail. At Cypress Cove, detour on the Old Veteran Trail to view the twisted Monterey cypress and the cove. The North Shore Trail ends in the coastal scrub at the trailhead to the Cypress Grove Trail (Hike 42) by the Sea Lion Point parking area. Return along the same trail.

The North Shore Trail curves around the north side of Whalers Knoll, a historic lookout for spotting whales. For a side trip, take the twisting Whalers Knoll Trail 200 feet up the hillside. At the summit is a bench and panoramic views.

Whalers Cabin is located on the park road 0.1 mile before the parking area. The cabin was built by Chinese fishermen in the 1850s.■

42. Cypress Grove Trail
POINT LOBOS STATE RESERVE

Hiking distance: 0.8 miles round trip
Hiking time: 30 minutes
Elevation gain: 100 feet
Maps: U.S.G.S. Monterey
　　　　　Point Lobos State Reserve map
Location: 2.5 miles south of Carmel

Summary of hike: The Cypress Grove Trail is a clifftop loop trail around Allan Memorial Grove in Point Lobos State Reserve. The trail passes through one of only two natural stands of Monterey cypress in the world. (The other occurs at Cypress Point on the west side of the Monterey Peninsula.) The hike loops

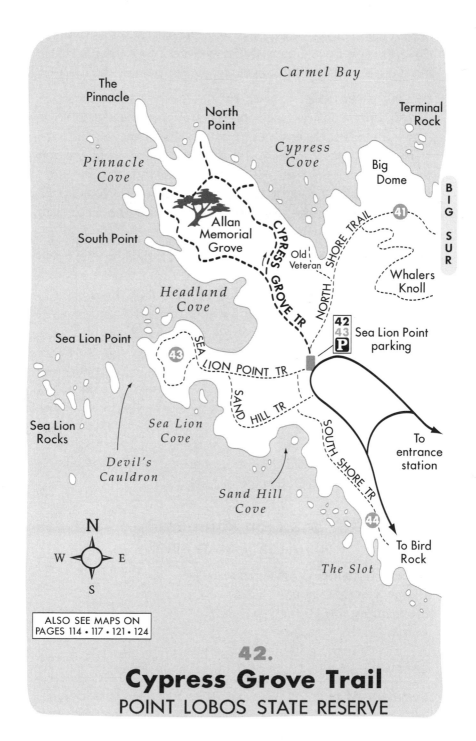

Carmel Bay

The Pinnacle

North Point

Terminal Rock

Pinnacle Cove

Cypress Cove

Big Dome

South Point

Allan Memorial Grove

CYPRESS GROVE TR

Old Veteran

NORTH SHORE TRAIL

BIG SUR

41

Whalers Knoll

Headland Cove

42
43
P
Sea Lion Point parking

Sea Lion Point

43

SEA LION POINT TR

SAND HILL TR

To entrance station

Sea Lion Rocks

Sea Lion Cove

SOUTH SHORE TR

Devil's Cauldron

Sand Hill Cove

44

N
W   E
S

To Bird Rock

The Slot

ALSO SEE MAPS ON
PAGES 114 • 117 • 121 • 124

42.

Cypress Grove Trail
POINT LOBOS STATE RESERVE

around rugged, weathered cliffs with stunning views of Cypress Cove, Pinnacle Cove, South Point, Headland Cove, and The Pinnacle, a narrow peninsula at the northernmost point in the reserve.

Driving directions: CARMEL. From Highway 1 and Rio Road in Carmel, drive 2.2 miles south on Highway 1 to the signed Point Lobos State Reserve entrance. Turn right (west) to the entrance station. Continue 0.7 miles to the Sea Lion Point parking area on the right side of the road. An entrance fee is required.

BIG SUR RANGER STATION. From the ranger station, located 27 miles south of Carmel, drive 24 miles north to the state park entrance and turn left.

Hiking directions: Two well-marked trails begin on the north end of the parking lot. To the right is the North Shore Trail (Hike 41). Take the Cypress Grove Trail to the left through coastal scrub 0.2 miles to a trail split. Begin the loop around Allan Memorial Grove to the right. Follow the edge of Cypress Cove to a short spur trail on the right, leading to an overlook of Cypress Cove and views of Carmel Bay. Back on the loop, pass through an indigenous Monterey cypress grove. A spur trail at the north end of the loop leads to the North Point overlook with views of The Pinnacle. Back on the main trail, granite steps lead up to Pinnacle Cove on a rocky promontory, where there are stunning views of South Point and Headland Cove. Continue past South Point and Headland Cove, completing the loop.■

43. Sea Lion Point Trail
POINT LOBOS STATE RESERVE

Hiking distance: 0.7 miles round trip
Hiking time: 30 minutes
Elevation gain: 50 feet
Maps: U.S.G.S. Monterey
　　　　Point Lobos State Reserve map
Location: 2.5 miles south of Carmel

Summary of hike: The Sea Lion Point Trail leads to a spectacular, surreal landscape on the coastal bluff above Headland Cove

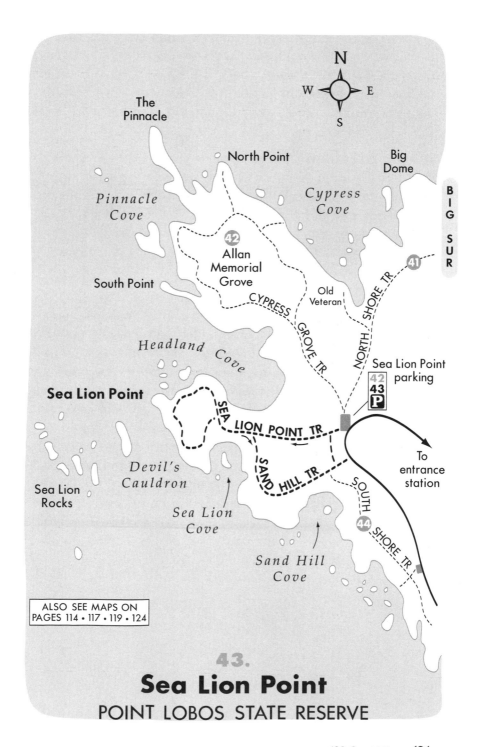

The Pinnacle

North Point

Big Dome

N
W E
S

Cypress Cove

Pinnacle Cove

42
Allan Memorial Grove

South Point

CYPRESS GROVE TR.

Old Veteran

NORTH SHORE TR.

41

BIG SUR

Headland Cove

Sea Lion Point

Sea Lion Point parking

42
43 P

SEA LION POINT TR.

SAND HILL TR.

Devil's Cauldron

Sea Lion Rocks

Sea Lion Cove

SOUTH SHORE TR.

44

To entrance station

Sand Hill Cove

ALSO SEE MAPS ON
PAGES 114 • 117 • 119 • 124

43.
Sea Lion Point
POINT LOBOS STATE RESERVE

in Point Lobos State Reserve. From the bluffs are vistas of Sea Lion Cove, Sea Lion Rocks, and the churning whitewater at Devil's Cauldron. The offshore sea stacks and rocky coves are often abundant with sea otters, harbor seals, and barking California sea lions. The return route follows the eroded cliffs between Sea Lion Cove and Sand Hill Cove.

Driving directions: CARMEL. From Highway 1 and Rio Road in Carmel, drive 2.2 miles south on Highway 1 to the signed Point Lobos State Reserve entrance. Turn right (west) to the entrance station. Continue 0.7 miles to the Sea Lion Point parking area on the right side of the road. An entrance fee is required.

BIG SUR RANGER STATION. From the ranger station, located 27 miles south of Carmel, drive 24 miles north to the state park entrance and turn left.

Hiking directions: From the far west end of the parking area, take the signed Sea Lion Point Trail. The path crosses through coastal scrub to a trail split. Stay to the right, heading toward the point. At the crest of the rocky bluffs is a trail junction and an incredible vista point. The views include South Point, The Pinnacle, Sea Lion Cove, Devil's Cauldron, and Sea Lion Rocks. On the right, descend the natural staircase of weathered rock to the headland. From the lower level, circle the point around Headland Cove to close up views of Devil's Cauldron and Sea Lion Rocks. Loop back around by the sandy beach at Sea Lion Cove. Return up the steps to the overlook. Proceed south on Sand Hill Trail, following the cliffs above Sea Lion Cove and Sand Hill Cove. Pass the South Shore Trail on the right (Hike 44), and complete the loop back at the parking area.■

44. South Shore Trail

POINT LOBOS STATE RESERVE

Hiking distance: 2 miles round trip
Hiking time: 1 hour
Elevation gain: 30 feet
Maps: U.S.G.S. Monterey
Point Lobos State Reserve map
Location: 2.5 miles south of Carmel

map next page

BIG SUR

Summary of hike: The South Shore Trail explores the eroded sandstone terrain along the jagged southern ridges and troughs of Point Lobos State Reserve. The trail begins near Bird Island and ends by Sea Lion Point, weaving past tidepools and rocky beach coves tucked between the cliffs. The beach coves include rock-enclosed Hidden Beach and Weston Beach, covered with multi-colored pebbles and flat rock slabs. The trail continues past The Slot (a narrow channel bound by rock) and the 100-foot cliffs at Sand Hill Cove.

Driving directions: CARMEL. From Highway 1 and Rio Road in Carmel, drive 2.2 miles south on Highway 1 to the signed Point Lobos State Reserve entrance. Turn right (west) to the entrance kiosk. Continue 1.6 miles to the Bird Rock parking area at the end of the road. An entrance fee is required.

BIG SUR RANGER STATION. From the ranger station, located 27 miles south of Carmel, drive 24 miles north to the state park entrance and turn left.

Hiking directions: The signed South Shore Trail begins at the north end of the parking area overlooking China Cove (Hike 45). Head north (right), walking along the edge of the cliffs to a junction with the Hidden Beach path on the left. Stone steps descend to the oval beach cove. Return to the main trail and follow the contours of the jagged coastline past numerous coves, tidepools, and rock islands. A few connector trails on the right lead to parking areas along the park road. At Sand Hill Cove, steps lead up to a T-junction with the Sand Hill Trail—Hike 43. This is the turn-around spot. Return along the same trail. ■

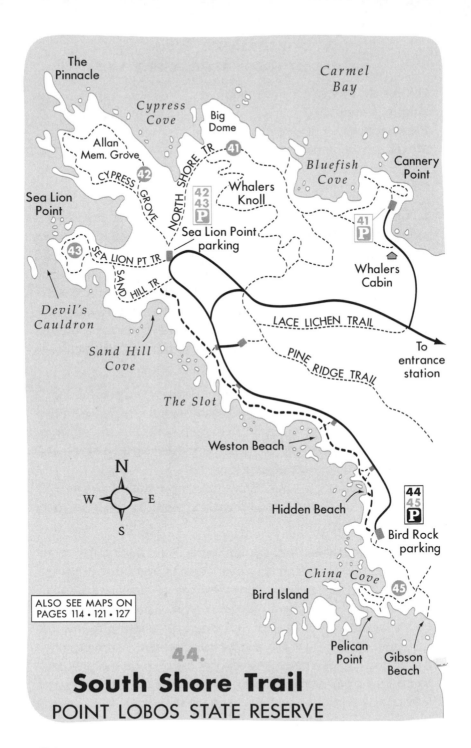

The
Pinnacle

*Carmel
Bay*

*Cypress
Cove*

Big
Dome

Allan
Mem. Grove

CYPRESS GROVE

NORTH SHORE TR

41

*Bluefish
Cove*

Cannery
Point

Sea Lion
Point

42

Whalers
Knoll

42
43
P

Sea Lion Point
parking

41
P

Whalers
Cabin

43

SEA LION PT TR

SAND HILL TR

LACE LICHEN TRAIL

To
entrance
station

*Devil's
Cauldron*

*Sand Hill
Cove*

PINE RIDGE TRAIL

The Slot

Weston Beach

N
W — E
S

Hidden Beach

44
45
P

Bird Rock
parking

China Cove

45

ALSO SEE MAPS ON
PAGES 114 • 121 • 127

Bird Island

Pelican
Point

Gibson
Beach

44.

South Shore Trail
POINT LOBOS STATE RESERVE

45. Bird Island Trail
China Cove — Pelican Point — Gibson Beach
POINT LOBOS STATE RESERVE

Hiking distance: 0.8 miles round trip
Hiking time: 30 minutes
Elevation gain: 20 feet
Maps: U.S.G.S. Monterey
   Point Lobos State Reserve map
Location: 2.5 miles south of Carmel

map
page 127

B
I
G

S
U
R

Summary of hike: The Bird Island Trail follows the rocky coastline through a Monterey pine forest along the clifftops overlooking the sea. The trail passes chasms, arches, sea caves, and the beautiful white sand beaches of China Cove and Gibson Beach. Both beach coves are surrounded by granite cliffs with staircase access. The hike then loops around Pelican Point, where off-shore Bird Island can be viewed. The island is inhabited by nesting colonies of cormorants and brown pelicans.

Driving directions: CARMEL. From Highway 1 and Rio Road in Carmel, drive 2.2 miles south on Highway 1 to the signed Point Lobos State Reserve entrance. Turn right (west) to the entrance kiosk. Continue 1.6 miles to the Bird Rock parking area at the end of the road. An entrance fee is required.

BIG SUR RANGER STATION. From the ranger station, located 27 miles south of Carmel, drive 24 miles north to the state park entrance and turn left.

Hiking directions: Ascend the steps at the south end of the parking lot, and head through a Monterey pine forest to an overlook of China Cove and Bird Island. Follow the cliffside path as it curves around the head of China Cove to a signed junction. A long set of stairs to the right descends the cliffs to the sandy beach and cave in China Cove. After exploring the beach, return to the Bird Island Trail. Continue along the cliffs to a posted T-junction and overlook of the crescent-shaped Gibson Beach below the Carmel Highlands. For a short detour to Gibson Beach, bear left on the South Plateau Trail a few yards to the posted beach access on the right. Descend a long flight of steps to the sandy beach at the base of the cliffs.

Returning to the T-junction, head west towards Pelican Point through coastal scrub to a trail split. The paths loop around the flat bench, overlooking Bird Island, the magnificent offshore rock outcroppings, chasms, sea caves, and China Cove. Complete the loop and return along the same route.■

46. Soberanes Point Trails
GARRAPATA STATE PARK

Hiking distance: 1.8 miles round trip
Hiking time: 1 hour
Elevation gain: 200 feet
Maps: U.S.G.S. Soberanes Point
　　　　Garrapata State Park map
Location: 7 miles south of Carmel off Highway 1

map
page 129

Summary of hike: The undeveloped Garrapata State Park stretches along four miles of scenic coastline and extends into the inland mountains. These coastal bluff trails along Soberanes Point lead to a myriad of crenelated coves, hidden beaches, and rocky points (cover photo).

Soberanes Point is a popular whale-watching spot. It is a serrated headland backed by Whale Peak, a 280-foot cone-shaped hill overlooking the Pacific. The trail circles the headland, then climbs Whale Peak. From the summit of Whale Peak are 360-degree panoramic views from Yankee Point in the north to Point Sur in the south.

Driving directions: CARMEL. From Highway 1 and Rio Road in Carmel, drive 6.8 miles south on Highway 1 to the unsigned parking turnouts on both sides of the road. The turnouts are located by a tin roof barn on the inland side of the highway.

BIG SUR RANGER STATION. From the ranger station, located 27 miles south of Carmel, drive 19.4 miles north to the parking turnouts.

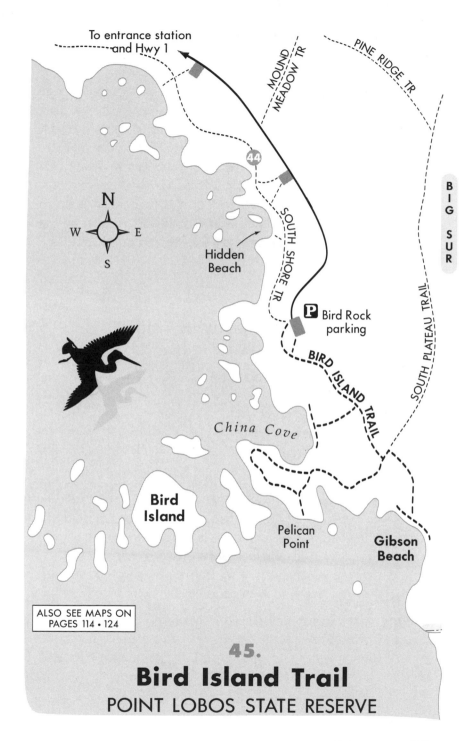

To entrance station
and Hwy 1

MOUND MEADOW TR

PINE RIDGE TR

44

SOUTH SHORE TR

Hidden
Beach

B I G   S U R

P Bird Rock
parking

BIRD ISLAND TRAIL

SOUTH PLATEAU TRAIL

China Cove

Bird
Island

Pelican
Point

Gibson
Beach

N
W E
S

ALSO SEE MAPS ON
PAGES 114 • 124

45.
Bird Island Trail
POINT LOBOS STATE RESERVE

Hiking directions: Walk through the trailhead gate on the ocean side of the highway, bearing left through a grove of cypress trees. Continue south towards Soberanes Point and Whale Peak, curving around the north side of the peak to an unsigned junction. The left fork circles the base of the hill. Take the right fork west along the coastal terrace to the northwest end of Soberanes Point. Follow the ocean cliffs to the southern point. From the south end, the trail returns toward Highway 1 by a gate. Stay on the footpath to the left, following the hillside trail to an unsigned junction. The left fork climbs a quarter mile up to the grassy ridge of Whale Peak. A trail follows the crest to the two summits. Return to the base of the hill, and continue to the north to complete the loop.■

47. Soberanes Canyon Trail
GARRAPATA STATE PARK

Hiking distance: 3 miles round trip
Hiking time: 1.5 hours
Elevation gain: 900 feet
Maps: U.S.G.S. Soberanes Point
      Garrapata State Park map
Location: 7 miles south of Carmel off Highway 1

map
page 131

Summary of hike: The Soberanes Canyon Trail follows Soberanes Creek up a wet, narrow canyon through magnificent stands of huge redwoods in Garrapata State Park. The trail crosses Soberanes Creek seven times before climbing up to the head of the canyon. At the top, the trail emerges onto the dry, chaparral-covered hillside with panoramic views.

Driving directions: CARMEL. From Highway 1 and Rio Road in Carmel, drive 6.8 miles south on Highway 1 to the unsigned parking turnouts on either side of the road. The turnouts are located by a tin roof barn on the inland side of the highway.

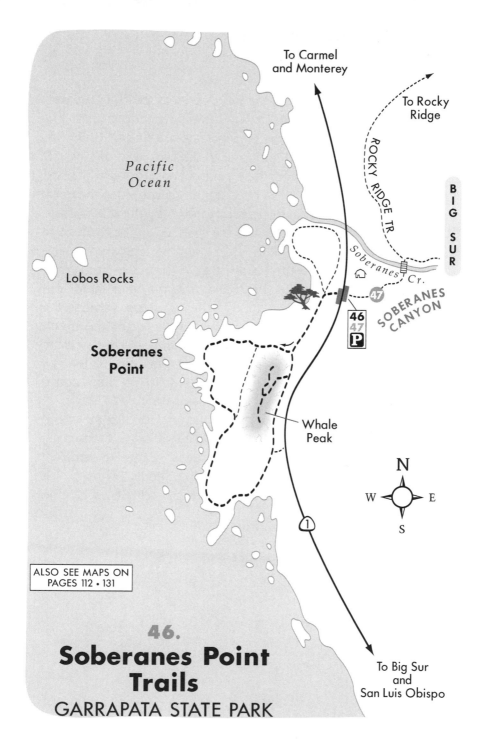

To Carmel
and Monterey

To Rocky
Ridge

*Pacific
Ocean*

ROCKY RIDGE TR

B
I
G

S
U
R

Lobos Rocks

Soberanes Cr.

47

**Soberanes
Point**

SOBERANES
CANYON

46
47
P

Whale
Peak

N
W E
S

1

ALSO SEE MAPS ON
PAGES 112 • 131

To Big Sur
and
San Luis Obispo

46.
Soberanes Point
Trails
GARRAPATA STATE PARK

BIG SUR RANGER STATION. From the ranger station, located 27 miles south of Carmel, drive 19.4 miles north to the parking turnouts.

Hiking directions: From the inland side of the highway, walk past the trailhead gate, following the old ranch road through a cypress grove. Curve left around the barn and down to Soberanes Creek. Cross the bridge to a signed junction. The left fork leads to Rocky Ridge, the rounded 1,435-foot peak to the north. Take the right fork and head up the canyon along the north side of the creek. Cross another footbridge and curve left, staying in Soberanes Canyon. Recross the creek on a third footbridge and head steadily uphill. Rock-hop over the creek, entering a beautiful redwood forest. Follow the watercourse through the redwoods to a lush grotto. The trail crosses the creek three consecutive times, then climbs a long series of steps. Traverse the canyon wall on a cliff ledge, climbing high above the creek. Switchbacks descend back to the creek. Climb up more steps to the head of the canyon. The lush canyon gives way to the dry sage-covered hills and an unsigned trail split, the turn-around point. Return down canyon along the same trail.

For an optional return hike, take the left fork up the steep slope towards Rocky Ridge and Doud Peak. The trail follows the dry, exposed hillside. The hike is strenuous, but the rewards are sweeping views of the ocean, coastline, and mountains. This return loop is the same distance back but adds an additional 1,000 feet in elevation.■

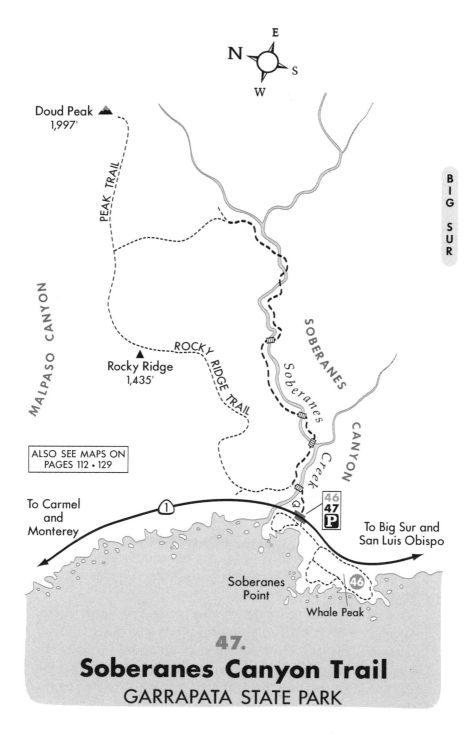

Doud Peak ▲
1,997'

N E S W

B I G S U R

PEAK TRAIL

MALPASO CANYON

SOBERANES CANYON

Soberanes Creek

ROCKY RIDGE TRAIL

Rocky Ridge ▲
1,435'

ALSO SEE MAPS ON
PAGES 112 • 129

To Carmel
and
Monterey

1

46
47
P

To Big Sur and
San Luis Obispo

46

Soberanes
Point

Whale Peak

47.
Soberanes Canyon Trail
GARRAPATA STATE PARK

48. Garrapata Beach and Bluff Trail

GARRAPATA STATE PARK

Hiking distance: 1—2.5 miles round trip
Hiking time: 1—1.5 hours
Elevation gain: 50 feet
Maps: U.S.G.S. Soberanes Point
       Garrapata State Park map
Location: 10 miles south of Carmel off Highway 1

Summary of hike: Garrapata Beach sits near the southern border of this 2,879-acre state park. The pristine beach is a half-mile crescent of white sand with rocky tidepools. At the south end, Garrapata Creek empties into the Pacific through a granite gorge. This trail follows the bluffs through an ice plant meadow above the beach. Stairways access the beach. The beautiful sandy strand is an unofficial clothing-optional beach.

Driving directions: CARMEL. From Highway 1 and Rio Road in Carmel, drive 9.6 miles south on Highway 1 to the unsigned parking turnouts on both sides of the highway. The turnouts are located between two historic bridges—1.2 miles south of the Granite Creek Bridge and 0.2 miles north of the Garrapata Creek Bridge.

BIG SUR RANGER STATION. From the ranger station, located 27 miles south of Carmel, drive 16.6 miles north to the turnouts.

Hiking directions: Walk through gate 19 and descend a few steps. Follow the path to the edge of the oceanfront cliffs and a trail split. To the left, steps lead down the cliffs to the sandy beach. From the beach, head south (left) a short distance to Garrapata Creek and the jagged rocks at the point. Return north and beachcomb for a half mile along the base of the cliffs to the north point.

Back at the blufftop junction, the bluff trail heads north, following the cliff's edge into a ravine. Steps lead down to Doud Creek and a trail split. The left path leads to Garrapata Beach. To the right, the trail crosses the drainage. Steps lead back up the bluffs to a junction. Take the left fork to continue along the bluffs. Choose your own turn-around point. ■

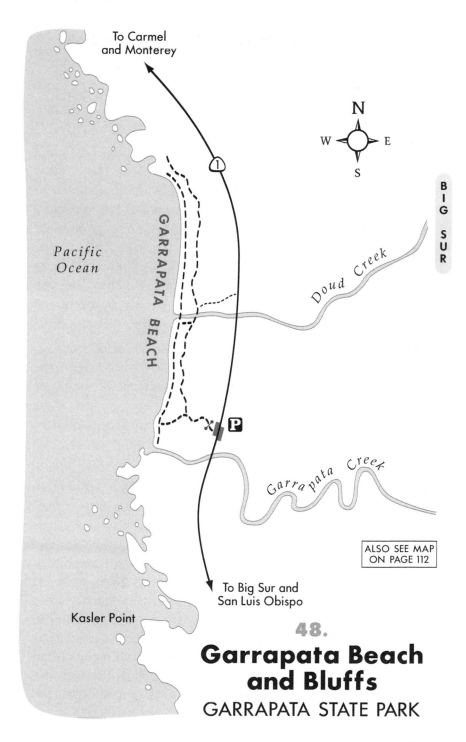

To Carmel
and Monterey

N
W · E
S

BIG SUR

Pacific
Ocean

GARRAPATA BEACH

Doud Creek

1

X P

Garrapata Creek

ALSO SEE MAP
ON PAGE 112

To Big Sur and
San Luis Obispo

Kasler Point

48.

Garrapata Beach
and Bluffs

GARRAPATA STATE PARK

49. Old Coast Road—NORTHERN ACCESS

Hiking distance: 11.5 miles round trip (or 10.2-mile shuttle)
Hiking time: 5.5 hours
Elevation gain: 2,000 feet
Maps: U.S.G.S. Point Sur and Big Sur
Location: 13 miles south of Carmel off Highway 1

map page 136

Summary of hike: The Old Coast Road was the original coastal route connecting Carmel with Big Sur before the Bixby Bridge was completed in 1932. The hike begins at the frequently photographed Bixby Bridge and follows the twisting, unpaved back road through a shaded canyon dense with coastal redwoods and lush ferns. The trail parallels Bixby Creek and Sierra Creek and crosses two bridges over the Little Sur River. The road is open to the public but is bordered by private property. The hike may be combined with Hike 50 for a 10.2-mile shuttle hike.

Driving directions: CARMEL. From Highway 1 and Rio Road in Carmel, drive 12.7 miles south on Highway 1 to the Bixby Bridge. The parking pullout is at the north end of the bridge on the ocean side of the highway.

BIG SUR RANGER STATION. From the ranger station, located 27 miles south of Carmel, drive 13.5 miles north to the parking pull-outs on the left just after crossing Bixby Bridge.

Hiking directions: From the north end of Bixby Bridge, take the signed Coast Road inland along the north side of Bixby Creek. At 0.3 miles, as the road curves right, is a great view down canyon of Bixby Bridge and the offshore rocks. Curve south and descend to the canyon floor. Cross a bridge over Bixby Creek. Gently ascend the lower reaches of Sierra Hill along the west wall of the canyon, passing homes tucked into the trees and numerous cliffside tributary streams. As the old road continues south through a lush redwood forest, Bixby Creek curves away to the east. The road continues to parallel Sierra Creek, a tributary of Bixby Creek. The road crosses the creek five consecutive times. At the sixth crossing, leave Sierra Creek on a hairpin right bend. Climb out of the shaded canyon to open rolling hillsides on the summit of the Sierra Grade. Descend 1,000 feet along the contours of the mountains on the chaparral slopes of the Sierra Grade. Pico Blanco, rising 3,710 feet, dominates the views to the southeast. At the bottom of the grade, walk through a stand of bishop pines to the Little Sur River. Two consecutive metal bridges cross the South Fork and Main Fork of the Little Sur River just above their confluence. Return along the same trail, or continue with the next hike for a one-way shuttle hike. ■

50. Old Coast Road—SOUTHERN ACCESS

Hiking distance: 9 miles round trip (or 10.2-mile shuttle)
Hiking time: 4 hours
Elevation gain: 1,650 feet
Maps: U.S.G.S. Big Sur

map
page 137

Location: 22 miles south of Carmel at Andrew Molera St. Park

Summary of hike: The Old Coast Road was the primary route of travel along this mountainous coastal stretch prior to 1932, when the 260-foot-high Bixby Bridge was opened. This hike begins at the Big Sur Valley in Andrew Molera State Park near the mouth of the Big Sur River. The winding, breathtaking route curves along hillsides with panoramic vistas of the coastline and interior mountains. The road slowly descends into a shaded canyon to the Little Sur River, rich with lush ferns and coastal redwoods. The road is open to the public, but the adjacent land is privately owned. The hike may be combined with Hike 49 for a 10.2-mile shuttle hike.

Driving directions: CARMEL. From Highway 1 and Rio Road in Carmel, drive 21.4 miles south on Highway 1 to the signed Andrew Molera State Park entrance. Turn right and drive down to the entrance kiosk and parking lot. A parking fee is required.

BIG SUR RANGER STATION. From the ranger station, located 27 miles south of Carmel, drive 4.8 miles north to the Andrew Molera State Park entrance and turn left.

Hiking directions: Walk back up to Highway 1, and cross the highway to the signed Coast Road. Head up the winding, unpaved road on a northern course to steadily improving coastal views. At 1.5 miles, weave through groves of oaks, sycamores and redwoods, reaching a 942-foot summit. Views extend to the coastal marine terrace, Andrew Molera State Park, inland to the South Fork Canyon, and across Dani Ridge to the towering 3,710-foot

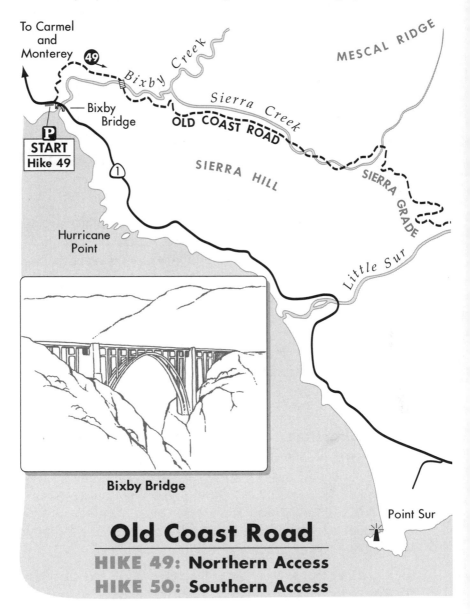

Bixby Bridge

Old Coast Road

HIKE 49: Northern Access
HIKE 50: Southern Access

Pico Blanco in the east. Slowly descend, passing a ranch on the left, and enter a lush redwood forest. Skirt around the west edge of Dani Ridge. Parallel the South Fork Little Sur River down the narrow, shaded canyon through oaks, maples, pines, redwoods, and an understory of ferns. At the canyon floor, two consecutive metal bridges cross the South Fork and Main Fork of the Little Sur River just above their confluence. Return along the same trail or continue with Hike 49 for a one-way shuttle hike. ■

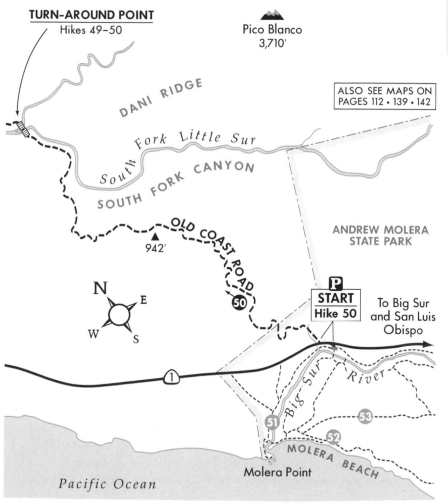

TURN-AROUND POINT
Hikes 49–50

Pico Blanco
3,710'

DANI RIDGE

ALSO SEE MAPS ON
PAGES 112 • 139 • 142

South Fork Little Sur

South

SOUTH FORK CANYON

ANDREW MOLERA
STATE PARK

OLD COAST ROAD

942'

START
Hike 50

To Big Sur
and San Luis
Obispo

N
E
W
S

1

Big Sur River

51

53

52

MOLERA BEACH

Molera Point

Pacific Ocean

51. Molera Point and Molera Beach
ANDREW MOLERA STATE PARK

Hiking distance: 2.5 miles round trip
Hiking time: 1.5 hours
Elevation gain: 70 feet
Maps: U.S.G.S. Big Sur
Andrew Molera State Park map
Location: 22 miles south of Carmel off Highway 1

Summary of hike: Andrew Molera State Park, the largest state park on the Big Sur coast, encompasses 4,800 acres and extends along both sides of Highway 1. The park has mountains, meadows, a 2.5-mile strand of beach, and over 15 miles of hiking trails.

This hike parallels the Big Sur River along ocean bluffs to Molera Point and Molera Beach. From the ridge are views of this diverse park, its numerous hiking trails, Molera Beach, the Point Sur Lighthouse, and Cooper Point at the south end of the bay. A side trip leads to Cooper Cabin. Built with redwood logs in 1861, the cabin is the oldest surviving ranch structure in Big Sur. The return trail meanders through a grassy meadow lined with sycamores.

Driving directions: CARMEL. From Highway 1 and Rio Road in Carmel, drive 21.4 miles south on Highway 1 to the signed Andrew Molera State Park entrance. Turn right and drive down to the entrance kiosk and parking lot. A parking fee is required.

BIG SUR RANGER STATION. From the ranger station, located 27 miles south of Carmel, drive 4.8 miles north to the state park entrance and turn left.

Hiking directions: The signed trail is at the far northwest end of the parking lot. Walk past the Trail Camp sign and up into a shady grove. Cross a footbridge over a tributary stream, and parallel the Big Sur River. At 0.3 miles, the trail merges with an old ranch road. Bear left, entering Trail Camp, and walk through the campground past large oaks and sycamores. Cooper Cabin is to the south in a eucalyptus grove. After viewing the historic cabin,

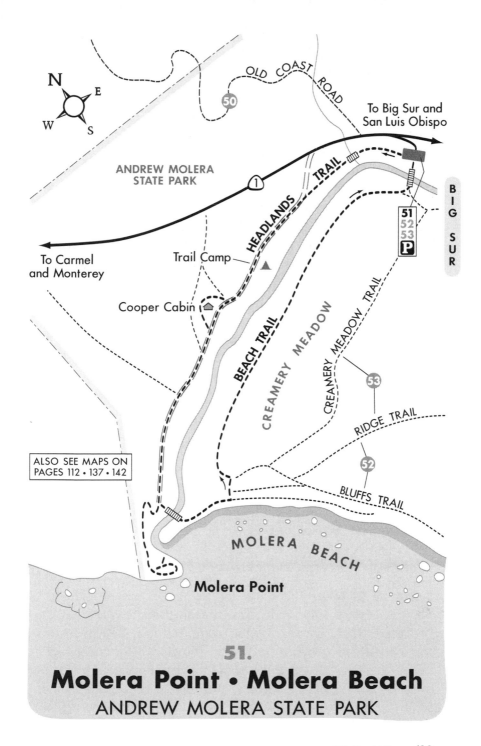

51.
Molera Point • Molera Beach
ANDREW MOLERA STATE PARK

continue southwest on the ranch road, following the river to a signed junction and map at one mile. The left fork leads to a seasonal bridge crossing the Big Sur River to Molera Beach—the return route. Take the right fork on the Headlands Trail up wooden steps to the ridge. Walk out to sea on the headlands, circling the point.

Return to the seasonal bridge, and head down to Molera Beach at the mouth of the Big Sur River. The beach extends south for two miles, but the tide often makes further access impossible. After exploring the beach, head to the back of the beach to the Beach Trail. Pass the Bluffs Trail and the Creamery Meadow Trail, both on the right. Stay left on the Beach Trail, and follow the river upstream a short distance. Soon the river veers left, and the footpath curves through the grassy meadow dotted with sycamore and cottonwood trees. The trail is separated from the river by dense willow thickets. Meander through Creamery Meadow to a junction with the River Trail and another seasonal bridge over the Big Sur River. Head left over the bridge, back to the parking lot.■

52. Bluffs—Panorama—Ridge Loop
ANDREW MOLERA STATE PARK

Hiking distance: 9-mile loop
Hiking time: 4.5 hours
Elevation gain: 1,100 feet

map
page 142

Maps: U.S.G.S. Big Sur
      Andrew Molera State Park map
Location: 22 miles south of Carmel off Highway 1

Summary of hike: This hike circles the western side of Andrew Molera State Park through a diverse cross-section of landscapes that include coastal bluffs, isolated beach coves, forested stream canyons, redwood forests, overlooks, meadows, and a river crossing. The long loop trail meanders for two miles on the flat marine terrace, then climbs up a ridge at the south park boundary to sweeping views of the coast and mountains. The trail descends along Pfeiffer Ridge through oak forests, massive redwood groves, and open grasslands with vistas of the Big Sur coastline.

Driving directions: Same as Hike 51.

Hiking directions: At the signed Beach Trail near the middle of the parking lot, cross the Big Sur River on the summer footbridge (or wade across if removed) to a trail fork. Stay to the left on the River Trail. Bear left again fifty yards ahead, staying on the River Trail to a posted junction at the base of the hillside. The River Trail curves left. Take the Creamery Meadow Trail right, and contour southwest along the base of the hill, skirting the edge of the meadow. At 0.8 miles is a junction with the Ridge Trail on the left. Take the Ridge Trail and leave the meadow, heading up the ridge to an open flat and trail fork a short distance ahead.

Begin the loop to the right on the Bluffs Trail. Cross the wide marine terrace between the jagged coastal cliffs and the inland hills. Pass several side paths that lead to the edge of the cliffs. Curve around a pair of eroding, spring-fed gullies. Dip in and out of another gulch to the end of the Bluffs Trail at a posted trail junction. The Spring Trail bears right, and zigzags down a draw to a small pocket beach. Continue on the Panorama Trail, dropping into a drainage. Climb out and steadily wind up the hillside to the park's south boundary and views of Pacific Valley and the Big Sur coast. Curve along the fenced boundary to the end of the Panorama Trail on the summit at 4.6 miles. A bench, set among the cypress trees, offers a respite with sweeping coastal views.

Take the posted Ridge Trail north, descending towards the towering redwoods ahead. The spongy, needle-covered path levels out and meanders through a shady grove of massive redwoods and twisted oaks draped with lace lichen. Pass the South Boundary Trail on the right, and follow Pfeiffer (Molera) Ridge across the exposed grass and chaparral. Cross two long, sweeping saddles to a junction with Hidden Trail. Continue down the seaward ridge, completing the loop at the base of the ridge on the Bluffs Trail. Retrace your steps along the Creamery Meadow Trail back to the parking lot. ■

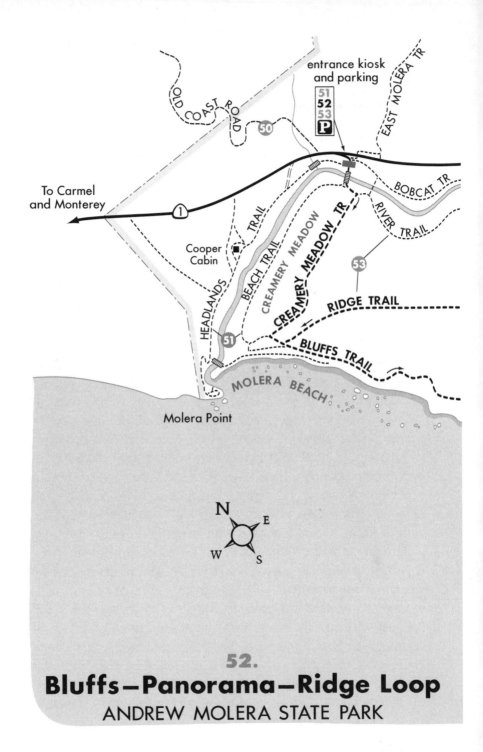

entrance kiosk
and parking

51
52
53
P

OLD COAST ROAD

50

EAST MOLERA TR

To Carmel
and Monterey

1

BOBCAT TR

RIVER TRAIL

53

Cooper
Cabin

TRAIL

BEACH TRAIL

CREAMERY MEADOW

CREAMERY MEADOW TR

RIDGE TRAIL

HEADLANDS

51

BLUFFS TRAIL

MOLERA BEACH

Molera Point

N
E
W
S

52.
Bluffs–Panorama–Ridge Loop
ANDREW MOLERA STATE PARK

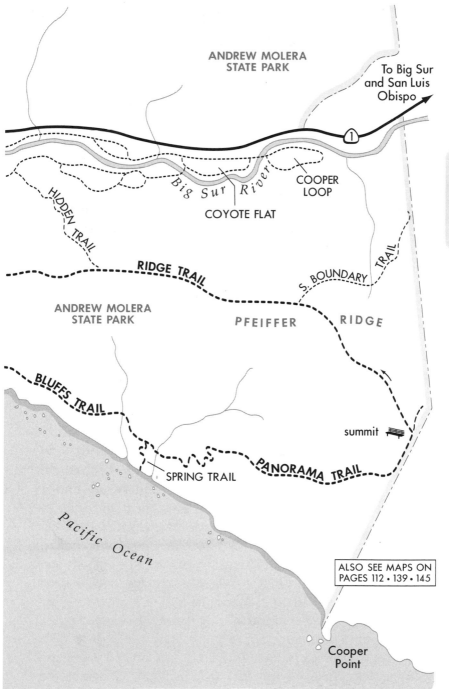

ANDREW MOLERA
STATE PARK

To Big Sur
and San Luis
Obispo

1

B I G S U R

Big Sur River

COOPER
LOOP

COYOTE FLAT

HIDDEN TRAIL

RIDGE TRAIL

S. BOUNDARY TRAIL

ANDREW MOLERA
STATE PARK

PFEIFFER RIDGE

BLUFFS TRAIL

summit

PANORAMA TRAIL

SPRING TRAIL

Pacific Ocean

ALSO SEE MAPS ON
PAGES 112 • 139 • 145

Cooper
Point

53. River Trail—Hidden Trail— Ridge Trail Loop
ANDREW MOLERA STATE PARK

Hiking distance: 3.6 mile loop
Hiking time: 2 hours
Elevation gain: 700 feet
Maps: U.S.G.S. Big Sur
Andrew Molera State Park map
Location: 22 miles south of Carmel off Highway 1

Summary of hike: The Hidden Trail climbs 570 feet to Pfeiffer (Molera) Ridge. The trail winds in and out of shady live oak glens and grassy coyote brush slopes. From the ridge are 360-degree panoramic views of the crenulated Pacific coastline, Point Sur, the Big Sur River canyon, Mount Manuel, and Pico Blanco. The path follows Pfeiffer Ridge—the backbone of Andrew Molera State Park—back down to Creamery Meadow and the Big Sur River.

Driving directions: Same as Hike 51.

Hiking directions: Take the posted Beach Trail across the Big Sur River to a trail split. (Wade across the Big Sur if the summer footbridge has been removed.) Follow the River Trail, bearing left at two consecutive junctions, to the foot of the hill and a trail split. The Creamery Meadow Trail goes to the right. Stay on the River Trail to the left, and curve right around the base of the hillside, following the Big Sur River upstream. Skirt the west edge of the meadow along the foot of the hillside. The path gains elevation through an oak canopy to the posted junction on the right. The River Trail continues straight. Instead, take the Hidden Trail to the right and ascend the hill, alternating between oak groves and small open meadows. Cross a two-plank bridge over a small gulch to the open chaparral. Along the Big Sur River below are distinct groves of redwoods towering above the oaks and pines. Along the trail, wooden steps aid in footing and help to curb erosion. The 0.7-mile Hidden Trail ends at a posted T-junction with the Ridge Trail. The left fork follows Pfeiffer Ridge to the

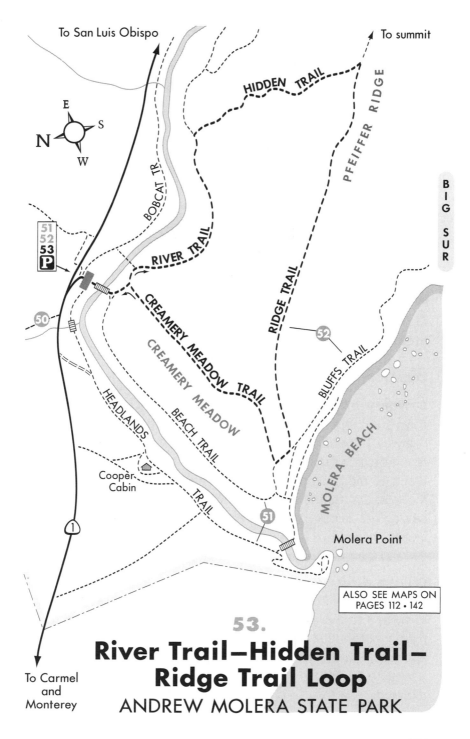

To San Luis Obispo

To summit

HIDDEN TRAIL

PFEIFFER RIDGE

BIG SUR

E
N S
W

BOBCAT TR

51
52
53
P

RIVER TRAIL

CREAMERY MEADOW TRAIL

RIDGE TRAIL

52

CREAMERY MEADOW

BLUFFS TRAIL

50

HEADLANDS

BEACH TRAIL

MOLERA BEACH

Cooper
Cabin

TRAIL

1

51

Molera Point

ALSO SEE MAPS ON
PAGES 112 • 142

To Carmel
and
Monterey

53.

River Trail–Hidden Trail–
Ridge Trail Loop
ANDREW MOLERA STATE PARK

1,050-foot summit—Hike 52. Take the right fork, following the ridge up a short hill to a level flat at 703 feet. There are grand coastal vistas of Molera Point and the Point Sur Lightstation. Descend along the seaward ridge, overlooking the state park, to a 3-way junction on a flat at the ridge bottom. The left fork follows the Bluffs Trail south (Hike 52). Take the right fork, dropping into Creamery Meadow. Bear right along the south edge of the meadow on the Creamery Meadow Trail, contouring the base of the hillside. Complete the loop at the River Trail.■

54. Pfeiffer Falls—Valley View Loop
PFEIFFER BIG SUR STATE PARK

Hiking distance: 2.2 miles round trip
Hiking time: 1 hour
Elevation gain: 450 feet
Maps: U.S.G.S. Big Sur
Pfeiffer Big Sur State Park map
Location: 27 miles south of Carmel off Highway 1

Summary of hike: Pfeiffer Big Sur State Park is home to lush forests and open meadows surrounding the Big Sur River along Highway 1. Pfeiffer Falls spills 60 feet over granite rock in a small fern grotto. This moist, fern-lined trail follows Pfeiffer-Redwood Creek up the canyon through a redwood forest to the base of the falls. On the return, the Valley View Trail climbs out of the canyon into an oak and chaparral woodland. From an overlook are sweeping views of the Santa Lucia Range, the Big Sur Valley, Point Sur, and the blue Pacific Ocean.

Driving directions: BIG SUR RANGER STATION. From the ranger station, located 27 miles south of Carmel, drive 0.5 miles north on Highway 1 to the signed Pfeiffer Big Sur State Park entrance. Turn right (inland) to the entrance station. Continue to a stop sign. Turn left and a quick right, following the trail signs 0.2 miles to the signed trailhead parking area on the right. An entrance fee is required.

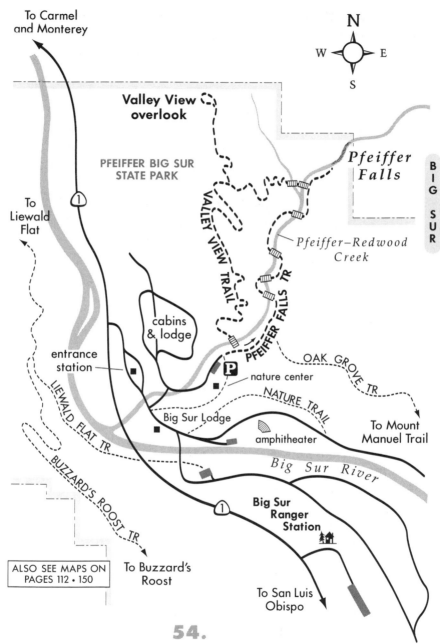

To Carmel
and Monterey

Valley View
overlook

PFEIFFER BIG SUR
STATE PARK

To
Liewald
Flat

①

*Pfeiffer
Falls*

B
I
G

S
U
R

VALLEY VIEW TRAIL

*Pfeiffer–Redwood
Creek*

PFEIFFER FALLS TR

cabins
& lodge

entrance
station

LIEWALD FLAT TR

Ⓟ

nature center

OAK GROVE TR

NATURE TRAIL

BUZZARD'S ROOST TR

Big Sur Lodge

amphitheater

To Mount
Manuel Trail

Big Sur River

①

Big Sur
Ranger
Station

ALSO SEE MAPS ON
PAGES 112 • 150

To Buzzard's
Roost

To San Luis
Obispo

54.

Pfeiffer Falls–Valley View Loop
PFEIFFER BIG SUR STATE PARK

Hiking directions: Take the trail at the far northeast end of the parking area. Head gradually uphill through the redwood forest. Parallel Pfeiffer-Redwood Creek to the signed Valley View Trail on the left. Begin the loop to the right. Ascend a long series of steps to a signed junction with the Oak Grove Trail on the right. Continue up the canyon towards Pfeiffer Falls as the path zigzags upstream over four wooden footbridges. After the fourth crossing is the second junction with the Valley View Trail on the left—the return route. Stay to the right, climbing two sets of stairs to a platform in front of Pfeiffer Falls.

Return to the junction and take the Valley View Trail, crossing a bridge over the creek and another bridge over a tributary stream. Switchbacks lead up the south-facing slope to a signed junction. Bear right towards the Valley View Overlook. Ascend the ridge 0.3 miles to a short loop at the overlook. Return back downhill to the junction, and bear right to the canyon floor on the Valley View Trail. Cross the bridge over the creek, completing the loop on the Pfeiffer Falls Trail. Return to the trailhead on the right.■

55. Mount Manuel Trail
PFEIFFER BIG SUR STATE PARK

Hiking distance: 10.4 miles round trip
Hiking time: 5.5 hours

Elevation gain: 3,200 feet
Maps: U.S.G.S. Big Sur and Pfeiffer Point
    Pfeiffer Big Sur State Park map
Location: 27 miles south of Carmel off Highway 1

map
page 150

Summary of hike: Mount Manuel is the towering mountain that dominates Pfeiffer Big Sur State Park. This hike climbs to a vista point near the 3,379-foot summit. The sweeping 360-degree panoramic views extend across the entire Big Sur area, from the Santa Lucia Mountains to the expansive crenelated coastline and sheer coastal cliffs. The hike up to the vista point is on exposed chaparral-covered hillsides that offer little shade.

Driving directions: BIG SUR RANGER STATION. From the ranger station, located 27 miles south of Carmel, drive 0.5 miles north on Highway 1 to the signed Pfeiffer Big Sur State Park entrance. Turn right (inland) past the entrance station to the stop sign. Continue straight through the intersection, passing Big Sur Lodge on the right, and bear left, following the signs towards the picnic area. At 0.7 miles is the signed trailhead parking area on the left. An entrance fee is required.

Hiking directions: Take the gated road past the trail sign into the shade of the old oak forest. At 0.1 mile is a junction at the Homestead Cabin. The right fork follows the Big Sur River along the Gorge Trail. Take the left fork to the Homestead Cabin and a trail fork. Go straight on the left fork on the Oak Grove Trail. Switchback up the hillside, alternating between shady oak woodlands and exposed chaparral. At 0.7 miles, the path levels out on a 560-foot saddle by a signed junction with the Mount Manuel Trail. Bear right up the steps, leaving the oak canopy, and begin zigzagging up the south flank of Mount Manuel above the Big Sur River Valley. Cross the arid, exposed mountainside amid low-growing scrub and forested gullies to a ridge. At 3 miles, the trail curves north and follows the ridge in the Ventana Wilderness, dipping in and out of more gullies. Views expand across Pfeiffer Ridge (Hike 52) to the ocean. Cross a forested saddle to a reflector. A short distance ahead is the rocky summit and vista point. After enjoying the expansive views, return along the same trail.■

55.
Mount Manuel Trail
PFEIFFER BIG SUR STATE PARK

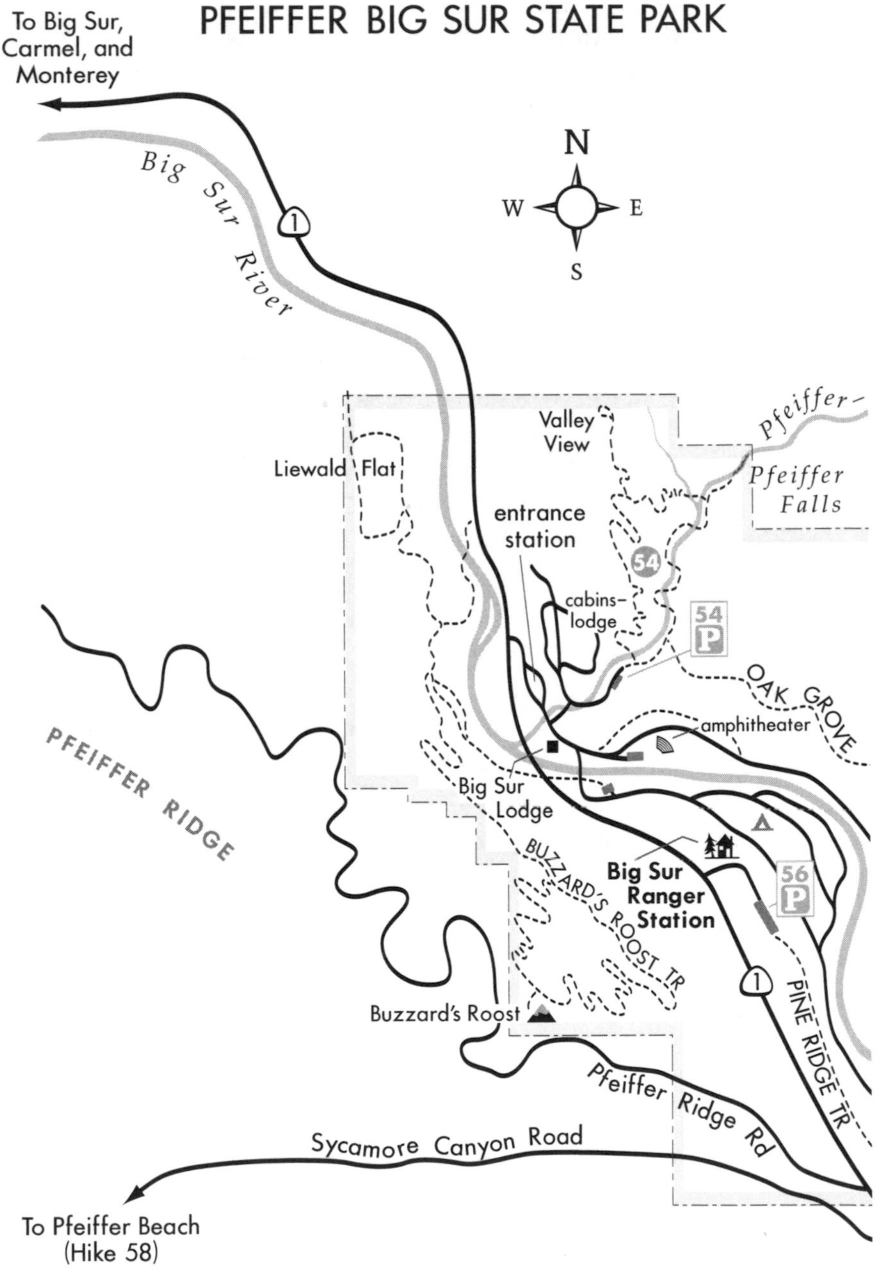

To Big Sur,
Carmel, and
Monterey

Big Sur River

①

N

W ✦ E

S

Valley
View

Liewald Flat

Pfeiffer

*Pfeiffer
Falls*

entrance
station

54

cabins-
lodge

54
P

OAK GROVE

amphitheater

PFEIFFER RIDGE

Big Sur
Lodge

BUZZARD'S ROOST TR

**Big Sur
Ranger
Station**

56
P

①

PINE RIDGE TR

Buzzard's Roost

Pfeiffer Ridge Rd

Sycamore Canyon Road

To Pfeiffer Beach
(Hike 58)

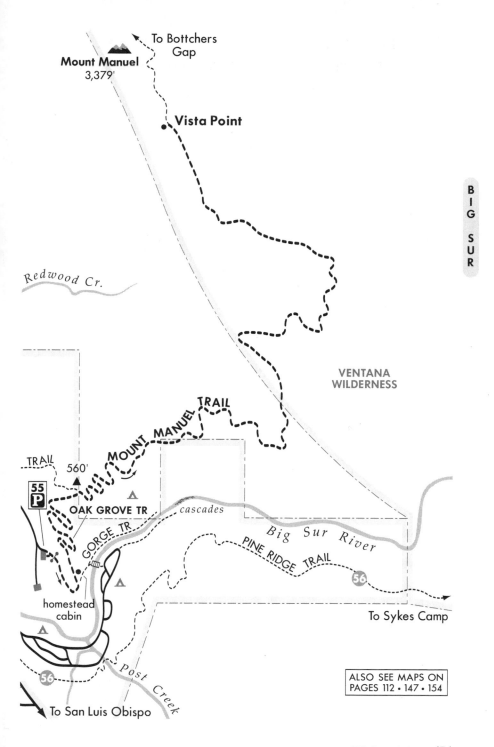

To Bottchers Gap

Mount Manuel
3,379'

Vista Point

B
I
G

S
U
R

Redwood Cr.

VENTANA
WILDERNESS

MOUNT MANUEL **TRAIL**

TRAIL

560'

55
P

OAK GROVE TR   *cascades*

GORGE TR

Big Sur River

PINE RIDGE TRAIL

56

homestead
cabin

To Sykes Camp

56

Post Creek

To San Luis Obispo

ALSO SEE MAPS ON
PAGES 112 • 147 • 154

120 Great Hikes – **151**

56. Pine Ridge Trail to Terrace Creek

PFEIFFER BIG SUR STATE PARK to VENTANA WILDERNESS

Hiking distance: 10.6 miles round trip

Hiking time: 5 hours

map
page 154

Elevation gain: 1,000 feet

Maps: U.S.G.S. Pfeiffer Point, Partington Ridge, Ventana Cross
Pfeiffer Big Sur State Park map

Location: 27 miles south of Carmel off Highway 1

Summary of hike: The Pine Ridge Trail is a key access route to numerous camps and trails throughout the expansive Ventana Wilderness. The trailhead is at the Big Sur Ranger Station in Pfeiffer Big Sur State Park. The most popular destination from the Pine Ridge Trail is the ten-mile overnight hike to the hot springs at Sykes Camp. This hike takes in the first 5.3 miles of the trail to Terrace Creek, traveling along the Big Sur River Valley 600—800 feet above the river. The hike may be combined with the Coast Ridge Trail (Hike 57) for a 12.5-mile loop.

Driving directions: BIG SUR RANGER STATION. The trail begins at the ranger station, located 27 miles south of Carmel. Turn inland and drive 0.2 miles to the far end of the parking area.

Hiking directions: Take the signed trail at the far end of the parking lot into the shaded forest. Cross the hillside above the Big Sur River through tanbark oak and redwood groves, skirting the edge of the Big Sur Campground to an unsigned trail split. The left fork descends into the campground. Stay to the right and cross a water-carved ravine along Pfeiffer Creek. Zigzag downhill and cross Post Creek. Climb out of the narrow canyon to vistas of the Big Sur Valley. Steadily gain elevation, traversing the cliffs above the Big Sur River Valley. The path alternates from exposed chaparral to shady draws. The Mount Manuel Trail (Hike 55) is visible across the canyon. At 2.5 miles, the trail leaves the state park and enters the Ventana Wilderness by a boundary sign. Continue up the river valley to a junction with the trail to Ventana Camp at 4 miles. The left fork descends 1.2 miles to the camp, situated in a horseshoe bend along the Big Sur River. Continue east on the Pine

Ridge Trail for 1.2 miles to Terrace Creek and a signed junction with the Terrace Creek Trail. Terrace Creek Camp sits above and to the right, straddling the creek in a beautiful grove of redwoods. This is the turn-around spot.

For the 12.5-mile loop, take the Terrace Creek Trail through the lush canyon for 1.6 miles to the Coast Ridge Road. Referencing the hiking directions of Hike 57, follow the Coast Ridge Road southwest back to the parking area. Return 1.7 miles along Highway 1 back to the Big Sur Ranger Station.■

57. Coast Ridge Road to Terrace Creek Trail

Hiking distance: 8 miles round trip
Hiking time: 4 hours
Elevation gain: 1,600 feet

map
page 155

Maps: U.S.G.S. Pfeiffer Point and Partington Ridge
Location: 28.7 miles south of Carmel off Highway 1

Summary of hike: The Coast Ridge Road is a public right-of-way for hikers that is on a private, unpaved road. The road switchbacks to the top of the coastal ridge and follows the ridge for 30 miles. This hike follows the first four miles to the Terrace Creek Trail. The trail offers spectacular views deep into the precipitous Ventana Wilderness, extending across the Big Sur Valley to the Pacific Ocean. The hike may be combined with the Pine Ridge Trail (Hike 56) for a 12.5-mile loop.

Driving directions: BIG SUR RANGER STATION. From the ranger station, located 27 miles south of Carmel, drive 1.7 miles south on Highway 1 to the signed Ventana Inn turnoff on the left. Turn left (inland) and drive 0.2 miles—staying to the right—to the signed Vista Point parking area on the right.

Hiking directions: Walk 0.1 mile up the paved road past Vista Point to the gated road on the right, where the paved road forks left. Pass the gate and take the unpaved Coast Ridge Road around Ventana Inn. The wooded road winds through the shaded oak, bay, and redwood forest. At one mile, curve sharply left, crossing the trickling headwaters of Post Creek. Pass a narrow 30-foot waterfall cascading off a vertical rock wall on the right. Emerge from the forest, overlooking the canyon filled with redwoods. Steadily climb the open hillside trail while enjoying the commanding coastal views. The road winds slowly upward, following the mountain contours to the ridge and a hairpin right bend just before 2 miles. The serpentine road continues a steady but gentle uphill grade, crossing a saddle with views into the Ventana Wilderness. Cross several shady gullies and rolling grassy hills. At 4 miles, on a saddle just beyond a gated side road, is a signed junction with the Terrace Creek Trail on the left. This is our turn-around spot.

For a 12.5-mile loop, take the Terrace Creek Trail through the lush, wooded canyon. Continue 1.6 miles to Terrace Creek Camp in a redwood grove by a junction with the Pine Ridge Trail—Hike 56. Bear left and return via the Pine Ridge Trail. (Reference the hiking directions for Hike 56). At the Big Sur Ranger Station, walk 1.7 miles southbound along Highway 1 back to the Ventana Inn turnoff.■

HIKE 56: **Pine Ridge Trail**

HIKE 57: **Coast Ridge Road**

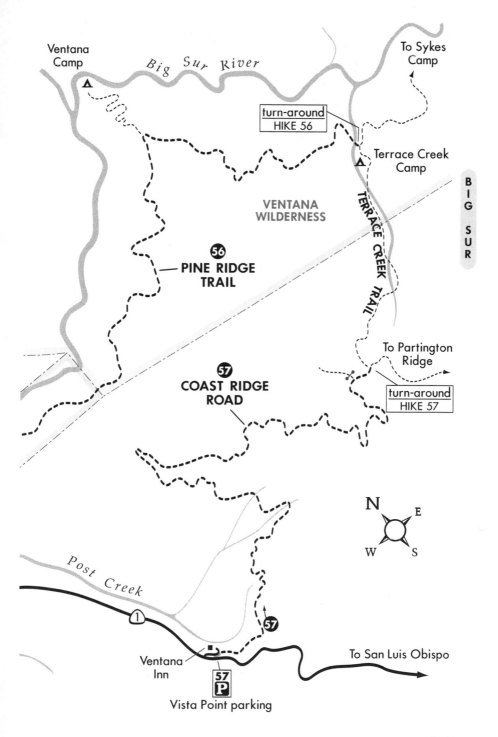

Ventana Camp

Big Sur River

To Sykes Camp

turn-around
HIKE 56

Terrace Creek Camp

VENTANA
WILDERNESS

TERRACE CREEK TRAIL

56
— PINE RIDGE
TRAIL

To Partington Ridge

57
COAST RIDGE
ROAD

turn-around
HIKE 57

N
E
W
S

Post Creek

1

57

Ventana
Inn

To San Luis Obispo

57
P

Vista Point parking

58. Pfeiffer Beach

Hiking distance: 1 mile round trip
Hiking time: 30 minutes
Elevation gain: Level
Maps: U.S.G.S. Pfeiffer Point
       Los Padres National Forest Northern Section Trail Map
Location: 27.5 miles south of Carmel off Highway 1

Summary of hike: Pfeiffer Beach is a white sand beach surrounded by towering headland cliffs within the Los Padres National Forest. Pfeiffer Point extends outward at the south end. Dramatic offshore sea stacks have been sculpted by the wind and pounding surf, creating sea caves, eroded natural arches, and blowholes. On the beach, Sycamore Creek forms a small lagoon as it empties into the Pacific. Leashed dogs are allowed.

Driving directions: BIG SUR RANGER STATION. From the ranger station, located 27 miles south of Carmel, drive 0.5 miles south on Highway 1 to the unsigned Sycamore Canyon Road. Turn right and drive 2.2 miles down the narrow, winding road through Sycamore Canyon to the parking lot. A parking fee is required.

From the signed Julia Pfeiffer Burns State Park entrance, Sycamore Canyon Road is 9.8 miles north.

RAGGED POINT. From Highway 1 at Ragged Point Inn, 1.5 miles south of the Monterey County line, drive 47 miles north to the unsigned Sycamore Canyon Road. It is located a half mile north of the post office.

Hiking directions: From the west end of the parking area, take the signed trail through a canopy of cypress trees along Sycamore Creek to the wide, sandy beach. The creek divides the beach, which forms a small lagoon. Straight ahead are giant rock formations with natural arches and sea caves. A short distance to the south are the steep cliffs of Pfeiffer Point. Beachcomb along the shore from the point to the cliffs at the far north end of the beach. An unmaintained trail heads up the cliffs to the north and follows the bluffs. Choose your own turn-around point.■

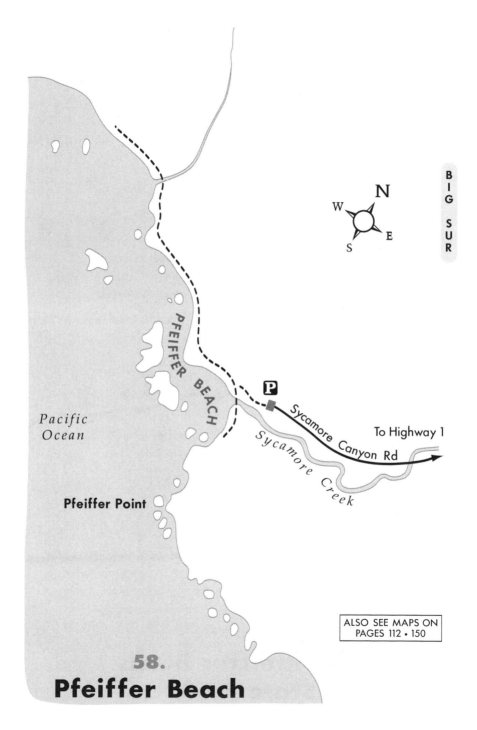

B
I
G

S
U
R

N
W ⟡ E
S

P

Sycamore Canyon Rd

To Highway 1

Sycamore Creek

PFEIFFER BEACH

Pacific
Ocean

Pfeiffer Point

ALSO SEE MAPS ON
PAGES 112 • 150

58.
Pfeiffer Beach

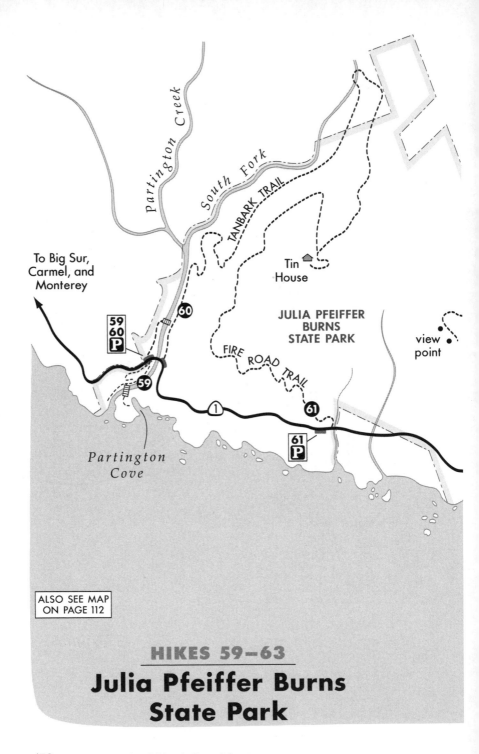

To Big Sur,
Carmel, and
Monterey

Partington Creek

South Fork

TANBARK TRAIL

Tin
House

JULIA PFEIFFER
BURNS
STATE PARK

view
point

**59
60
P**

60

FIRE ROAD TRAIL

59

1

61

**61
P**

*Partington
Cove*

ALSO SEE MAP
ON PAGE 112

HIKES 59–63

Julia Pfeiffer Burns
State Park

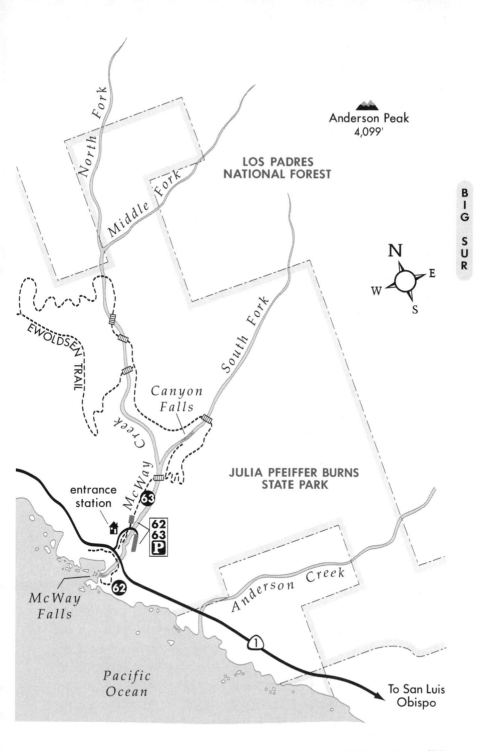

North Fork

Middle Fork

EWOLDSEN TRAIL

South Fork

Anderson Peak
4,099'

LOS PADRES
NATIONAL FOREST

Canyon
Falls

McWay Creek

entrance
station

JULIA PFEIFFER BURNS
STATE PARK

63

62
63
P

62

McWay
Falls

Anderson Creek

1

Pacific
Ocean

To San Luis
Obispo

N
W E
S

BIG SUR

59. Partington Cove

JULIA PFEIFFER BURNS STATE PARK

Hiking distance: 1 mile round trip
Hiking time: 1 hour
Elevation gain: 280 feet
Maps: U.S.G.S. Partington Ridge
Julia Pfeiffer Burns State Park map
Location: 35.5 miles south of Carmel off Highway 1

Summary of hike: Partington Cove sits at the northern boundary of Julia Pfeiffer Burns State Park along a pristine and rugged section of the Big Sur coastline. The trail to the enclosed cove descends down Partington Canyon on an old dirt road. The creek, which carved the canyon, empties into the ocean at the rocky west cove. A 120-foot tunnel was cut through the cliffs over 100 years ago, leading to the east cove and Partington Landing. The tunnel was a transit route to haul tanbark to the ships moored in Partington Cove. The historical landing was used as a shipping dock in the 1880s by homesteader John Partington.

Driving directions: BIG SUR RANGER STATION. From the ranger station, located 27 miles south of Carmel, drive 8.5 miles south on Highway 1 to the wide parking pullouts on both sides of the highway by Partington Bridge, where the road curves across Partington Creek and the canyon.

RAGGED POINT. From Highway 1 at Ragged Point Inn, located 1.5 miles south of the Monterey County line, drive 39 miles north to the parking pullouts. The pullouts are 1.9 miles north of the signed entrance for Julia Pfeiffer Burns State Park.

Hiking directions: Head west on the ocean side of Highway 1 past the trailhead gate. Descend on the eroded granite road along the north canyon wall, high above Partington Creek. The old road weaves downhill to the creek and a junction with an interpretive sign. The left fork follows Partington Creek upstream under a dense forest canopy. Take the right fork 50 yards to a second junction. The left route crosses a wooden footbridge over Partington Creek and leads to the tunnel carved through the granite wall. The tunnel ends at the east cove, where remnants of Partington Landing remain.

Return to the junction by the bridge, and take the path that is now on your left. Follow the north bank of Partington Creek to an enclosed beach cove surrounded by the steep cliffs of Partington Point. Return along the same trail. ■

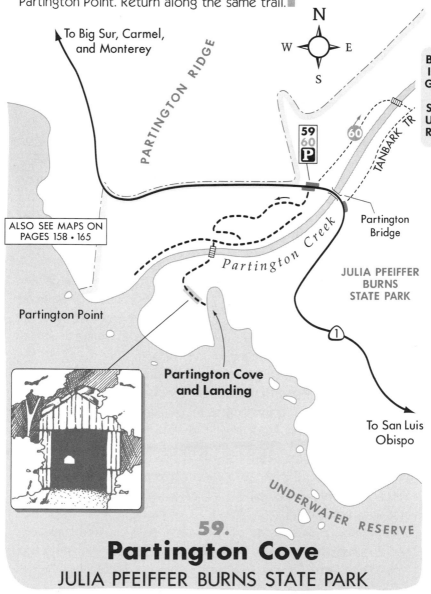

ALSO SEE MAPS ON PAGES 158 • 165

59.
Partington Cove
JULIA PFEIFFER BURNS STATE PARK

60. Tanbark Trail to Tin House
JULIA PFEIFFER BURNS STATE PARK

Hiking distance: 6.4 miles round trip
Hiking time: 4 hours
Elevation gain: 1,900 feet
Maps: U.S.G.S. Partington Ridge
      Julia Pfeiffer Burns State Park map
Location: 35.5 miles south of Carmel off Highway 1

*map
page 165*

Summary of hike: The 3,762-acre Julia Pfeiffer Burns State Park lies along ten miles of beautiful Big Sur coast backed by 3,000-foot ridges. The Tanbark Trail is a steep climb up Partington Canyon to a grassy meadow with spectacular coastal views from the abandoned Tin House. The path parallels Partington Creek through a dense forest of huge redwoods, tanbark oaks, and a lush understory of ferns. Switchbacks lead up the canyon wall to the ridge separating Partington and McWay Canyons in the heart of the park. The hike can be combined with the Fire Road Trail—Hike 61—for a 6.4-mile loop.

Driving directions: BIG SUR RANGER STATION. From the ranger station, located 27 miles south of Carmel, drive 8.5 miles south on Highway 1 to the wide parking pullouts on both sides of the highway by Partington Bridge, where the road curves across Partington Creek and the canyon.

RAGGED POINT. From Highway 1 at Ragged Point Inn, located 1.5 miles south of the Monterey County line, drive 39 miles north to the parking pullouts. The pullouts are 1.9 miles north of the signed entrance for Julia Pfeiffer Burns State Park.

Hiking directions: From the inland side of the road, take the path leading into the steep-walled canyon from either side of the bridge. Both trails join together by a wooden footbridge crossing over Partington Creek. The Tanbark Trail continues upstream on the east side of the creek, passing huge rock formations, redwood groves, pools, cascades, waterfalls, ferns, and mossy boulders. Cross a tributary stream by McLaughlin Grove, and head up the canyon wall on a few switchbacks, leaving the creek and canyon floor. Weave up the mountain to a sharp left switchback. A short detour to the right leads to a ridge over-looking Partington Point.

Return to the trail and traverse the canyon wall through tanbark oaks and redwoods. Cross planks over the South Fork of Partington Creek. Sharply switchback to the right, and recross the creek by a bench in a redwood grove. Continue uphill towards the south, reaching the high point of the hike at a trail sign. Descend to a T-junction with the Fire Road Trail (Hike 61). Bear left on the unpaved road, and descend a short distance, curving to the right to the abandoned Tin House. Below the house is a grassy meadow with inspiring views of the Big Sur Coast.

Return along the same trail, or combine this hike with the Fire Road Trail for a 6.4-mile loop. The loop requires returning 0.9 miles along Highway 1 back to the trailhead.■

61. Fire Road Trail to Tin House
JULIA PFEIFFER BURNS STATE PARK

Hiking distance: 4.6 miles round trip
Hiking time: 2.5 hours
Elevation gain: 1,600 feet

map
page 165

Maps: U.S.G.S. Partington Ridge
      Julia Pfeiffer Burns State Park map
Location: 36.3 miles south of Carmel off Highway 1

Summary of hike: The Fire Road Trail is a shorter and slightly easier route up the coastal ridge to the Tin House. From the house are panoramic views of the ocean and Julia Pfeiffer Burns State Park from an elevation of 1,950 feet. The Fire Road Trail resembles more of a trail than a road. The wide trail begins on the coastal cliffs and heads inland, weaving in and out of gullies to Partington Canyon. The path contours the east wall of the canyon, rich with coastal redwoods, tanbark oaks, and shade-loving plants. The trail ends at the Tin House, a boarded up tin building on the high ridge separating Partington and McWay Canyons. This hike can be combined with the Tanbark Trail—Hike 60—for a 6.4-mile loop.

Driving directions: BIG SUR RANGER STATION. From the ranger station, located 27 miles south of Carmel, drive 9.3 miles south on Highway 1 to the signed Vista Point parking pullout on the right.

RAGGED POINT. From Highway 1 at Ragged Point Inn, located 1.5 miles south of the Monterey County line, drive 38 miles north to the signed Vista Point parking pullout on the left. The pullout is 1.1 miles north of the signed entrance for Julia Pfeiffer Burns State Park.

Hiking directions: Head 75 yards southbound on Highway 1 to the gated Fire Road on the inland side of the highway. Walk around the trail gate into a shady redwood grove, paralleling a trickling stream on the right. Curve left, emerging from the trees, and climb to an overlook of the coast and offshore rocks. The trail follows the coastal cliffs along the oceanfront mountains. As you near Partington Canyon, a thousand feet above Partington Cove, curve right and enter the canyon. The views extend across the canyon to homes on the south-facing cliffs. Curve along the contours of the mountain, winding uphill on the serpentine path through redwoods and tanbark oaks. A few switchbacks aid in the climb through the shady forest. The road tops out at a signed junction with the Tanbark Trail (Hike 60) on the left. Continue straight ahead and gently descend for a short distance, looping to the right. The trail ends at the abandoned Tin House and the grassy meadow overlook just below the building.

Return along the same trail, or combine this hike with the Tanbark Trail for a 6.4-mile loop. The loop requires returning 0.9 miles along Highway 1 back to the Vista Point pullouts. ▪

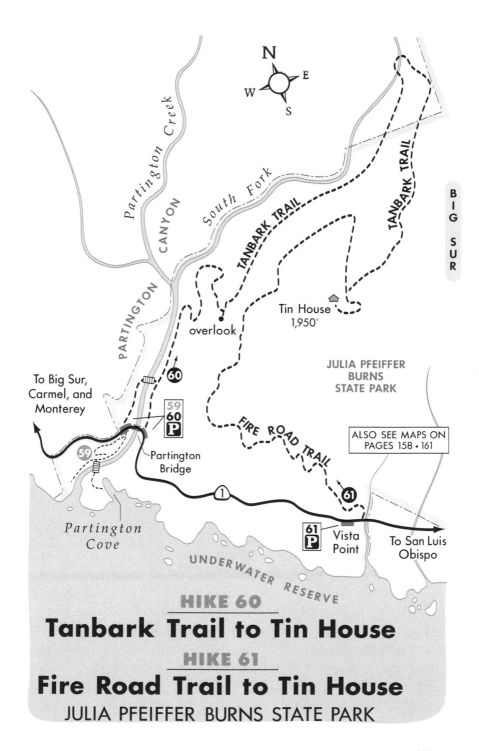

N
E
W
S

Partington Creek

South Fork

Partington Canyon

TANBARK TRAIL

TANBARK TRAIL

BIG SUR

Tin House
1,950'

overlook

PARTINGTON

To Big Sur,
Carmel, and
Monterey

JULIA PFEIFFER
BURNS
STATE PARK

FIRE ROAD TRAIL

ALSO SEE MAPS ON
PAGES 158 • 161

60

59
60
P

59

Partington
Bridge

1

61

61
P
Vista
Point

To San Luis
Obispo

Partington
Cove

UNDERWATER RESERVE

HIKE 60
Tanbark Trail to Tin House
HIKE 61
Fire Road Trail to Tin House
JULIA PFEIFFER BURNS STATE PARK

62. McWay Falls and Saddle Rock
JULIA PFEIFFER BURNS STATE PARK

Hiking distance: 0.7 miles round trip
Hiking time: 30 minutes
Elevation gain: 50 feet
Maps: U.S.G.S. Partington Ridge
       Julia Pfeiffer Burns State Park map
Location: 37.4 miles south of Carmel off Highway 1

Summary of hike: McWay Falls pours 80 feet onto the sand along the edge of the Pacific at the mouth of McWay Canyon. The incredibly scenic waterfall drops off the granite bluff in a wooded beach cove lined with offshore rocks. A handicap accessible trail leads to a viewing area of McWay Cove and the cataract on the 100-foot high bluffs. The pristine beach itself is not accessible. On the south side of the bay is a footpath to a scenic overlook at a cypress-shaded picnic area adjacent to Saddle Rock.

Driving directions: BIG SUR RANGER STATION. From the ranger station, located 27 miles south of Carmel, drive 10.4 miles south on Highway 1 to the signed Julia Pfeiffer Burns State Park. Turn left (inland) and park in the day-use parking lot.

RAGGED POINT. From Highway 1 at Ragged Point Inn, located 1.5 miles south of the Monterey County line, drive 37 miles north to the signed Julia Pfeiffer Burns State Park.

Hiking directions: Descend the steps across the road from the restrooms. At the base of the steps, bear right and head southwest on the signed Waterfall Trail. Follow the north canyon wall above the creek, and walk through the tunnel under Highway 1 to a T-junction. The left fork leads to the Saddle Rock Overlook. For now, take the right fork along the cliffs. Cross a wooden footbridge, with great views of McWay Falls pouring onto the sand. Beyond the bridge is an observation deck with expansive coastal views.

After enjoying the sights, return to the junction and take the footpath towards the south end of the bay. Walk through a canopy of old-growth eucalyptus trees high above the falls. Descend to the trail's end at a 206-foot overlook in a cypress grove by a picnic area and an environmental camp.■

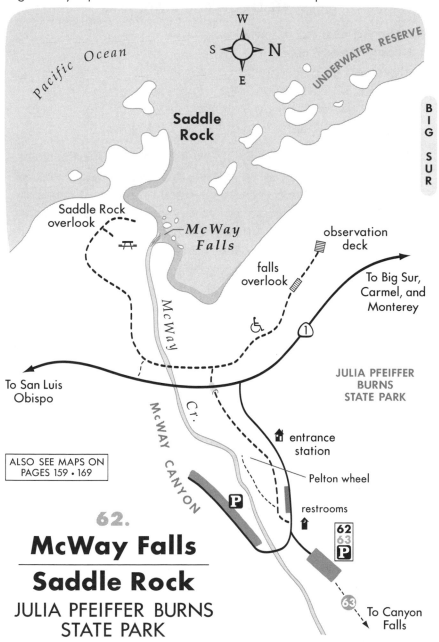

Pacific Ocean

UNDERWATER RESERVE

B I G

S U R

Saddle Rock

Saddle Rock
overlook

McWay Falls

observation deck

falls overlook

To Big Sur, Carmel, and Monterey

McWay

To San Luis
Obispo

JULIA PFEIFFER
BURNS
STATE PARK

ALSO SEE MAPS ON
PAGES 159 • 169

McWay Cr.

McWAY CANYON

entrance
station

Pelton wheel

restrooms

62
63
P

62.

McWay Falls
Saddle Rock

JULIA PFEIFFER BURNS
STATE PARK

63 To Canyon Falls

63. Ewoldsen Trail
to Canyon Falls and Overlook
JULIA PFEIFFER BURNS STATE PARK

Hiking distance: 4.7-mile loop
Hiking time: 3 hours
Elevation gain: 1,600 feet
Maps: U.S.G.S. Partington Ridge
Julia Pfeiffer Burns State Park map
Location: 37.4 miles south of Carmel off Highway 1

Summary of hike: The Ewoldsen Trail in Julia Pfeiffer Burns State Park leads through a dense coastal redwood forest in McWay Canyon. The trail crosses several bridges as it heads up to the steep ridge separating McWay and Partington Canyons. From the grassy coastal cliffs are amazing overlooks perched on the edge of the cliffs. The views extend across the park and far beyond, showcasing the jagged coastline and endless mountain ridges and valleys. En route to the ridgetop overlooks is Canyon Falls, a long, narrow, two-tiered waterfall on the South Fork of McWay Creek. The 70-foot cataract cascades off fern-covered rock cliffs in a lush grotto at the back of a serene canyon.

Driving directions: BIG SUR RANGER STATION. From the ranger station, located 27 miles south of Carmel, drive 10.4 miles south on Highway 1 to the signed Julia Pfeiffer Burns State Park. Turn left (inland) and park in the day-use parking lot.

RAGGED POINT. From Highway 1 at Ragged Point Inn, located 1.5 miles south of the Monterey County line, drive 37 miles north to the signed Julia Pfeiffer Burns State Park.

Hiking directions: From the upper end of the parking area, take the signed Canyon and Ewoldsen Trails into a dark redwood forest. Follow McWay Creek upstream past the picnic area. Cross a wooden footbridge over the creek to the east bank, just below the confluence of the South Fork and Main Fork of McWay Creek. A short distance upstream is a posted junction. Take the left fork on the Canyon Trail, staying close to the creek. The narrow, cliffside path ends at the base of Canyon Falls.

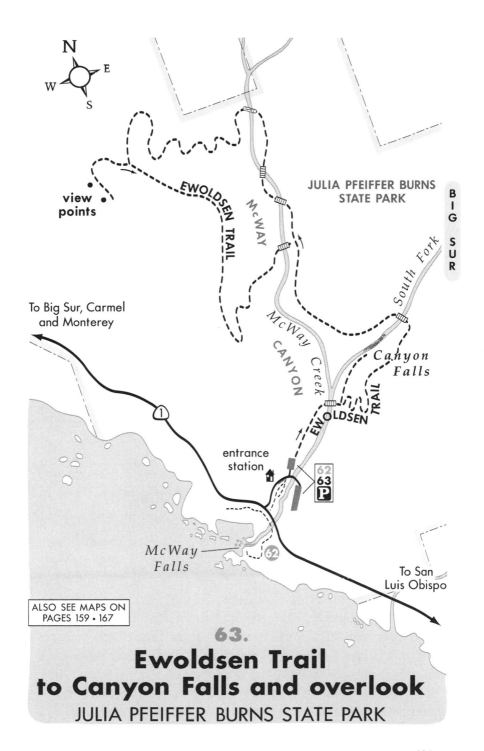

N
W · E
S

view
points

EWOLDSEN TRAIL

McWAY

JULIA PFEIFFER BURNS
STATE PARK

BIG SUR

South Fork

McWay Creek

CANYON

Canyon
Falls

To Big Sur, Carmel
and Monterey

EWOLDSEN TRAIL

1

entrance
station

62
63
P

McWay
Falls

62

To San
Luis Obispo

ALSO SEE MAPS ON
PAGES 159 • 167

63.
Ewoldsen Trail
to Canyon Falls and overlook
JULIA PFEIFFER BURNS STATE PARK

Return back to the juction, and continue on the Ewoldsen Trail up the switchback, leaving the canyon floor and creek. Zigzag up the south wall of the canyon, and cross another footbridge over the South Fork. Traverse the hillside up the mountain contours, and rejoin the Main Fork of McWay Creek, where views extend down canyon to the sea. Follow the watercourse above the creek to a signed junction at one mile, beginning the loop. Take the right fork along the east bank of the creek. Cross two bridges over the creek, passing cascades, small waterfalls, pools, out-croppings, and moss-covered boulders. Cross a log bridge over the creek, and ascend the west canyon wall. Enter an oak wood-land and follow the hillside path to a signed junction. Detour to the right a quarter mile to the viewpoint on the 1,800-foot oceanfront cliffs. Take a break and enjoy the vistas. Return to the junction and continue on the loop. The winding path descends along the oceanfront cliffs, then curves left into the forested canyon. Complete the loop at the bridge over McWay Creek, and retrace your steps back to the right.■

64. The Limekilns and Limekiln Falls
LIMEKILN STATE PARK

Hiking distance: 1—2.4 miles round trip
Hiking time: 30 minutes—1.5 hours
Elevation gain: 200 feet
Maps: U.S.G.S. Lopez Point
　　　　　Limekiln State Park map
Location: 52 miles south of Carmel off Highway 1

Summary of hike: Limekiln State Park is a magnificent 716-acre park and campground along the Big Sur coastline at the south end of the Ventana Wilderness. Three year-round creeks flow through the park under the shade of towering coastal redwoods with a lush mix of sycamores, oaks, and maples. The Redwood Trail leads to four massive stone and steel kilns used to purify quar-ried limestone into powdered lime in the 1880s. The lime was

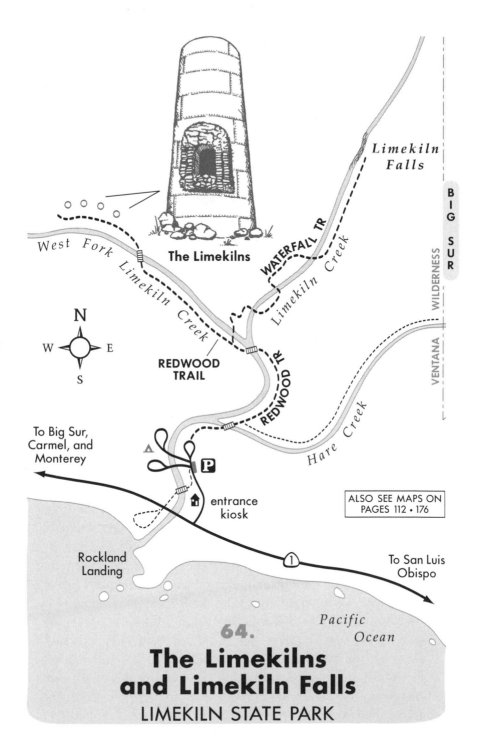

Limekiln
Falls

West Fork Limekiln Creek

The Limekilns

WATERFALL TR

Limekiln Creek

N
W E
S

REDWOOD
TRAIL

REDWOOD TR

Hare Creek

To Big Sur,
Carmel, and
Monterey

P

entrance
kiosk

ALSO SEE MAPS ON
PAGES 112 • 176

Rockland
Landing

1

To San Luis
Obispo

Pacific
Ocean

BIG SUR

VENTANA WILDERNESS

64.

The Limekilns
and Limekiln Falls
LIMEKILN STATE PARK

used as an ingredient in cement. The Redwood Trail follows the old wagon route used to haul barrels of lime slacked from the furnaces. The hike follows Limekiln Creek and the West Fork up the canyon to the giant limekilns.

A side trip leads to Limekiln Falls. The waterfall cascades 100 feet off a vertical limestone wall and fans out more than 25 feet wide in a narrow box canyon.

Driving directions: BIG SUR RANGER STATION. From the ranger station, located 27 miles south of Carmel, drive 25.3 miles south on Highway 1 to the signed Limekiln State Park. Turn left (inland) to the entrance kiosk. Park 30 yards ahead in the day use parking area on the right. An entrance fee is required.

RAGGED POINT. From Highway 1 at Ragged Point Inn, located 1.5 miles south of the Monterey County line, drive 22.2 miles north to the state park on the right.

Hiking directions: Walk up the campground road to the road's north end near the confluence of Limekiln Creek and Hare Creek. Cross the footbridge over Hare Creek in the dense redwood forest to a posted trail fork. The right fork parallels the north side of Hare Creek to the park boundary. Instead, take the left fork on the Redwood Trail, following the contours of Limekiln Creek through the shady redwood forest. Cross a second footbridge where Limekiln Creek and the West Fork merge. To get to the limekilns, follow the west bank of the West Fork past the Waterfall Trail on the right. Continue on the Redwood Trail to a third bridge by cascades and a small waterfall. Head gradually uphill along the east side of the creek, skirting past a large rock outcropping. Thirty yards beyond the rock are the four enormous metal cylinders on the right. On the left are waterfalls and pools.

For a side trip on the return, take the Waterfall Trail down log steps, and boulder hop across the West Fork. Head up the side canyon, and cross Limekiln Creek to its east bank. Pass a magnificent triple-trunk redwood tree, and head upstream past endless cascades, pools, and waterfalls. After crossing the creek two more times, the path reaches the end of the lush canyon at the base of the majestic cataract. ∎

65. Vicente Flat
from Kirk Creek Campground

Hiking distance: 10.6 miles round trip
Hiking time: 6 hours
Elevation gain: 1,700 feet
Maps: U.S.G.S. Cape San Martin and Cone Peak
     Ventana Wilderness Map
Location: 54 miles south of Carmel off Highway 1

map
page 176

Summary of hike: Vicente Flat is a large, beautiful camp on the banks of Hare Creek in the Ventana Wilderness. The camp sits in a grove of majestic redwoods and a sunny meadow the size of a football field. The Vicente Flat Trail (also known as the Kirk Creek Trail) is one of the most scenic and diverse hikes in the Ventana Wilderness. There are sweeping views from the ocean to Cone Peak as well as deep, forested canyons.

The trail begins at the coast and crosses scrub-covered coastal slopes above Pacific Valley. The trail leads to Hare Canyon, where the path follows the south wall of the canyon into wood-shaded ravines and meadowlands. The trail reaches Hare Creek under a canopy of towering redwoods. This hike can be combined with Hike 66 for a 7.4-mile, one-way shuttle hike (downhill starting from Cone Peak Road).

Driving directions: BIG SUR RANGER STATION. From the ranger station, located 27 miles south of Carmel, drive 27.2 miles south on Highway 1 to the Kirk Creek Campground on the right. The posted trail is on the left (inland side), directly across from the campground. Park in a pullout alongside the highway.

RAGGED POINT. From Highway 1 at Ragged Point Inn, 1.5 miles south of the Monterey County line, drive 20.4 miles north to the Kirk Creek Campground and trailhead.

Hiking directions: Climb the exposed, brush-covered coastal slope toward the saddle. The magnificent coastal views from above Pacific Valley improve with every step. Just before reaching the saddle, bear left and cross the sloping grassland to the posted Ventana Wilderness boundary. Cross a gully below the

B
I
G

S
U
R

sheer rock cliffs, and curve west to the west tip of the ridge, with sweeping panoramas from north to south. Climb the ridge and curve north. Traverse the upper mountain slope, wending in and out of mature redwood and bay groves. Contour around three more sizeable gullies to the south wall of Hare Canyon at 3 miles. The views extend up Limekiln Canyon and Hare Canyon to Cone Peak. Curve east and follow the level path through redwood groves along the south wall of Hare Canyon. Continue to Espinosa Camp on a small shoulder to the left. The camp is 20 yards off the trail on a flat, grassy ridge with an ocean view. A quarter mile after the camp, cross a redwood-lined stream. Continue through the forest on a moderate grade for 2 miles, then begin a steady descent to Hare Creek on the canyon floor. Cross the creek to a posted junction with the Stone Ridge Trail on the left. Bear to the right and enter Vicente Flat. Campsites line the creek among the towering redwoods. Return along the same trail.

Vicente Flat is also the destination for Hike 66. For a one-way shuttle hike along the Vicente Flat Trail, begin the hike from Cone Peak Road—Hike 66—and continue 7.4 miles down to the Kirk Creek Campground.■

66. Vicente Flat from Cone Peak Road

Hiking distance: 4.5 miles round trip
Hiking time: 3 hours
Elevation gain: 1,600 feet
Maps: U.S.G.S. Cone Peak
      Ventana Wilderness Map
Location: 54 miles south of Carmel and 11 miles off Highway 1

map
page 176

Summary of hike: Vicente Flat is a spacious camp with a large open meadow along the banks of Hare Creek. Campsites line the serene streamside glade under a canopy of majestic redwoods. The well-graded Vicente Flat Trail descends from its upper east end at Cone Peak Road. The path drops into wooded Hare

Canyon, with exceptional views down the 3,000-foot deep canyon to the sea. The downhill path parallels Hare Creek beneath the shade of massive redwoods. This trail may be combined with Hike 65 for a 7.4-mile, one-way downhill shuttle hike.

Driving directions: BIG SUR RANGER STATION. From the ranger station, located 27 miles south of Carmel, drive 27.4 miles south to Nacimiento-Fergusson Road. The road is 0.2 miles south of Kirk Creek Campground. Turn inland and wind up the paved mountain road 7.1 miles to the South Coast Ridge Road on the right. Turn left on the narrow, unpaved Central Coast Ridge Road (also known as Cone Peak Road), and drive 3.7 miles to the posted trail on the left. Park in the pullout on the left, just past the trailhead. Cone Peak Road is impassable in wet weather.

RAGGED POINT. From Highway 1 at Ragged Point Inn, 1.5 miles south of the Monterey County line, drive 20.2 miles north to Nacimiento-Fergusson Road, located 4.2 miles north of the Pacific Valley Ranger Station. Continue with the directions above.

Hiking directions: Walk up the hill and curve around to the south side of the knoll. Descend from the head of Hare Canyon. At a quarter mile, the path steeply zigzags down the south wall of the canyon and temporarily levels out on a small grassy ridge. Curve to the right and continue down switchbacks to Hare Creek in the shaded redwood grove. Follow the creek downstream through lush riparian vegetation, climbing over and stooping under a few fallen redwoods while crossing Hare Creek five times. The fifth crossing is at the upper reaches of Vicente Flat, with campsites on each side of the creek. Stroll through the dense grove of redwoods along the west side of the creek to the heart of Vicente Flat by a grassy meadow. A lower path borders the creek to several campsites. Just beyond the meadow is a posted junction, our turn-around spot. The Vicente Flat Trail bears to the left and descends another 5 miles to Highway 1 at Kirk Creek Campground. The Stone Ridge Trail, straight ahead on the right fork, leads to Goat Camp and the Gamboa Trail.

To hike the 7.4-mile shuttle hike, continue on the Vicente Flat Trail down to the Kirk Creek Campground—Hike 65 in reverse.■

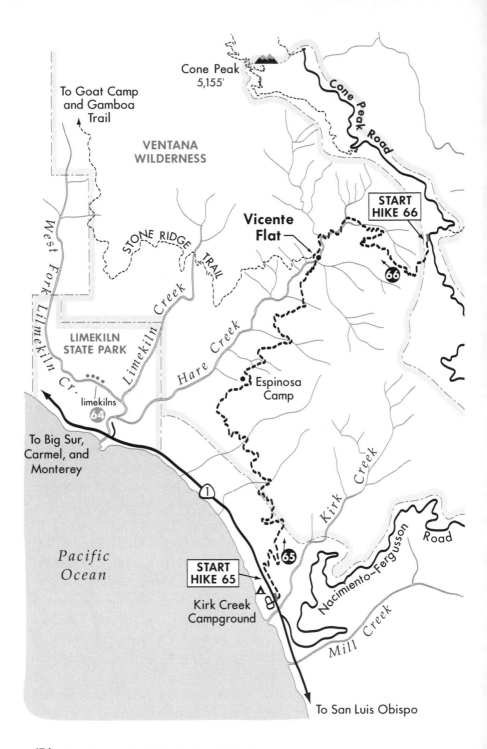

Cone Peak
5,155'

To Goat Camp
and Gamboa
Trail

VENTANA
WILDERNESS

Cone Peak Road

START
HIKE 66

Vicente
Flat

66

STONE RIDGE TRAIL

West Fork Lilmekiln Cr.

Limekiln Creek

LIMEKILN
STATE PARK

Hare Creek

Espinosa
Camp

limekilns
64

To Big Sur,
Carmel, and
Monterey

1

Kirk Creek

Nacimiento-Fergusson Road

65

Pacific
Ocean

START
HIKE 65

Kirk Creek
Campground

Mill Creek

To San Luis Obispo

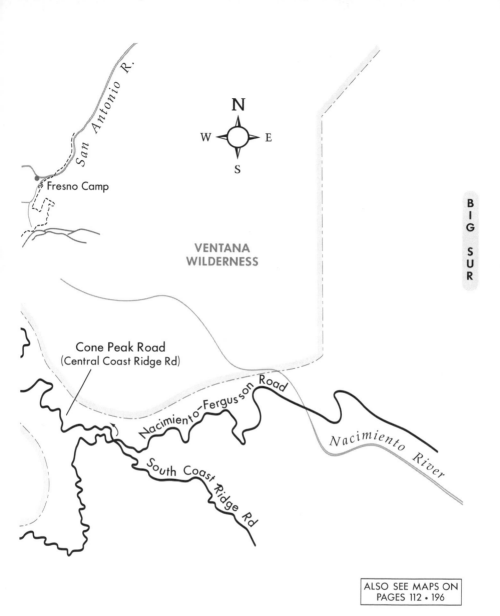

San Antonio R.

Fresno Camp

VENTANA
WILDERNESS

Cone Peak Road
(Central Coast Ridge Rd)

Nacimiento-Fergusson Road

Nacimiento River

South Coast Ridge Rd

ALSO SEE MAPS ON
PAGES 112 • 196

Vicente Flat

HIKE 65: from Kirk Creek Campground
HIKE 66: from Cone Peak Road

67. Pacific Valley Flats

Hiking distance: 2 miles round trip
Hiking time: 1 hour
Elevation gain: 50 feet
Maps: U.S.G.S. Cape San Martin
Los Padres National Forest Northern Section Trail Map
Location: 59 miles south of Carmel; 39 miles north of Cambria

Summary of hike: Pacific Valley is a flat, four-mile-long marine terrace along the southern Monterey County coastline. The broad expanse extends west from the steep slopes of the Santa Lucia Mountains to the serrated bluffs above the Pacific Ocean. This hike crosses the grassy coastal terrace to the eroded coastline a hundred feet above the ocean. There are dramatic views of Plaskett Rock, offshore rock formations with natural arches, and the scalloped coastal cliffs. Numerous access points lead to the grassland terrace. This hike begins at the Pacific Valley Ranger Station.

Driving directions: BIG SUR RANGER STATION. From the ranger station, located 27 miles south of Carmel, drive 31.5 miles south on Highway 1 to the Pacific Valley Ranger Station on the left. The trailhead is across the highway from the ranger station. Park in the pullouts on either side of the road or in the parking lot at the station.

RAGGED POINT. From Highway 1 at the Ragged Point Inn, located 23 miles north of Cambria, drive 16 miles north on Highway 1 to the Pacific Valley Ranger Station on the right.

Hiking directions: The hike begins directly across the road from the ranger station. Step up and over the trail access ladder. Head west across the grassy expanse and past rock outcroppings on the left. Near the point is a rolling sand dune with numerous trails and great overlooks. The main trail stays to the north of the dune, leading to the edge of the cliffs along the jagged coastline high above the pounding surf. At one mile, the trail ends at a fenceline above Prewitt Creek. The trails around the dunes connect with the bluff trail south for one mile to Sand Dollar

Beach (Hike 68), then circle back to the first junction at the cliff's edge. Return along the same trail. ■

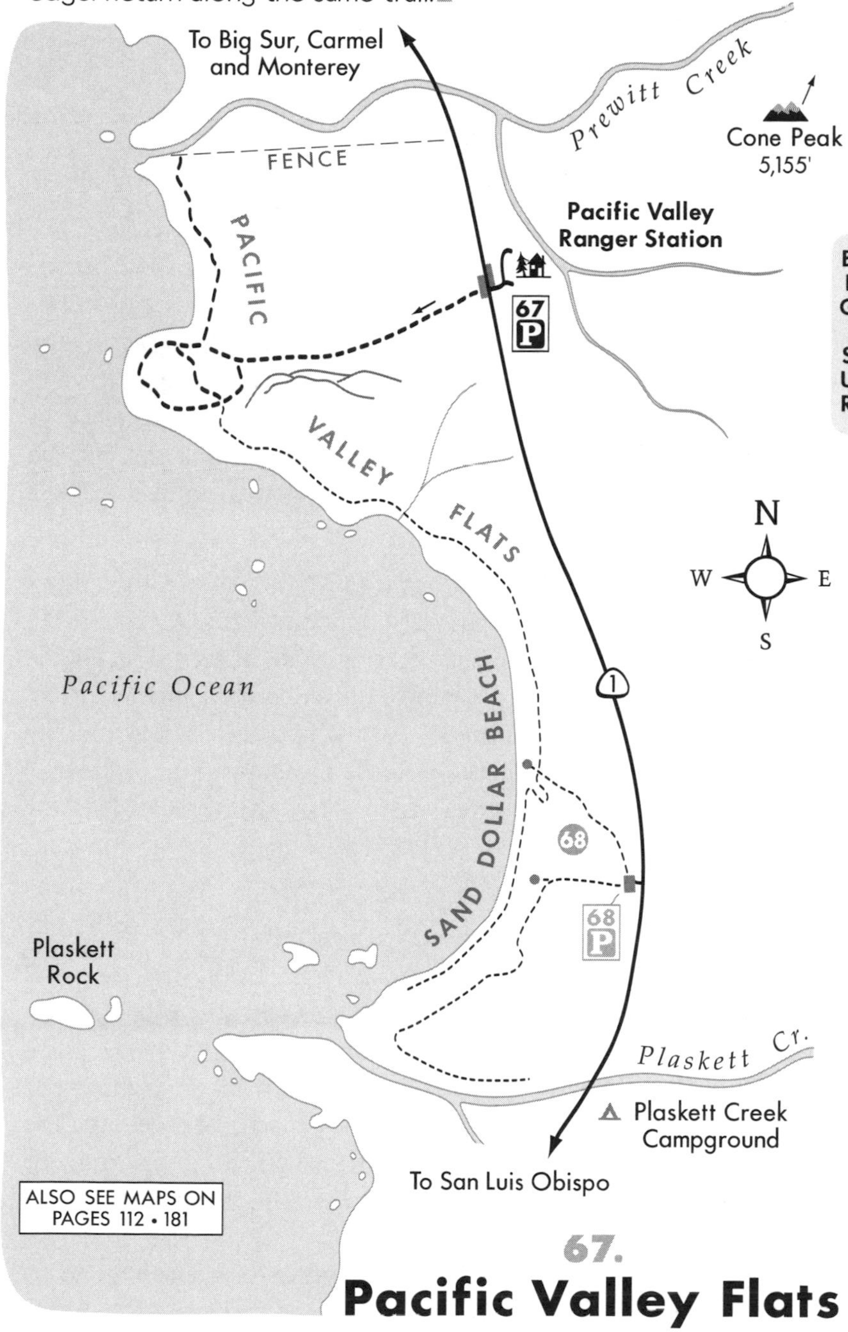

To Big Sur, Carmel and Monterey

Prewitt Creek

Cone Peak
5,155'

FENCE

Pacific Valley
Ranger Station

PACIFIC

67
P

B
I
G

S
U
R

VALLEY

FLATS

N

W ◆ E

S

Pacific Ocean

1

SAND DOLLAR BEACH

68

68
P

Plaskett
Rock

Plaskett Cr.

▲ Plaskett Creek
Campground

To San Luis Obispo

ALSO SEE MAPS ON
PAGES 112 • 181

67.
Pacific Valley Flats

68. Sand Dollar Beach

Hiking distance: 1.5 miles round trip
Hiking time: 1 hour
Elevation gain: 150 feet
Maps: U.S.G.S. Cape San Martin
      Los Padres National Forest Northern Section Trail Map
Location: 60 miles south of Carmel; 38 miles north of Cambria

Summary of hike: Sand Dollar Beach is a protected horse-shoe-shaped sand and rock beach between two rocky headlands that jut into the Pacific Ocean. The trail passes a picnic area lined with Monterey cypress trees to the steep eroded cliffs and an overlook with interpretive signs. There are great coastal views of large offshore rock outcroppings. Plaskett Rock sits off the southern point. Cone Peak can be seen inland along the Santa Lucia Range.

Driving directions: BIG SUR RANGER STATION. From the ranger station, located 27 miles south of Carmel, drive 32.4 miles south on Highway 1 to the parking lot on the right (ocean) side. Park in the lot (entrance fee) or in the pullouts along the highway (free).

RAGGED POINT. From Highway 1 at the Ragged Point Inn, located 23 miles north of Cambria, drive 15 miles north on Highway 1 to the parking lot on the left (ocean) side, just north of Plaskett Creek Campground. Park in the lot (entrance fee) or in the pullouts along the highway (free).

Hiking directions: The signed trailhead is at the north end of the parking lot. Walk up and over the step ladder, then descend through a shady picnic area. Cross the grasslands to a junction by a wooden fence. The right fork leads 30 yards to an overlook with an interpretive sign about wildlife. Return to the junction and take the left fork down the switchbacks and a staircase to the shoreline. After exploring the crescent-shaped cove, return to the bluffs. An optional cliffside path heads one mile north to Pacific Valley (Hike 67).

A second trail leaves from the center of the parking lot to Plaskett Creek. Climb up and over the ladder, and cross the grassy coastal terrace to a cliffside overlook. The meandering path follows the grassy bluffs less than a half mile south to the deep ravine carved by Plaskett Creek.■

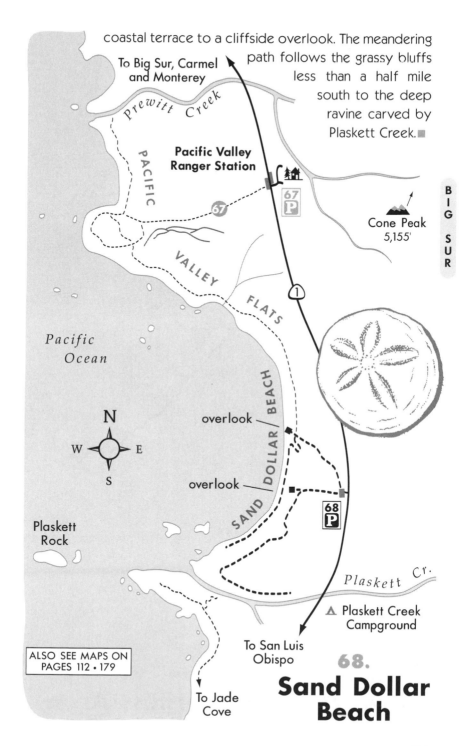

To Big Sur, Carmel and Monterey

Prewitt Creek

Pacific Valley Ranger Station

PACIFIC

67

67
P

Cone Peak
5,155'

B I G   S U R

VALLEY FLATS

1

Pacific Ocean

N
W ⊕ E
S

overlook

SAND DOLLAR BEACH

overlook

Plaskett Rock

68
P

Plaskett Cr.

△ Plaskett Creek Campground

To San Luis Obispo

To Jade Cove

ALSO SEE MAPS ON PAGES 112 • 179

68.

Sand Dollar Beach

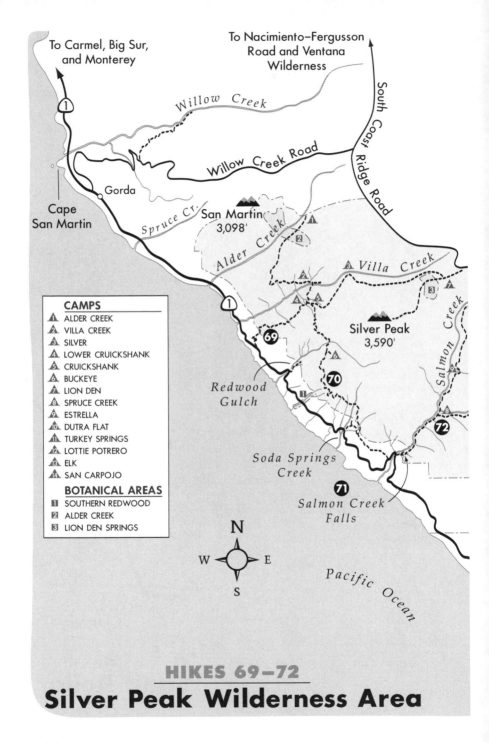

To Carmel, Big Sur, and Monterey

To Nacimiento–Fergusson Road and Ventana Wilderness

Willow Creek

Willow Creek Road

South Coast Ridge Road

Cape San Martin

Gorda

Spruce Cr.

San Martin 3,098'

Alder Creek

Villa Creek

Silver Peak 3,590'

Salmon Creek

Redwood Gulch

Soda Springs Creek

Salmon Creek Falls

Pacific Ocean

N W E S

CAMPS
- 🔺 ALDER CREEK
- 🔺 VILLA CREEK
- 🔺 SILVER
- 🔺 LOWER CRUICKSHANK
- 🔺 CRUICKSHANK
- 🔺 BUCKEYE
- 🔺 LION DEN
- 🔺 SPRUCE CREEK
- 🔺 ESTRELLA
- 🔺 DUTRA FLAT
- 🔺 TURKEY SPRINGS
- 🔺 LOTTIE POTRERO
- 🔺 ELK
- 🔺 SAN CARPOJO

BOTANICAL AREAS
- 1 SOUTHERN REDWOOD
- 2 ALDER CREEK
- 3 LION DEN SPRINGS

HIKES 69–72
Silver Peak Wilderness Area

The rugged Silver Peak Wilderness, established in 1992, is located in the Santa Lucia Range of the Los Padres National Forest. This remote 14,500-acre wilderness at the southwestern corner of Monterey County is home to California's southernmost coastal redwoods. Three year-round creeks—Villa Creek, Salmon Creek, and San Carpoforo Creek—flow from the upper mountain reaches to the sea. A group of steep intersecting trails weave through this wilderness from the ocean to the mountain ridge, gaining nearly 3,600 feet within a couple of miles. The trails wind through open meadows, forest groves, stream-fed canyons, and ridgelines with sweeping coastal views.

B
I
G

S
U
R

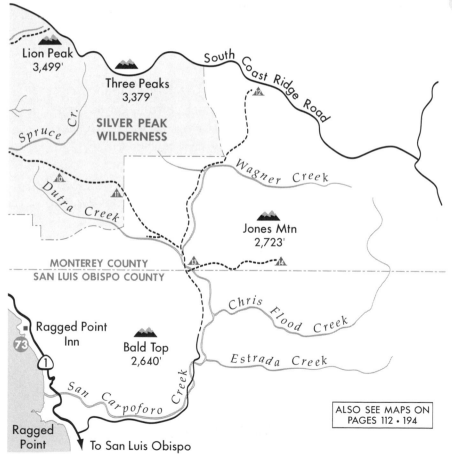

ALSO SEE MAPS ON
PAGES 112 • 194

69. Cruickshank Trail to Cruickshank Camp

SILVER PEAK WILDERNESS AREA

Hiking distance: 5 miles round trip
Hiking time: 3 hours
Elevation gain: 1,200 feet
Maps: U.S.G.S. Villa Creek
          Los Padres National Forest Northern Section Trail Map
Location: 67 miles south of Carmel; 31 miles north of Cambria

*map
page 187*

Summary of hike: The Cruickshank Trail in the Silver Peak Wilderness begins from Highway 1 and climbs the exposed oceanfront hillside to magnificent coastal vistas before dropping into Villa Creek Canyon. The lush canyon path winds through giant redwood groves to the Cruickshank Camps in an oak-shaded grassland.

Driving directions: BIG SUR RANGER STATION. From the ranger station, located 27 miles south of Carmel, drive 39.6 miles south on Highway 1 to the grassy parking pullout on the east (inland) side of the road by the signed Cruickshank trailhead.

RAGGED POINT. From Highway 1 at the Ragged Point Inn, located 23 miles north of Cambria, drive 7.9 miles north on Highway 1 to the grassy parking pullout on the east (inland) side of the road by the signed Cruickshank trailhead.

Hiking directions: From the signed trailhead, climb switchbacks up the brushy mountain slope. Wind through the thick coastal scrub overlooking the ocean and offshore rocks. More switchbacks lead up the exposed south-facing slope to a ridge with sweeping coastal vistas at 900 feet. Descend a short distance into Villa Creek Canyon above the coastal redwoods carpeting the canyon floor. Traverse the south canyon slope through lush vegetation under oak and redwood groves. Pass the unexplained "Hjalmur's Loop" sign, and continue through the shade of the redwoods. Emerge from the forest to a picturesque view of the ocean, framed by the V-shaped canyon walls. Reenter the forest, passing a tall stand of narrow eucalyptus trees on the left. Cross a log plank over a seasonal stream to Lower Cruickshank Camp fifty yards ahead, a small camp with room for one tent. A quarter mile farther is the upper Cruickshank Camp in a large oak flat. This is the turn-around spot for a 5-mile round-trip hike.

To extend the hike, two trails depart from the upper camp. To the left (north), the Buckeye Trail crosses a stream by a giant redwood and descends 0.6 miles to Villa Creek Camp in a dense redwood grove at Villa Creek. To the right, the combined Cruickshank and Buckeye Trails cross through the camp to an oak-dotted grassland and a posted junction. The Buckeye Trail bears right and heads 1.5 miles south to Buckeye Camp (Hike 70). To the left, the Cruickshank Trail climbs 500 feet in 1 mile to Silver Camp and 1,500 feet in 3 miles to Lion Den Camp. (See the map on page 182 for camp locations.)▪

B
I
G

S
U
R

70. Buckeye Trail to Buckeye Camp
SILVER PEAK WILDERNESS AREA

Hiking distance: 7 miles round trip
Hiking time: 4 hours
Elevation gain: 1,600 feet

map
page 187

Maps: U.S.G.S. Burro Mountain and Villa Creek
      Los Padres National Forest Northern Section Trail Map
Location: 71 miles south of Carmel; 27 miles north of Cambria

Summary of hike: Buckeye Camp sits in a large meadow rimmed with oaks and pines in the mountainous interior of the Silver Peak Wilderness. The camp has a developed spring, a picnic bench, and a rock fire pit under the canopy of an immense bay tree with expansive overhanging branches. The trail begins from the abandoned Salmon Creek Ranger Station and climbs the exposed coastal slopes to sweeping views of the Pacific and Salmon Creek Falls. The path weaves in and out of several small canyons with shaded oak groves and passes an ephemeral 30-foot waterfall.

Driving directions: BIG SUR RANGER STATION. From the ranger station, located 27 miles south of Carmel, drive 43.7 miles south on Highway 1 to the paved parking area on the inland side of the road by the abandoned Salmon Creek Ranger Station.

RAGGED POINT. From Highway 1 at the Ragged Point Inn, located 23 miles north of Cambria, drive 3.8 miles north on Highway 1 to the paved parking area on the inland side of the road by the Salmon Creek Ranger Station.

Hiking directions: Walk through the trailhead gate at the north end of the parking area. Ascend the hillside on a few short switchbacks, passing through a second trail gate. Climb through the chaparral and grasslands, passing a trough and underground spring to a third gate. The path levels out on a grassy plateau that overlooks the ocean and Salmon Creek Falls (Hike 71). Traverse the hillside high above the ocean, and pass through a gate to a posted Y-fork at 1 mile. The Soda Springs Trail bears left, returning to Highway 1 at Soda Springs Creek. Take the Buckeye Trail to the right. Cross a stream-fed gully with a seasonal waterfall off a sheer, moss-covered rock wall. Climb out of the gully, following the contours of the mountains in and out of small oak-shaded canyons. Cross Soda Springs Creek at 2 miles to a grassy ridge a half mile ahead, where there are far-reaching vistas from the coastline and across to the ridges and canyons of the Santa Lucia Range. Follow the exposed ridge uphill to an elevated perch in an open pine grove above Redwood Gulch. Curve inland and descend into the rolling mountainous interior, reaching Buckeye Camp at 3.5 miles. Return along the same trail.

To extend the hike, the Buckeye Trail continues 1.5 miles north to the upper Cruickshank Camp (Hike 69).■

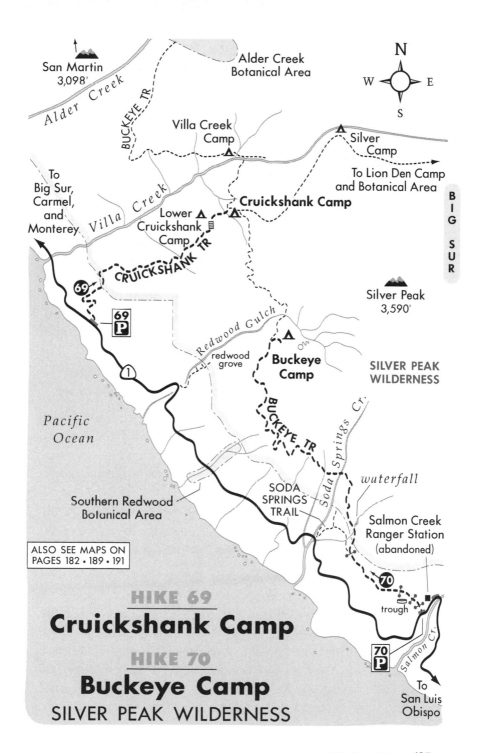

San Martin
3,098'

Alder Creek

BUCKEYE TR.

Alder Creek
Botanical Area

Villa Creek
Camp

Silver
Camp

To
Big Sur,
Carmel,
and
Monterey

Villa Creek

To Lion Den Camp
and Botanical Area

Cruickshank Camp

Lower
Cruickshank
Camp

CRUICKSHANK TR.

**B
I
G

S
U
R**

69

69
P

Redwood Gulch

redwood
grove

Silver Peak
3,590'

**Buckeye
Camp**

BUCKEYE TR.

SILVER PEAK
WILDERNESS

Soda Springs Cr.

*Pacific
Ocean*

waterfall

1

SODA
SPRINGS
TRAIL

Southern Redwood
Botanical Area

Salmon Creek
Ranger Station
(abandoned)

ALSO SEE MAPS ON
PAGES 182 • 189 • 191

70

trough

Salmon Cr.

70
P

To
San Luis
Obispo

HIKE 69

Cruickshank Camp

HIKE 70

Buckeye Camp

SILVER PEAK WILDERNESS

71. Salmon Creek Falls
from Salmon Creek Trail
SILVER PEAK WILDERNESS AREA

Hiking distance: 0.6 miles round trip
Hiking time: 20 minutes
Elevation gain: 150 feet
Maps: U.S.G.S. Burro Mountain
Location: 71 miles south of Carmel; 27 miles north of Cambria

Summary of hike: The Salmon Creek Trail runs through the deep interior of the Silver Peak Wilderness in the Santa Lucia Mountains. The trail connects the coastline with the 3,000-foot South Coast Ridge Road. This hike follows a short section at the beginning of the trail to the dynamic Salmon Creek Falls, where a tremendous volume of water plunges from three chutes. The beautiful waterfall drops more than 100 feet off the vertical rock face, crashing onto the rocks and pools below. A cool mist sprays over the mossy green streamside vegetation under a shady landscape of sycamores, maples, alders, and bay laurels.

Driving directions: BIG SUR RANGER STATION. From the ranger station, located 27 miles south of Carmel, drive 43.8 miles south on Highway 1 to the signed Salmon Creek trailhead at a sweeping horseshoe bend in the road. Park in the wide pullout on the left by the guardrail.

RAGGED POINT. From Highway 1 at the Ragged Point Inn, located 23 miles north of Cambria, drive 3.7 miles north on Highway 1 to the signed Salmon Creek trailhead on the right.

Hiking directions: Walk alongside the guardrail to the signed trailhead on the south side of Salmon Creek. Salmon Creek Falls can be seen from the guardrail. Take the Salmon Creek Trail up the gorge into the lush, verdant forest. Pass an old wooden gate, and cross a small tributary stream. Two hundred yards ahead is a signed junction. The right fork continues on the Salmon Creek Trail (Hike 72). Take the left fork towards the falls. Cross another small stream, then descend around huge boulders towards Salmon

Creek at the base of the falls. Head towards the thunderous sound of the waterfall. Climb around the wet, mossy boulders to explore the various caves and overlooks. ■

To Spruce Creek Camp and Estrella Camp

SILVER PEAK WILDERNESS

B I G   S U R

Salmon Creek Falls

SALMON CREEK TRAIL

72

To Soda Springs Creek and Buckeye Camp

70 BUCKEYE TR

Salmon Creek Ranger Station (abandoned)

71
72
P

To Big Sur, Carmel, and Monterey

70
P

1

Salmon Creek

N
W ○ E
S

ALSO SEE MAPS ON
PAGES 182 • 187 • 191

To San Luis Obispo

Pacific Ocean

71.
Salmon Creek Falls
SILVER PEAK WILDERNESS

72. Salmon Creek Trail
to Spruce Creek Camp and Estrella Camp
SILVER PEAK WILDERNESS AREA

Hiking distance: 6.5 miles round trip
Hiking time: 3.5 hours
Elevation gain: 1,300 feet
Maps: U.S.G.S. Burro Mountain
   Los Padres National Forest Northern Section Trail Map
Location: 71 miles south of Carmel; 27 miles north of Cambria

Summary of hike: The Salmon Creek Trail begins at Salmon Creek Falls (Hike 71) and follows the southeast wall of the V-shaped canyon through forests and open slopes. There are far-reaching views up the canyon and down to the ocean. The trail, which cuts across the Silver Peak Wilderness to the South Coast Ridge Road, leads to Spruce Creek Camp and Estrella Camp. Estrella Camp sits in a large grassy meadow under the shade of oak, pine, and madrone trees. After crossing Spruce Creek, the cliffside path parallels Salmon Creek, overlooking endless cascades, small waterfalls, and pools.

Driving directions: Same as Hike 71.

Hiking directions: Head up the forested canyon on the south side of Salmon Creek to a junction at 200 yards. The left fork drops down a short distance to Salmon Creek Falls— Hike 71. Take the right fork, heading up the hillside to an overlook of Highway 1 and the Pacific. The path winds through the fir forest, steadily gaining elevation to a clearing high above Salmon Creek. The sweeping vistas extend up Salmon Creek canyon and back down across the ocean. Follow the contours of the south canyon wall, with small dips and rises, to a posted junction with the Spruce Creek Trail at 1.9 miles. Stay to the left and descend a quarter mile to Spruce Creek Camp on the banks of Spruce Creek. Cross Spruce Creek on a log bridge just above its confluence with Salmon Creek. Follow Salmon Creek upstream on the southeast canyon slope, overlooking a long series of cascades, pools, and waterfalls. Continually ascend the hillside contours above the creek, crossing an old mudslide. The trail levels out on a grassy flat with scattered oaks and enters the shady Estrella Camp at 1,500 feet. Descend 50 yards to the Estrella Fork of Salmon Creek, just beyond the camp. This is our turn-around area.

The trail continues past the creek, climbing 1,800 feet in 2.5 miles to the South Coast Ridge Road.■

ALSO SEE MAPS ON
PAGES 182 • 187 • 189

72.
Salmon Creek Trail
SILVER PEAK WILDERNESS

San Luis Obispo County

San Luis Obispo County is located where the white sand beaches of Central California merge with the dramatic Big Sur coastline. The county's beautiful coastline stretches for 84 miles and includes wide, sandy beaches; windswept coastal dunes; rocky coves; jagged bluffs; grassy coastal terraces; protected bays and tidepools; wildlife sanctuaries; and a fertile 1,400-acre estuary at Morro Bay.

Heading inland from the Pacific Ocean are oak-studded hills, verdant farmland, and the Santa Lucia Range of the Los Padres National Forest. A chain of nine extinct volcanoes, 23 million years old, form a spine of peaks extending from the city of San Luis Obispo to the ocean at Morro Bay. San Luis Obispo rests in a beautiful valley amongst these volcanic morros and the rolling foothills of the Santa Lucia Mountain Range.

Highlights along the San Luis Obispo coast include vista points overlooking the crashing surf, accessible tidepools, grassy coastal terraces for viewing offshore wildlife, Morro Rock at Morro Bay, the spectacular Montaña De Oro State Park, and huge coastal dunes.

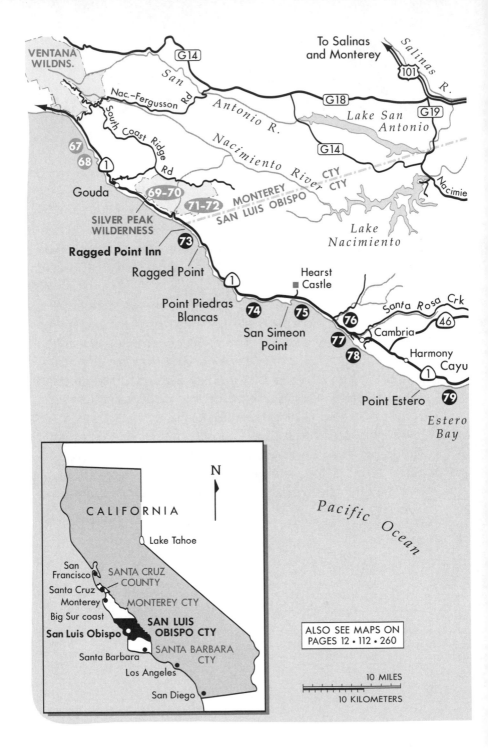

VENTANA WILDNS.

G14

To Salinas and Monterey

Salinas R.

101

San Antonio R.

Nac.-Fergusson Rd

South Coast Ridge

G18

G19

Lake San Antonio

G14

67
68
1

Gouda

Rd

69-70

71-72

MONTEREY
SAN LUIS OBISPO

Nacimiento River CTY

CTY

Nacimie

SILVER PEAK WILDERNESS

Lake Nacimiento

Ragged Point Inn

73

Ragged Point

1

Hearst
■ Castle

Point Piedras
Blancas

74

75

Santa Rosa Crk

76

46

San Simeon
Point

77

Cambria

78

Harmony
Cayu

1

Point Estero

79

Estero
Bay

N

CALIFORNIA

Lake Tahoe

San
Francisco

SANTA CRUZ
COUNTY

Santa Cruz

Monterey

MONTEREY CTY

Big Sur coast

**SAN LUIS
OBISPO CTY**

San Luis Obispo

SANTA BARBARA
CTY

Santa Barbara

Los Angeles

San Diego

Pacific Ocean

ALSO SEE MAPS ON
PAGES 12 • 112 • 260

10 MILES

10 KILOMETERS

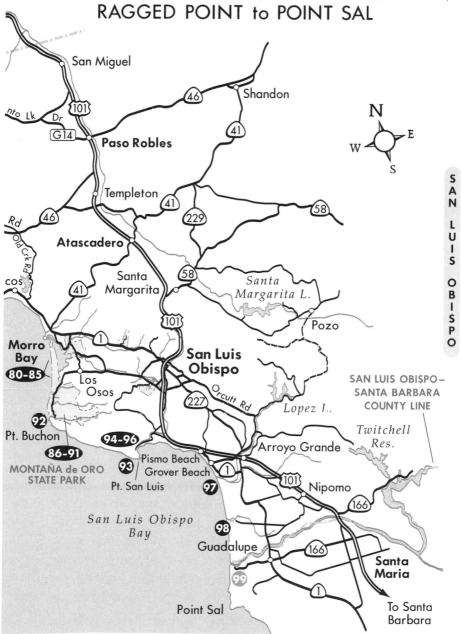

San Miguel

46 Shandon

nto Lk Dr
101
G14 **Paso Robles**

46 41

N
W E
S

Templeton 41
46 Rd 229 58
Old Crk Rd
Atascadero
cos 41 Santa
Margarita 58 *Santa
Margarita L.*
101
Pozo
**Morro
Bay** 1
80-85 Los
Osos San Luis
Obispo
227 Orcutt Rd
92 *Lopez L.*
Pt. Buchon
86-91 94-96
MONTAÑA de ORO 93 Pismo Beach
STATE PARK Grover Beach 1
Pt. San Luis 97 Nipomo
101
166
*San Luis Obispo
Bay* 98
Guadalupe 166
99
Santa
Maria
Point Sal 1 To Santa
Barbara

SAN LUIS OBISPO-
SANTA BARBARA
COUNTY LINE

*Twitchell
Res.*

Arroyo Grande

S
A
N

L
U
I
S

O
B
I
S
P
O

73. Ragged Point Inn
CLIFFSIDE and NATURE TRAILS

Hiking distance: 1 mile round trip
Hiking time: 30 minutes
Elevation gain: 300 feet
Maps: U.S.G.S. Burro Mountain
Location: 23 miles north of Cambria

Summary of hike: The Ragged Point Inn is the last stop in San Luis Obispo County, just 1.5 miles south of Monterey County. The Ragged Point Cliffside Trail begins at the inn and cuts across the edge of a steep, rugged cliff where the San Luis Obispo coast turns into the Big Sur coast. The trail ends at the black sand beach and rocky shore at the base of Black Swift Falls, a 300-foot tiered waterfall. Benches are perched on the cliff for great views of the sheer coastal mountains plunging into the sea.

The Ragged Point Nature Trail follows the perimeter of the peninsula along the high blufftop terrace. There are several scenic vista points and an overlook of the crashing surf and waterfalls. (The actual Ragged Point land formation is located 1.8 miles south of the Ragged Point Inn.)

Driving directions: CAMBRIA. From Cambria, drive 23 miles north on Highway 1 to the Ragged Point Inn and Restaurant on the left. Turn left and park in the paved lot.

Hiking directions: Take the gravel path west between the snack bar and gift shop. Walk across the level, grassy terrace towards the point. Fifty yards ahead is a signed junction at an overlook 300 feet above the ocean, with views of the dramatic Big Sur coast. The Nature Trail continues straight ahead, circling the blufftop terrace through windswept pine and cypress trees. At the northwest point is a viewing platform. Waterfalls can be seen cascading off the cliffs on both sides of the promontory. Back at the junction, the Cliffside Trail descends down the steps over the cliff's edge past a bench and across a wooden bridge. Switchbacks cut across the edge of the steep north-facing cliff

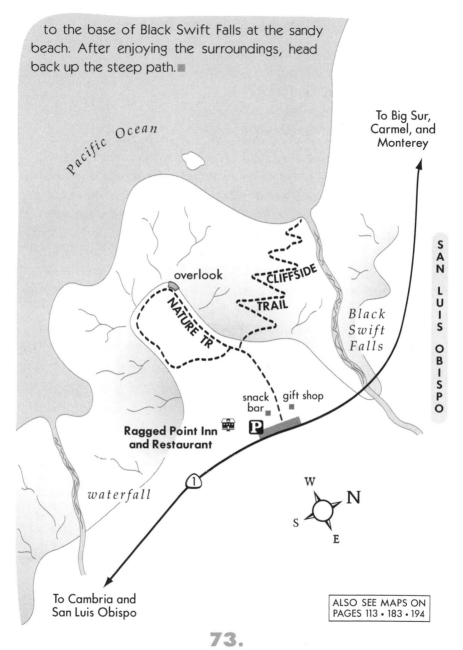

to the base of Black Swift Falls at the sandy
beach. After enjoying the surroundings, head
back up the steep path.■

Pacific Ocean

To Big Sur,
Carmel, and
Monterey

SAN LUIS OBISPO

overlook

CLIFFSIDE
TRAIL

NATURE TR

*Black
Swift
Falls*

snack bar

gift shop

**Ragged Point Inn
and Restaurant**

P

waterfall

1

W N S E

To Cambria and
San Luis Obispo

ALSO SEE MAPS ON
PAGES 113 • 183 • 194

73.
Ragged Point Inn
NATURE and CLIFFSIDE TRAILS

74. Piedras Blancas Bluffs

Hiking distance: 4.5 miles round trip
Hiking time: 2.5 hours
Elevation gain: 50 feet
Maps: U.S.G.S. Piedras Blancas
Location: 11.5 miles north of Cambria

Summary of hike: Piedras Blancas, meaning white rocks, was named by Juan Cabrillo in 1572 for the offshore rocks covered by centuries of bird guano. Piedras Blancas Lighthouse, built in 1874, sits on windswept Point Piedras Blancas near the northern end of San Luis Obispo County. For a few months every winter and spring, thousands of elephant seals colonize the beaches and coves south of the lighthouse for breeding, birthing, and molting. This hike follows the Piedras Blancas Bluffs, a marine terrace backed by the western slopes of the Santa Lucia Mountains. The coastal trail overlooks the scalloped shoreline and rocky beaches past elephant seals, tidepools, outcroppings, natural arches, and the 74-foot lighthouse.

Driving directions: CAMBRIA. From Cambria, drive 11.5 miles north on Highway 1 to the signed Vista Point parking lot on the left.

RAGGED POINT. From Highway 1 at the Ragged Point Inn, located 1.5 miles south of the Monterey County line, drive 10 miles south on to the signed parking lot.

Hiking directions: From the main (southern) parking lot and wildlife viewing area, head 0.2 miles southeast past the elephant seal interpretive displays. The bluff path extends 0.2 miles to the fenced overlook of the beach and coastline.

Return to the opposite end of the parking lot and take the footpath along the edge of the cliffs, parallel to Highway 1. At a quarter mile the path reaches the northern vista point parking lot. At the upper end of the parking lot, climb over the gate and follow the contours of the jagged coastline on the low bluffs. Pass a series of beach pockets, tidepools, and outcroppings. Wind through low dunes covered with ice plants. To avoid ending up on the beach and disturbing the elephant seals, stay on the inland side of the dunes. The lighthouse is in full view on Point Piedras Blancas. The trail fades across the blufftop meadow. Pick your own path towards the lighthouse through pockets of ice plants, reaching the lighthouse road by the powerpoles. This is the turn-around point for a 4.5-mile round-trip hike.

To extend the hike, follow the road left towards the light-house. Near the buildings, leave the road and head north along the fence. Continue on the faint path covered with ice plants to a pocket beach where the coastline nears the highway.■

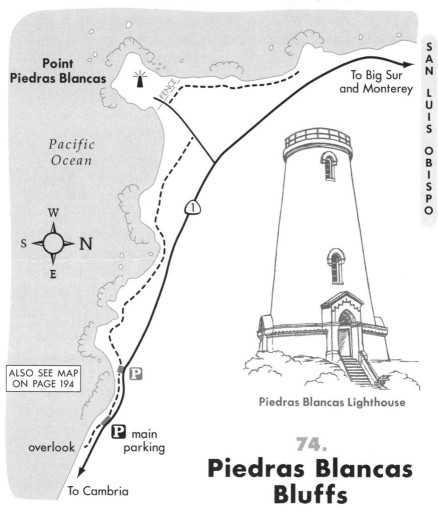

Piedras Blancas Lighthouse

74.

Piedras Blancas Bluffs

75. San Simeon Point
WILLIAM R. HEARST STATE BEACH

Hiking distance: 2.5 miles round trip
Hiking time: 1 hour
Elevation gain: 50 feet
Maps: U.S.G.S. San Simeon
Location: 8 miles north of Cambria

Summary of hike: The San Simeon Bay Trail begins at William R. Hearst State Beach along a crescent of white sand. The hike leads from the protected bay to the tip of San Simeon Point, a peninsula of striated sandstone extending a half mile into the ocean. At the point are beach coves, dramatic rock formations, natural arches, tidepools, and coastal views to Point Estero and Point Buchon in the south. The trail follows the bluffs through a beautiful forest of eucalyptus, pine, cedar, and cypress trees. Sections of the bluff top cliffs are unstable and caution is advised.

Driving directions: CAMBRIA. From Cambria, drive 8 miles north on Highway 1 to William R. Hearst State Beach on the left (oceanside), across from the turnoff to Hearst Castle. Turn left on San Simeon Road, and turn left again at 0.1 miles into the state park parking lot by the pier. An alternative trailhead starts from the parking pullouts 0.1 miles ahead (before crossing the bridge). Pullouts are on both sides of the road by the eucalyptus grove.

Hiking directions: From the parking lot, walk down to the sandy beach between the pier and Arroyo del Puerto Creek. From the pullouts, walk through the gated entrance in the chainlink fence, and follow the path through the eucalyptus grove to the ocean, just west of the pier. Head west along the sand and cross Arroyo del Puerto Creek. Continue towards the forested point. As the beach curves south, take the distinct footpath up to the wooded bluffs. Follow the path through the eucalyptus grove along the edge of the bluffs overlooking the ocean. At the beginning of San Simeon Point, the path joins an unpaved road. Head south across the promontory to the southeast tip. Various trails lead around the headland to endless vistas, beach coves, rock formations, and tidepools. The trail continues around the west side of the peninsula through a shady tunnel of tall cedar, juniper, and cypress trees. This is the turn-around spot. Return along the same path.

To hike farther, the trail emerges on an open coastal plateau with views of the Piedras Blancas Lighthouse, then descends onto dunes to the beach.■

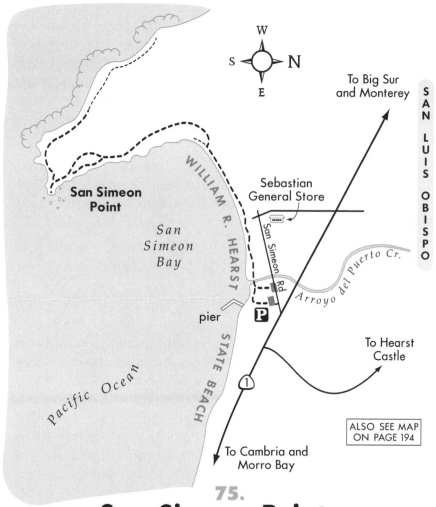

75.
San Simeon Point
WILLIAM R. HEARST STATE BEACH

76. San Simeon Trail
SAN SIMEON BEACH STATE PARK

Hiking distance: 4-mile loop
Hiking time: 2 hours
Elevation gain: 200 feet
Maps: U.S.G.S. Cambria
Location: 2 miles north of Cambria

Summary of hike: The San Simeon Trail loops through the state park with a diverse landscape of coastal scrub, grassy meadows, wetlands, a Monterey pine forest, a eucalyptus grove, and riparian woodlands. This loop hike includes footbridges and boardwalks; interpretive displays; outcroppings; vernal pools of winter rainfall; and Whitaker Flats, an old dairy ranch dating back to the 1860s.

Driving directions: CAMBRIA. From Highway 1 in Cambria, drive 2 miles north to the San Simeon Beach State Park turnoff on the right. Turn right and park in the Washburn Day Use Area parking lot.

Hiking directions: From the boardwalk, detour left and head west under Highway 1 to sandy San Simeon State Beach along the south bank of San Simeon Creek.

Return and follow the boardwalk east to the campground access road and bridge. Bear right on the signed gravel path through the coastal scrub. Cross a footbridge over the wetlands to the edge of the forested hillside. Ascend steps and follow Pine Ridge east through the forest of Monterey pines. At one mile, descend the hillside into Fern Gully, a lush riparian area. Cross the valley floor on Willow Bridge, a 500-foot bridge over the stream and marshland under a canopy of trees. Continue across the grassy slope along the eastern park boundary to a trail fork at the Washburn Campground. The left fork parallels the campground road, returning to the trailhead. Take the right fork across a grassy mesa to a bench and overlook at the Mima Mounds and vernal pools. Bear left, traversing the hillside above San Simeon Creek to a massive forested outcropping. Continue past the formation and head downhill into a eucalyptus grove at the old ranch site at Whitaker Flats. Ascend the hillside, joining the trail from the campground. Bear right, parallel to the campground road, back to the boardwalk and trailhead. ■

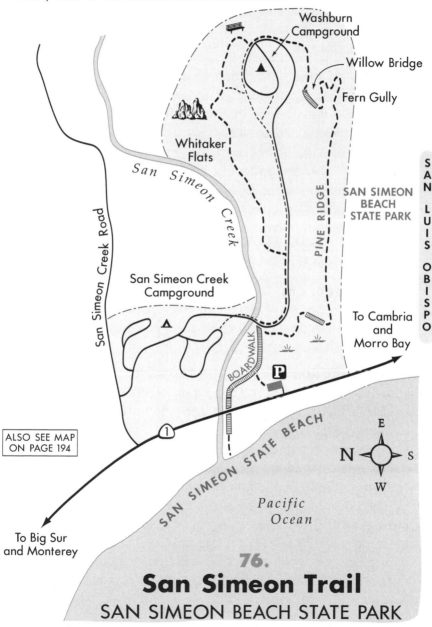

Washburn Campground

Willow Bridge

Fern Gully

Whitaker Flats

San Simeon Creek

San Simeon Creek Road

PINE RIDGE

SAN SIMEON BEACH STATE PARK

SAN LUIS OBISPO

San Simeon Creek Campground

BOARDWALK

To Cambria and Morro Bay

ALSO SEE MAP ON PAGE 194

SAN SIMEON STATE BEACH

To Big Sur and Monterey

Pacific Ocean

E
N — S
W

76.
San Simeon Trail
SAN SIMEON BEACH STATE PARK

77. Moonstone Beach Trail

Hiking distance: 2.5 miles round trip
Hiking time: 1.5 hours
Elevation gain: Level
Maps: U.S.G.S. Cambria
Location: Cambria

Summary of hike: The Moonstone Beach Trail follows the rocky shoreline at the edge of the windswept ocean cliffs in Cambria. On the 20-foot eroded bluffs along the oceanfront corridor, several staircases lead down to the sandy beach. Along the shore are smooth, translucent, milky white moonstone agates. Leffingwell Creek and Santa Rosa Creek carried the rocks to the shore, where they were rounded and polished by the surf. The trail leads past small coves, rock formations, and tidepools to scenic overlooks. There are views up the coast to San Simeon Point and the Piedras Blancas Lighthouse. This is an excellent vantage point to watch migrating gray whales.

Driving directions: CAMBRIA. From Highway 1 in Cambria, turn west on Windsor Boulevard and a quick right onto Moonstone Beach Drive. Continue 0.3 miles to the Santa Rosa Creek parking lot on the left. Turn left and park.

Hiking directions: The trail begins near the mouth of Santa Rosa Creek on the north end of the parking lot. Head north on the sandstone bluffs overlooking the ocean and offshore rocks while walking parallel to Moonstone Beach Drive. Steps descend to the sandy beach. Return up to the bluffs, crossing small wooden footbridges. At one mile, the old highway bridge spans Leffingwell Creek. Bear left down a ramp to the beach and cross the sand. Ascend the grassy slope to a picnic area and cypress grove at Leffingwell Landing, part of San Simeon State Park. Cross the parking lot, picking up the trail again on the bluffs, and wind through groves of Monterey pine and cypress. At 1.5 miles is an overlook on the left at the north end of Moonstone Beach Drive. Past the overlook, steps lead down to the beach. Return along the same path. ■

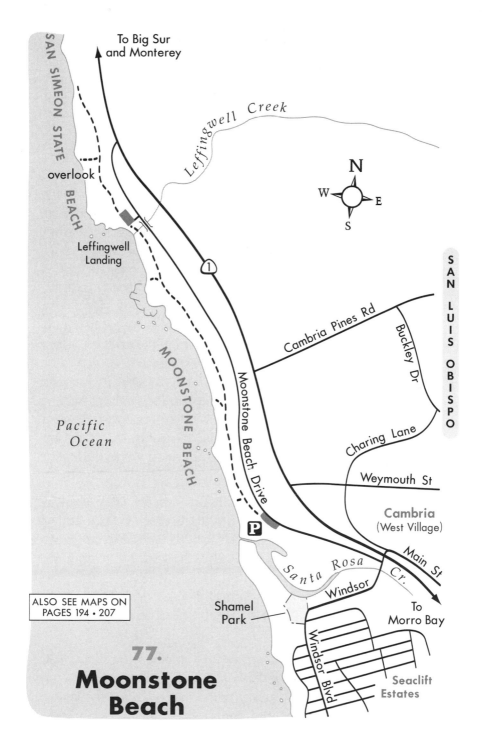

To Big Sur
and Monterey

SAN SIMEON STATE

Leffingwell Creek

N
W   E
S

overlook

BEACH

Leffingwell
Landing

1

Cambria Pines Rd

Buckley Dr

MOONSTONE BEACH

Pacific
Ocean

Moonstone Beach Drive

Charing Lane

Weymouth St

SAN LUIS OBISPO

Cambria
(West Village)

Main St

P

Santa Rosa Cr.

Windsor

To
Morro Bay

ALSO SEE MAPS ON
PAGES 194 • 207

Shamel
Park

Windsor Blvd.

Seaclift
Estates

77.
Moonstone
Beach

78. Fiscalini Bluff Trail
EAST WEST RANCH

Hiking distance: 2 miles round trip
Hiking time: 1 hour
Elevation gain: 50 feet
Maps: U.S.G.S. Cambria
Location: Cambria

Summary of hike: East West Ranch is a 430-acre reserve in the center of Cambria. The undeveloped open space extends from the oceanfront bluffs to the east side of Highway 1. The dog-friendly public land has a network of trails weaving through coastal bluffs, marine terraces, riparian creek habitats, rolling grasslands, and tree-covered hills, including stands of coast live oaks and rare native Monterey pines.

The Fiscalini Bluff Trail, a boardwalk and packed-earthen path, follows the edge of eroded 40-foot bluffs above the rocky shoreline and tidepools of the East West Ranch coast. En route are two bridge crossings, a handcrafted wooden shelter, and several unique driftwood benches. The mile-long trail crosses the ranch, connecting the two ends of Windsor Boulevard. There is no beach access along the trail, but the views are fantastic. During the winter migration, gray whales swim within 200 yards of the shoreline.

Driving directions: CAMBRIA: South Trailhead: From Highway 1 in Cambria, wind 1.6 miles west on Ardath Drive to Marlborough Lane. Turn right and continue a half mile to Wedgewood Street. Turn left and go one block to Windsor Boulevard. Turn right and park in the trailhead spaces.

CAMBRIA: North Trailhead: From Highway 1, drive 1 mile southwest on Windsor Boulevard to the trailhead at the end of the road. Park along the curb.

Hiking directions: Starting from the southern trailhead, walk north from the end of lower Windsor Boulevard through the trailhead gate. Cross the flat grassy bluffs that overlook the jagged shoreline, tidepools, and the ocean. Cross the wooden footbridge over a stream, curving along the edge of the eroded bluffs. Cross a second bridge over a small arroyo, then head past benches and a wooden shelter. The trail ends at the southern end of Windsor Boulevard by Abalone Cove and Seaclift Estates. Return along the same trail.■

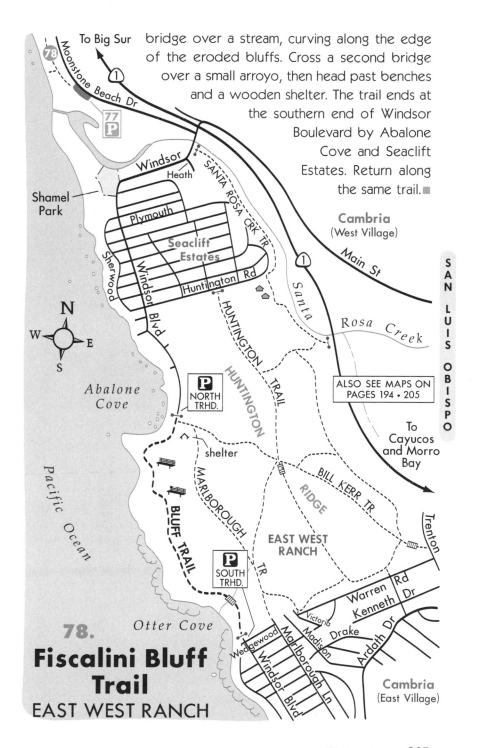

ALSO SEE MAPS ON PAGES 194 • 205

78.
Fiscalini Bluff Trail
EAST WEST RANCH

79. Estero Bluffs State Park

Hiking distance: 5 miles round trip
Hiking time: 2.5 hours
Elevation gain: 50 feet
Maps: U.S.G.S. Cayucos
Location: Cayucos

Summary of hike: Estero Bluffs State Park encompasses 355 acres at the north end of crescent-shaped Estero Bay, between the town of Cayucos and Villa Creek. The undeveloped park stretches 3.5 miles along the grassy coastal terrace and rocky shoreline from Highway 1 to the ocean. Six waterways flow from the Santa Lucia foothills through the rolling grasslands. The hike follows the craggy, windswept palisade, passing sea-battered rocks, sheltered coves, small sandy beaches, promontories, clefts, and rolling knolls.

Driving directions: CAYUCOS. From downtown Cayucos, drive 1 mile north on Highway 1 to the large dirt pullout on the left—the southern access to Estero Bluffs. The pullout is 0.1 miles past the end of the divided section of Highway 1. Heading north on Highway 1, four additional trailheads access the coastal bluffs over the next 1.6 miles. The northern-most access is located 1.6 miles south of Villa Creek Road.

Hiking directions: From the southern access, descend the slope from the south end of the parking area. Follow the path across the grassy marine terrace to the edge of the 40-foot bluffs. Take the path to the right, and stroll along the scalloped coastline. Cross an eroded gully and continue past coves, pocket beaches, offshore rocks, and tidepools. Cross San Geronimo Creek in a recessed sandy cove. Climb back to the bluffs by three huge eucalyptus trees. Pass a rounded 100-foot grassy knoll on the right to Red Rock, a 30-foot weather-sculpted rock formation surrounded by a jumble of boulders. A short distance ahead is Cayucos Point by an offshore sea stack. Cross a gully and pass more small, sandy coves and numerous rocks jutting out of the sea. Walk by eroding cliffs with finger-shaped points of land and a huge offshore rock with a grassy slope. Curve north, following the contours of the coastline toward Highway 1. Veer west toward the prominent 120-foot rounded hill on the vertical bluffs. Cross three minor draws along the south flank of the hill. At the west end of the knoll, a distinct path heads inland, parallel to Swallow Creek on the northern trail access. This is the turnaround spot.

To extend the hike, continue on the blufftop trail. The wetland terrace from Swallow Creek to Villa Creek is closed for resource protection except for the blufftop trail.■

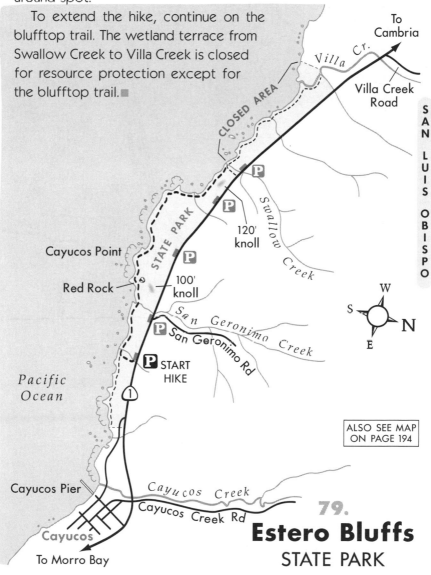

To Cambria

Villa Creek Road

**S
A
N

L
U
I
S

O
B
I
S
P
O**

CLOSED AREA

P

P

Swallow Creek

120' knoll

Cayucos Point

100' knoll

Red Rock

STATE PARK

P

San Geronimo Creek

P

San Geronimo Rd

P START HIKE

Pacific Ocean

①

W

S

N

E

ALSO SEE MAP ON PAGE 194

Cayucos Pier

Cayucos Creek

Cayucos Creek Rd

Cayucos

To Morro Bay

**79.
Estero Bluffs**
STATE PARK

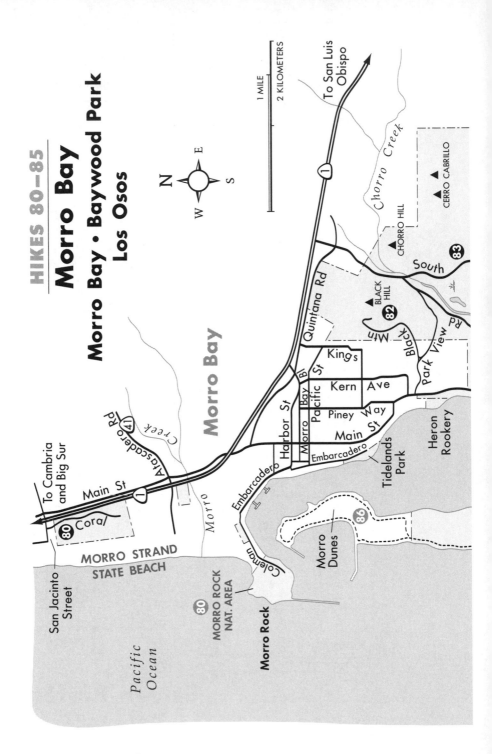

N
W E
S

1 MILE
2 KILOMETERS

To San Luis Obispo

Chorro Creek

CERRO CABRILLO

CHORRO HILL

South

Rd

BLACK HILL

Black Mtn

Park View Rd

Quintana Rd

Kings St

Kern Ave

Morro Bay Bl

Pacific St

Piney Way

Harbor St

Main St

Morro Bay

Embarcadero

Heron Rookery

Tidelands Park

Morro Dunes

Atascadero Rd

Morro Creek

To Cambria and Big Sur

Main St

Coral

MORRO STRAND STATE BEACH

San Jacinto Street

Pacific Ocean

MORRO ROCK NAT. AREA

Morro Rock

Coleman

Embarcadero

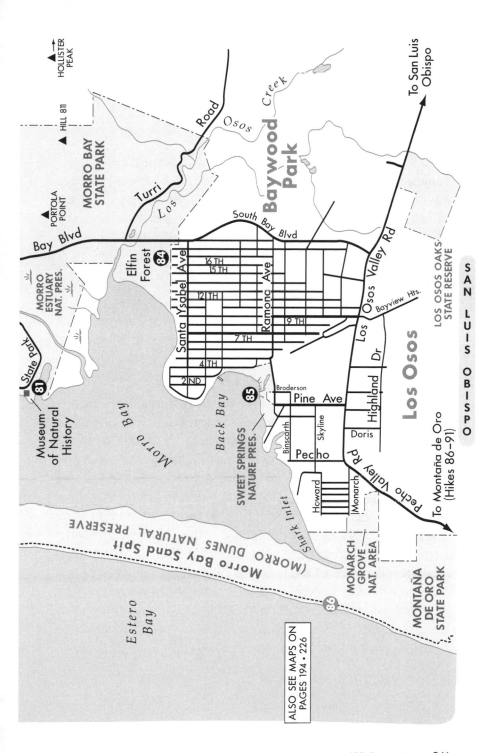

ALSO SEE MAPS ON
PAGES 194 • 226

80. Cloisters Wetland to Morro Rock

Hiking distance: 3.5 miles round trip
Hiking time: 1.5 hours
Elevation gain: Level
Maps: U.S.G.S. Morro Bay North and Morro Bay South
Location: Morro Bay

Summary of hike: The Cloisters Wetland is a 2.6-acre wildlife habitat with a freshwater lagoon. A trail with interpretive signs circles the lagoon. The hike crosses Morro Strand State Beach to Morro Rock, a dome-shaped volcanic plug rising from the ocean at the mouth of the harbor. This ancient 578-foot monolithic outcropping sits amidst a 30-acre wildlife preserve which is a protected nesting site for the peregrine falcon.

Driving directions: MORRO BAY. From Highway 1 in Morro Bay, head 2 miles north to San Jacinto Street and turn left. Drive to the first street and turn left again on Coral Avenue. Continue 0.3 miles and park in the Cloisters Community Park parking lot on the right.

Hiking directions: Take the paved path through the developed park along the south side of the lagoon. At the dunes is a junction. The right fork circles the Cloisters Wetland, a freshwater lagoon. Bear left and follow the path between the dunes and the park meadow towards the prominent Morro Rock. The trail curves through the dunes, crossing a wooden footbridge. Bear right and walk parallel to a row of pine trees to the end of the boardwalk at the sandy beach. Follow the shoreline of Morro Strand State Beach directly towards Morro Rock. Cross the sand isthmus to the base of the rock. Walk across the parking area and follow Coleman Drive (the paved road) clockwise around the perimeter of Morro Rock along the edge of the bay. At the west end of the rock is a sandy beach and breakwater at the entrance to the bay. Return along the same route.■

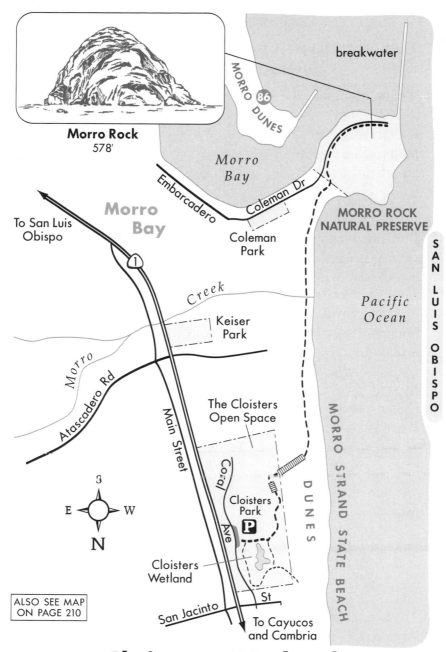

Morro Rock
578'

breakwater

MORRO DUNES 86

Morro Bay

Embarcadero

Coleman Dr

Morro Bay

To San Luis Obispo

1

Coleman Park

MORRO ROCK NATURAL PRESERVE

Creek

Morro

Keiser Park

Pacific Ocean

S A N   L U I S   O B I S P O

Atascadero Rd

Main Street

The Cloisters Open Space

Coral Ave

Cloisters Park

P

MORRO STRAND STATE BEACH

DUNES

Cloisters Wetland

San Jacinto St

ALSO SEE MAP ON PAGE 210

E — W
N

To Cayucos and Cambria

80. Cloisters Wetland Morro Rock

81. White Point

from the MUSEUM to the HERON ROOKERY and MARINA
MORRO BAY STATE PARK

Hiking distance: 2 miles round trip
Hiking time: 1 hour
Elevation gain: 80 feet
Maps: U.S.G.S. Morro Bay South
Location: Morro Bay

map page 217

Summary of hike: Morro Bay State Park is located along the lush inland side of Morro Bay. The 2,345-acre state park includes a massive estuary; a protected bird sanctuary; a heron rookey; a salt marsh; mudflats; dunes, pines, chaparral and riparian habitats; a golf course; campground; a small boat marina used to launch sailboats, canoes and kayaks; and a history museum.

The Heron Rookery Natural Preserve at Fairbank Point is a refuge for egrets, cormorants, and great blue herons, which nest atop the eucalyptus and cypress trees. The protected rookery is the only remaining large rookery between San Francisco and Mexico.

The Museum of Natural History is perched on White Point, overlooking the bay and Morro Rock. There is an observation deck and interpretive exhibits about the bay's history, wildlife, ecology, geology, and Native American life.

The Morro Estuary Natural Preserve within the state park extends four miles, linking the communities of Morro Bay, Baywood Park, and Los Osos. The estuary, where fresh and salt water mix, is fed by Chorro Creek and Los Osos Creek. It is protected from the ocean by the 4-mile-long Morro Dunes

Sand Spit. The estuary is teeming with migratory waterfowl, shorebirds, and wading birds. It is among the earth's richest and most productive bird habitats.

This hike begins at the museum and follows the shoreline to the heron rookery and along the northwest corner of the estuary by the marina.

Driving directions: LOS OSOS. From the intersection of Los Osos Valley Road and South Bay Boulevard in Los Osos, drive 3.2 miles north on South Bay Boulevard to State Park Road. Turn left and continue 1.2 miles, following the north edge of the Morro Bay Estuary to the Museum of Natural History. Turn left and park.

MORRO BAY. From Highway 1 in Morro Bay, take the Los Osos/Baywood Park exit. Drive 0.7 miles south on South Bay Boulevard to State Park Road and turn right. Continue with the directions above.

Hiking directions: After visiting the Museum of Natural History, walk back down the ramp and pick up the footpath in the cypress grove between the park road and Morro Bay. Head north along the bay toward Morro Rock. Climb a slope through the fragrant eucalyptus grove to the east edge of the protected heron rookery on Fairbank Point. The area allows observation, but access into the rookery is closed.

Return to the museum and follow the paved, rock-lined walkway around forested White Point, 40 feet above the bay. The paved path ends at the south end of the parking lot. Descend steps toward the Morro Bay State Park Marina, or curve right through the eucalyptus grove, parallel to the park road. At the south end of the marina, pick up the posted footpath on the edge of the estuary. Cross the south end of the marina to a trail split. Begin the loop to the right, and head west to the tip of the spit protecting the marina. Circle Marina Point and return along the estuary on one of the parallel paths, determined by the tide level. Curve left to complete the loop, and return to the museum. ■

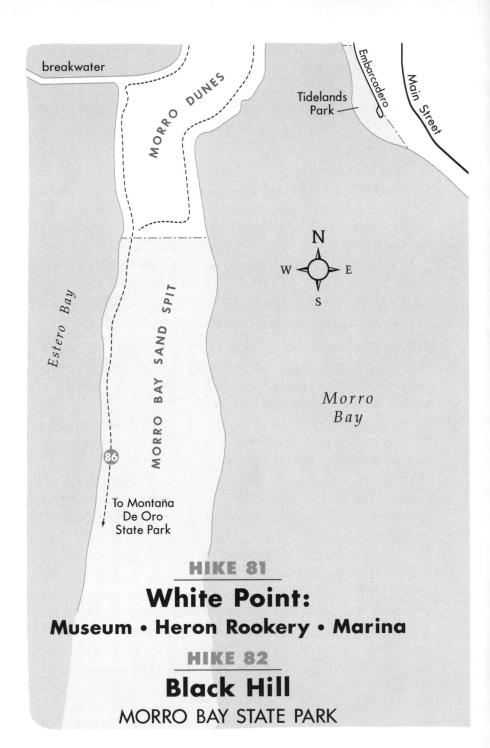

breakwater

MORRO DUNES

Embarcadero

Main Street

Tidelands
Park

N
W E
S

Estero Bay

MORRO BAY SAND SPIT

Morro
Bay

86

To Montaña
De Oro
State Park

HIKE 81
White Point:
Museum • Heron Rookery • Marina

HIKE 82
Black Hill
MORRO BAY STATE PARK

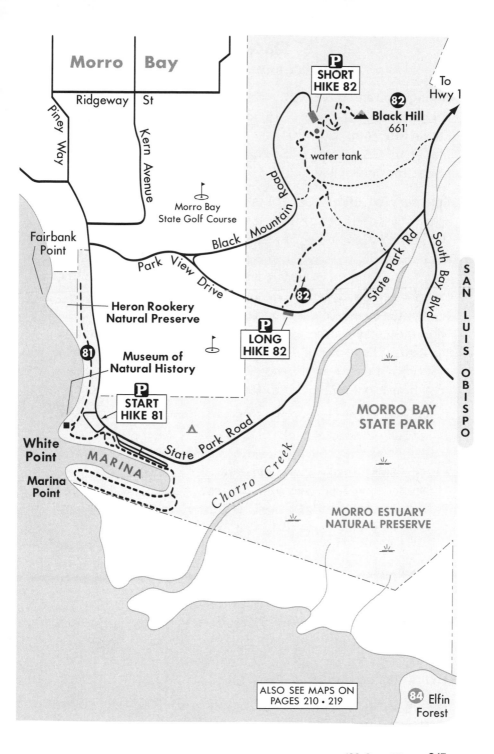

Morro Bay

Ridgeway St

Piney Way

Kern Avenue

P SHORT HIKE 82

82 ▲ Black Hill 661'

To Hwy 1

water tank

Morro Bay State Golf Course

Black Mountain Road

Fairbank Point

Park View Drive

State Park Rd

South Bay Blvd

Heron Rookery Natural Preserve

82

81

P LONG HIKE 82

Museum of Natural History

P START HIKE 81

White Point

MARINA

State Park Road

MORRO BAY STATE PARK

Marina Point

Chorro Creek

MORRO ESTUARY NATURAL PRESERVE

ALSO SEE MAPS ON PAGES 210 • 219

84 Elfin Forest

S A N   L U I S   O B I S P O

82. Black Hill
MORRO BAY STATE PARK

Hiking distance: 0.6—2.6 miles round trip
Hiking time: 30 minutes—1.5 hours
Elevation gain: 180—540 feet
Maps: U.S.G.S. Morro Bay South
Location: Morro Bay

map
page 217

Summary of hike: Black Hill (also known as Black Mountain) is an ancient 661-foot volcanic peak in Morro Bay State Park. It is the second in the chain of nine morros, stretching from Morro Rock (Hike 80) to Islay Hill in San Luis Obispo. There is a short easy trail to the rocky summit and a longer forested route. The longer route climbs up the western face through the shade of a eucalyptus forest, an oak woodland, and Monterey pine groves. From the rocky summit are panoramic views of Morro Bay and the estuary, Estero Point, Cayucos, Chorro Valley, and the nearby morros of Cerro Cabrillo and Hollister Peak. The ocean views span from Montaña De Oro to San Simeon.

Driving directions: SAN LUIS OBISPO. From Highway 101 south of San Luis Obispo, take the Los Osos Valley Road exit, and head 9.6 miles west to South Bay Boulevard. Turn right and continue 3.2 miles to State Park Road and turn left.

MORRO BAY. From Highway 1 in Morro Bay, take the Los Osos/Baywood Park exit. Head 0.7 miles south on South Bay Boulevard to State Park Road and turn right.

FOR THE LONG HIKE, bear right 0.1 mile ahead at a road fork, and head up Park View Drive for 0.3 miles to a parking pullout on the left.

FOR THE SHORT HIKE, bear right 0.1 mile ahead at a road fork and head 0.6 miles up Park View Drive to the unsigned Black Mountain Road and turn right. Continue 0.7 miles through the Morro Bay State Golf Course to the trailhead parking area at the end of the road.

Hiking directions: For the long hike, walk 100 yards up the road to the trail on the right with the "no bikes" sign. Head north across a meadow, dropping into a ravine to a T-junction. Bear left through a eucalyptus grove past an intersecting trail on the right. A short distance ahead is a third junction. Bear right, gaining elevation through an oak woodland. At one mile, loop around the right side of a cement water tank to the upper trailhead parking lot. This is where the short hike begins. Head northeast up several switchbacks to the summit. After marveling at the views, return by retracing your steps. ■

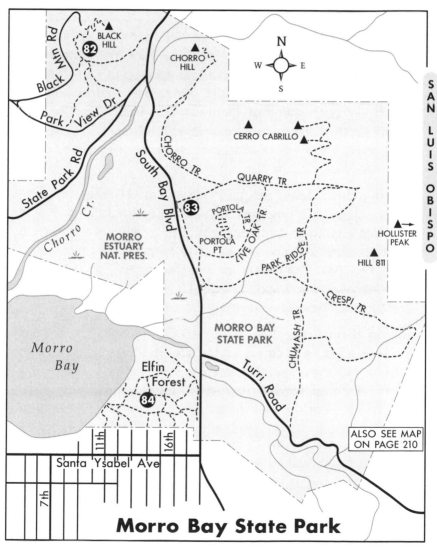

Morro Bay State Park

83. Portola Point

MORRO BAY STATE PARK

Hiking distance: 2-mile loop
Hiking time: 1 hour
Elevation gain: 320 feet
Maps: U.S.G.S. Morro Bay South
The Mountain Biking Map for San Luis Obispo
Location: Morro Bay

Summary of hike: Portola Hill is a 329-foot rounded volcanic hill on the east side of Morro Bay State Park. The route loops around the base of the hill. A spur trail leads up to Portola Point, offering sweeping views of the surrounding morros and the Morro Bay Estuary, one of the most vital and productive bird habitats in the country. The hike follows the Quarry and Live Oak Trails across rolling native grassland and through oak groves thriving in the shelter of the hills.

Driving directions: SAN LUIS OBISPO. From Highway 101 south of San Luis Obispo, take the Los Osos Valley Road exit, and head 9.6 miles west to South Bay Boulevard. Turn right and continue 2.6 miles to the trailhead parking lot on the right.

MORRO BAY. From Highway 1 in Morro Bay, take the Los Osos/Baywood Park exit. Drive 1.4 miles south on South Bay Boulevard to the trailhead parking lot on the left.

Hiking directions: Take the signed Quarry Trail uphill through the sage scrub. Head east along the south-facing slopes of Cerro Cabrillo to a signed junction at 0.5 miles. Take the Live Oak Trail to the right, descending across a grassy meadow towards Portola Hill. Near the base of the hill is a signed trail fork. Bear right on the Portola Trail, and ascend the hill past an oak grove. Switchbacks lead up to a trail split, circling the point to various overlooks and a resting bench. Complete the loop and return to the Live Oak Trail. Go right and descend into the draw between Portola Hill and Hill 811. At 1.5 miles is a signed trail split. Bear right, contouring around Portola Hill on the Live Oak Trail. Return to the parking lot.■

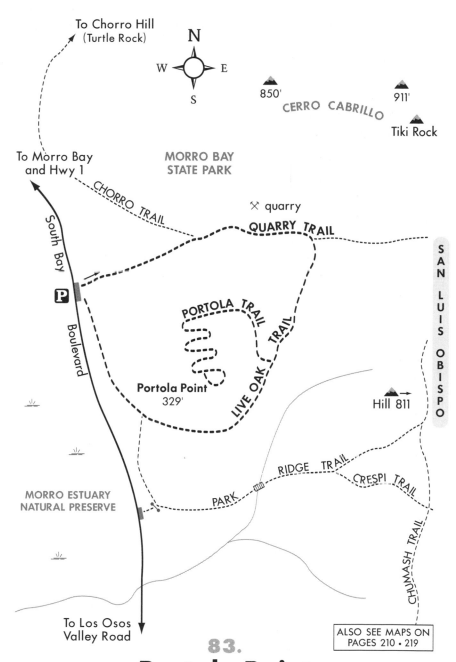

To Chorro Hill
(Turtle Rock)

N
W ⬥ E
S

850'   911'
CERRO CABRILLO
Tiki Rock

To Morro Bay
and Hwy 1

MORRO BAY
STATE PARK

CHORRO TRAIL

⚒ quarry

QUARRY TRAIL

South Bay

P

Boulevard

PORTOLA TRAIL

LIVE OAK TRAIL

Portola Point
329'

Hill 811

S
A
N

L
U
I
S

O
B
I
S
P
O

RIDGE TRAIL

CRESPI TRAIL

MORRO ESTUARY
NATURAL PRESERVE

PARK

CHUMASH TRAIL

To Los Osos
Valley Road

ALSO SEE MAPS ON
PAGES 210 • 219

83.
Portola Point
MORRO BAY STATE PARK

84. Elfin Forest Natural Area

Hiking distance: 1.5 miles round trip
Hiking time: 1 hour
Elevation gain: 100 feet
Maps: U.S.G.S. Morro Bay South
Location: Baywood Park

Summary of hike: The Elfin Forest Natural Area is a 90-acre refuge on an ancient sand dune on the shore of Morro Bay. A mile of wooden walkways with two viewing platforms and overlooks form an oval loop around the coastal slope. The area includes a salt marsh, coastal dune scrub, morro manzanita, riparian woodlands, and dense stands of dwarfed, 500-year-old pygmy oaks. The gnarled, windswept oaks, stunted by the coastal dune environment, have room-like openings and are draped with moss and lichen.

Driving directions: SAN LUIS OBISPO. From Highway 101 south of San Luis Obispo, take the Los Osos Valley Road exit, and head 9.6 miles west to South Bay Boulevard. Turn right and continue 1.4 miles to Santa Ysabel Avenue on the left. Turn left and drive to 16th Street. Turn right and park at the end of the block. The trail system can also be accessed from the north ends of 11th through 17th Streets.

MORRO BAY. From Highway 1 in Morro Bay, take the Los Osos/Baywood Park exit. Drive 2.7 miles south on South Bay Boulevard to Santa Ysabel Avenue. Turn right and follow the directions above.

Hiking directions: Head north at the end of 16th Street on the Monterey pine boardwalk. Walk through the dense sage scrub to the ridge overlooking the Morro Bay estuary. Bear left (west), following the Ridge Trail boardwalk to an overlook at the west end. Sandy paths return to the street accesses. From the overlook, return east 150 yards to a junction and bear left. Descend to the Celestial Meadow Trail. The left fork leads to another overlook platform at the edge of the estuary. The right fork heads uphill to a junction with the Ridge Trail. En route, natural paths on the left explore the ancient pygmy oaks. At the east end of the boardwalk is a view of Hollister Peak. The right fork completes the loop on the ridge by 16th Street. ■

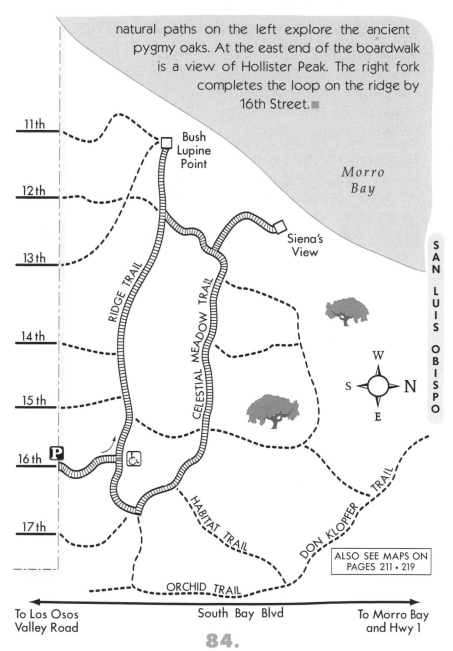

To Los Osos
Valley Road

South Bay Blvd

To Morro Bay
and Hwy 1

ALSO SEE MAPS ON
PAGES 211 • 219

84.
Elfin Forest
NATURAL AREA

85. Sweet Springs Nature Preserve

Hiking distance: 0.5 to 1 mile round trip
Hiking time: 30 minutes
Elevation gain: Level
Maps: U.S.G.S. Morro Bay South
Location: Baywood Park

Summary of hike: Sweet Springs Nature Preserve is a 24-acre wetland sanctuary for nesting and migrating birds. The preserve is located in Baywood Park on the southeast shore of Morro Bay. There are two serene freshwater ponds, a saltwater marsh at the bay, Monterey cypress, and eucalyptus groves. The eucalyptus groves are home to monarch butterflies during the winter months. The preserve is managed by the Morro Coast Audubon Society.

Driving directions: SAN LUIS OBISPO. From Highway 101 south of San Luis Obispo, take the Los Osos Valley Road exit, and head 10.1 miles west to 9th Street (0.5 miles past South Bay Boulevard). Turn right and drive 0.6 miles to Ramona Avenue, curving to the left. Continue 0.5 miles to the nature preserve on the right. Park along the road.

MORRO BAY. From Highway 1 in Morro Bay, take the Los Osos/Baywood Park exit. Drive 4 miles south on South Bay Boulevard to Los Osos Valley Road and turn right. Continue 0.5 miles to 9th Street and turn right. Continue with directions above.

Hiking directions: From the preserve entrance gate, walk past the trail sign and cross a wooden footbridge over the pond. Bear left to a second wooden bridge. Towards the right is a maze of waterways winding through the estuary. After crossing the bridge, the trail weaves through a eucalyptus grove. At the west end of the preserve is a junction. The left fork returns to the road at Broderson Street. The right fork leads to an overlook of the bay and marshy tidelands. Morro Rock can be seen at the north end of the bay. Return to the first bridge. Bear to the left, heading east alongside the pond. The trail loops back through another eucalyptus grove and returns to the park entrance.■

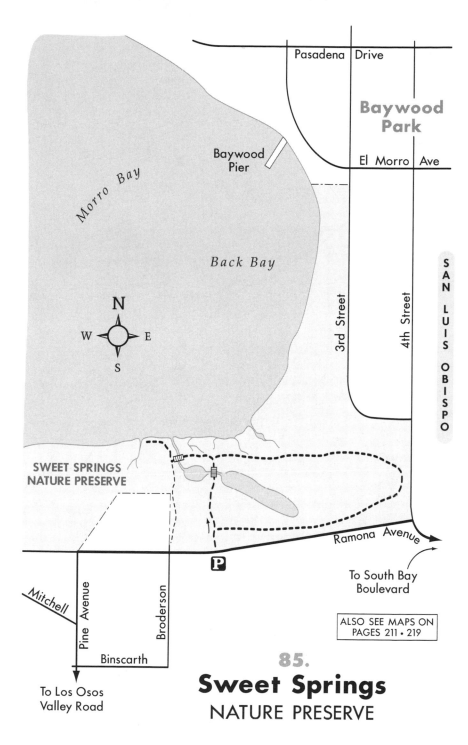

Pasadena Drive

Baywood Park

Baywood
Pier

El Morro Ave

Morro Bay

Back Bay

N
W — E
S

3rd Street

4th Street

S A N   L U I S   O B I S P O

SWEET SPRINGS
NATURE PRESERVE

Ramona Avenue

To South Bay
Boulevard

P

Mitchell

Pine Avenue

Broderson

Binscarth

To Los Osos
Valley Road

ALSO SEE MAPS ON
PAGES 211 • 219

85.
Sweet Springs
NATURE PRESERVE

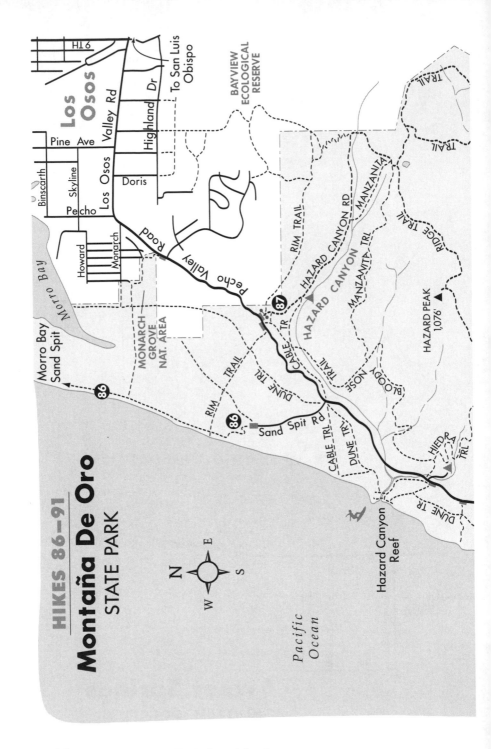

HIKES 86–91

Montaña De Oro
STATE PARK

Los Osos

H16

Pine Ave

Binscarth

Skyline

Pecho

Howard

Monarch

Los Osos

Valley Rd

Highland Dr

To San Luis Obispo

Doris

Pecho Valley Road

Morro Bay Sand Spit

Morro Bay

MONARCH GROVE NAT. AREA

RIM TRAIL

DUNE TRL

CABLE TR

Sand Spit Rd

CABLE TRL

DUNE TRL

DUNE TRL

BAYVIEW ECOLOGICAL RESERVE

TRAIL

TRAIL

TRAIL

RIM TRAIL

HAZARD CANYON RD

MANZANITA

RIDGE TRAIL

MANZANITA TRL

HAZARD CANYON

BLOODY NOSE

HAZARD PEAK
1,076'

HIEDRA

TRL

DUNE TR

Hazard Canyon Reef

Pacific Ocean

N
W — E
S

87

86

86

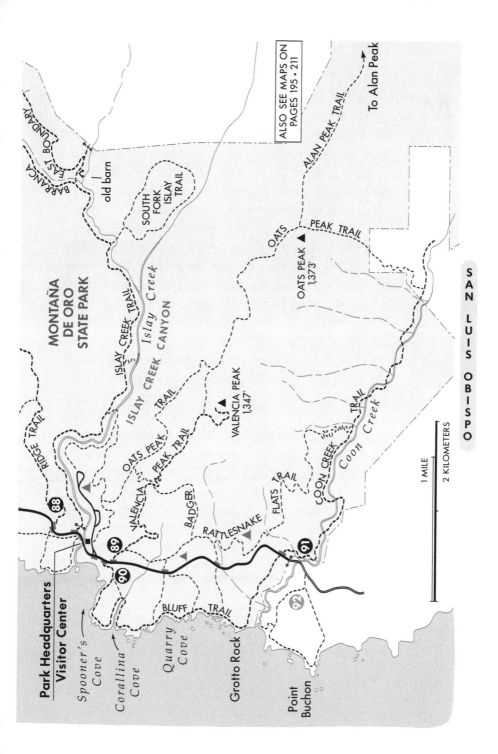

ALSO SEE MAPS ON
PAGES 195 - 211

To Alan Peak

ALAN PEAK TRAIL

SAN LUIS OBISPO

OATS PEAK TRAIL

OATS PEAK
1,373'

SOUTH FORK ISLAY TRAIL

old barn

EAST BOUNDARY

BARRANCA

MONTAÑA
DE ORO
STATE PARK

ISLAY CREEK TRAIL

Islay Creek

ISLAY CREEK CANYON

VALENCIA PEAK
1,347'

RIDGE TRAIL

OATS PEAK

VALENCIA PEAK TRAIL

BADGER

RATTLESNAKE

FLATS TRAIL

COON CREEK TRAIL

Coon Creek

88

89

90

91

92

1 MILE

2 KILOMETERS

Park Headquarters
Visitor Center

Spooner's Cove

Corallina Cove

Quarry Cove

BLUFF TRAIL

Grotto Rock

Point Buchon

Montaña De Oro State Park
HIKES 86–91

Montaña De Oro State Park (meaning *mountain of gold*) is a protected wilderness area on the west end of the Irish Hills, 2.5 miles south of Los Osos. It is a dramatic meeting of land and sea, where grassy coastal terraces sweep sharply back to 1,500-foot hills. Some of the most scenic coastline in Central California can be found along the park's waterfront.

The 8,400-acre state park stretches along 7 miles of wave-pounded coastline, with a myriad of weather-sculpted sea stacks rising offshore. Three major creeks flow from the interior mountains into the ocean—Coon Creek, Islay Creek, and Hazard Creek. Cool, wooded creek canyons emerge to sand dunes, coves, and beaches with beautiful tidepools. The year-round streams and secluded coves attract many species of wildlife.

A unique feature of the park is the long, narrow Morro Bay Sand Spit. The remote peninsula extends for three miles at the north end of the park, separating Morro Bay from the Pacific Ocean. Access to the preserve is from the north end of the park.

Montaña De Oro remains largely undeveloped with the exception of a few recreational amenities. Primitive campsites, horse facilities, and day-use facilities are available, as well as more than 50 miles of hiking, biking, and horse trails. The visitor center is housed in the original Spooner Ranch house from 1892, located in a grove of cypress trees overlooking the beach at Spooner's Cove.

Hikes 86–91 offer a cross-section of landscapes throughout the park, from coastal bluffs to expansive overlooks.

86. Morro Bay Sand Spit

MORRO DUNES NATURAL PRESERVE
MONTAÑA DE ORO STATE PARK

Hiking distance: 8—9.5 miles round trip
Hiking time: 3—5 hours
Elevation gain: 50 feet

map
page 231

Maps: U.S.G.S. Morro Bay South
Montaña De Oro State Park map
Location: Los Osos

Summary of hike: The Morro Dunes Sand Spit is a three-mile-long narrow vein of land that separates Morro Bay and the estuary from the waters of Estero Bay and the Pacific Ocean. A fragile 80-foot sand dune ridge, stabilized by scrubs, grasses, and succulents, runs the length of the preserve. Along the striated dunes are ancient Chumash Indian shell mounds known as middens. This hike follows the remote peninsula, offering a quiet opportunity for beach combing, wildlife viewing, and surf fishing along the ocean side of the dunes. The hike begins in Montaña De Oro State Park and heads north along the spit through the Morro Dunes Natural Preserve.

Driving directions: LOS OSOS. From the intersection of Los Osos Valley Road and South Bay Drive in Los Osos, drive 2.5 miles southwest on Los Osos Valley Road to the Montaña De Oro State Park entrance sign. (En route, Los Osos Valley Road becomes Pecho Valley Road.) From the entrance sign, continue 0.8 miles to Sand Spit Road and turn right. Drive 0.5 miles to the parking lot at the end of the road.

Hiking directions: Take the footpath past the information boards, and head west across the scrub-covered sand dunes. The path reaches the ocean at 0.2 miles. Head north along the hard-packed sand, staying close to the shoreline for easier walking. The coastline has an abundance of sea shells. At 4 miles is the first of two breakwaters guarding the bay entrance. Morro Rock, a 578-foot volcanic rock, dominates the landscape to the north. This is the turn-around point for an 8-mile round-trip hike.

SAN LUIS OBISPO

To add an additional 1.5 miles to the hike, continue following the shoreline to a second breakwater. Curve east towards Morro Bay, and follow the bay south about one mile. The trail curves west, crossing the soft sands of the dunes back to the ocean. Return along the same route.■

87. Hazard Canyon Road to East Boundary—Barranca Loop
MONTAÑA DE ORO STATE PARK

Hiking distance: 7.5-mile loop
Hiking time: 4 hours
Elevation gain: 600 feet
Maps: U.S.G.S. Morro Bay South
      Montaña De Oro State Park map
Location: Los Osos

map
page 233

Summary of hike: This hike includes a variety of scenery through the northeast side of Montaña De Oro State Park. The trail begins from the coastal terrace, heads up Hazard Canyon on an old ranch road, and continues up to a ridge with scenic views back down the canyon to the ocean. Once atop the ridge, the hike weaves through the Irish Hills and heads down into the adjacent canyon—Islay Creek Canyon—and past the old Spooner Ranch barn, an abandoned tin-roof barn. The hike makes a loop at the head of the canyons via the Barranca and East Boundary Trails, crossing two springs that feed year-round Islay Creek. The hike returns back down Hazard Canyon.

Driving directions: LOS OSOS. From the intersection of Los Osos Valley Road and South Bay Drive in Los Osos, drive 2.5 miles southwest on Los Osos Valley Road to the Montaña De Oro State Park entrance sign. (En route, Los Osos Valley Road becomes Pecho Valley Road.) From the entrance sign, continue 0.1 mile to the posted "Horse Camp" turnoff on the left. Park in the dirt pullout next to (but not blocking) the gated road/trail. If the area is full, park just beyond the trailhead in a pullout on the right.

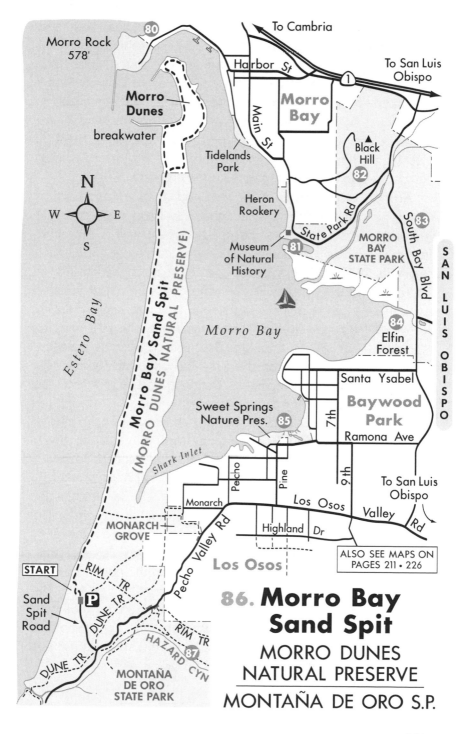

Morro Rock
578'

To Cambria

Harbor St

To San Luis
Obispo

**Morro
Dunes**

breakwater

Tidelands
Park

**Morro
Bay**

Main St

Black
Hill

82

State Park Rd

N

W — E

S

Heron
Rookery

Museum
of Natural
History

81

MORRO
BAY
STATE PARK

83

South Bay Blvd

Estero Bay

Morro Bay Sand Spit

(MORRO DUNES NATURAL PRESERVE)

Morro Bay

Elfin
Forest

84

SAN LUIS OBISPO

Santa Ysabel

Shark Inlet

Sweet Springs
Nature Pres.

85

7th

**Baywood
Park**

Ramona Ave

Pecho

Pine

9th

To San Luis
Obispo

Monarch

Los Osos

Valley

Rd

MONARCH
GROVE

Pecho Valley Rd

Highland

Dr

START

RIM TR

Los Osos

ALSO SEE MAPS ON
PAGES 211 • 226

Sand
Spit
Road

P

DUNE TR

RIM TR

87

HAZARD CYN

DUNE TR

MONTAÑA
DE ORO
STATE PARK

86. **Morro Bay
Sand Spit**

MORRO DUNES
NATURAL PRESERVE

MONTAÑA DE ORO S.P.

Hiking directions: Pass the trailhead gate and head southeast on the dirt campground road. Walk through a eucalyptus grove on the north wall of Hazard Canyon, and descend to the horse camp on the right. Continue straight, staying in Hazard Canyon. Pass a second trail gate to a posted junction with the Manzanita Trail on the right at 0.8 miles. Take either trail, as both routes head up the drainage and rejoin near the east boundary. The Manzanita Trail follows the north wall of a small side canyon. The Hazard Canyon Road stays on the dirt road through the chaparral.

At the fenced border at the east end of the Hazard Canyon Road, bear right on the East Boundary Trail and cross over the transient stream. Wind up the south canyon wall, with views down canyon to the ocean. Across the canyon, a zig-zagging trail with 28 switchbacks can be seen climbing to the Rim Trail at the park's north boundary. At 1.8 miles, pass the upper junction with the Manzanita Trail in a saddle and stay left, leaving Hazard Canyon. One hundred yards ahead, the Manzanita Trail goes to the right. Veer left to the Ridge Trail (which ascends from the right). Bear left, staying on the East Boundary Trail, and pass a seasonal pond in a depression on the right. Cross a saddle to the Barranca Trail on the right.

Begin the 3.3-mile loop to the left, and stroll through an oak grove high above Islay Creek Canyon. Traverse the rolling grasslands across the head of the canyon near the fenced boundary of the state park. Cross two wood bridges over springs, and follow the contours of the canyon along the cliffs. Descend to the floor of Islay Creek Canyon at the north side of the creek. Go right 200 yards to the old ranch barn, and continue another 200 yards to the posted Barranca Trail. Bear right on the Barranca Trail, and wind up the south-facing wall, following the ridge between two drainages. Near the top, pass oak groves to a trail split. The right fork leads 25 yards to a coastal overlook on the knoll with a bench. Complete the loop on the Barranca Trail, continuing to a saddle at the East Boundary Trail. Retrace your steps to the left (west), returning back down Hazard Canyon. ■

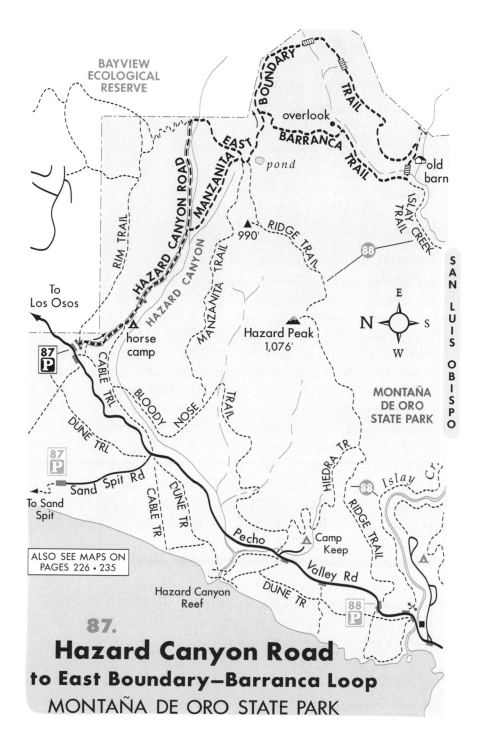

BAYVIEW
ECOLOGICAL
RESERVE

BOUNDARY TRAIL

overlook

EAST

BARRANCA TRAIL

pond

old barn

HAZARD CANYON ROAD

MANZANITA

RIM TRAIL

990'

RIDGE TRAIL

ISLAY CREEK TRAIL

88

HAZARD CANYON

MANZANITA TRAIL

To
Los Osos

horse camp

Hazard Peak
1,076'

E

N

S

W

CABLE TRL

BLOODY NOSE

TRAIL

MONTAÑA
DE ORO
STATE PARK

S A N   L U I S   O B I S P O

DUNE TRL

87
P

HIEDRA TR

88

Islay Cr.

Sand Spit Rd

CABLE TR

DUNE TR

RIDGE TRAIL

87
P

To Sand
Spit

Pecho

Camp
Keep

ALSO SEE MAPS ON
PAGES 226 • 235

Valley Rd

Hazard Canyon
Reef

DUNE TR

88
P

87.
Hazard Canyon Road
to East Boundary—Barranca Loop
MONTAÑA DE ORO STATE PARK

88. Hazard Peak—Islay Creek Canyon Loop

RIDGE TRAIL—BARRANCA TRAIL—ISLAY CREEK TRAIL

MONTAÑA DE ORO STATE PARK

Hiking distance: 7.9-mile loop
Hiking time: 4 hours
Elevation gain: 1,050 feet
Maps: U.S.G.S. Morro Bay South
Montaña De Oro State Park map
Location: Los Osos

Summary of hike: This hike offers expansive mountain vistas and sweeping views of the ocean from the heart of Montaña De Oro State Park. The route makes a large loop through the center of the park, traversing up a panoramic ridge and descending through lush Islay Creek Canyon. Islay Creek is a major drainage from the Irish Hills, entering the ocean at Spooner's Cove. The Ridge Trail follows the ridgeline between Island Creek Canyon and Hazard Canyon up to 1,076-foot Hazard Peak. The strenuous climb to the peak leads to great vistas of the rugged coastline. After the peak, the trail descends into the Islay Creek drainage, passing an overlook of Hazard Canyon, Morro Bay, and the Santa Lucia Range. The return along Islay Creek follows an old ranch road through the wooded canyon beneath the shadow of Valencia Peak and Oats Peak. The trail passes a waterfall tumbling out of a rock outcropping and fertile Reservoir Flats near the Islay Creek canyon bottom.

Driving directions: LOS OSOS. From the intersection of Los Osos Valley Road and South Bay Drive in Los Osos, drive 2.5 miles southwest on Los Osos Valley Road to the Montaña De Oro State Park entrance sign. (En route, Los Osos Valley Road becomes Pecho Valley Road.) From the entrance, continue 2.3 miles to the signed trailhead on the left. There are parking areas on both sides of the road. The visitor center is 0.3 miles ahead.

Hiking directions: Head up the posted Ridge Trail on an easy

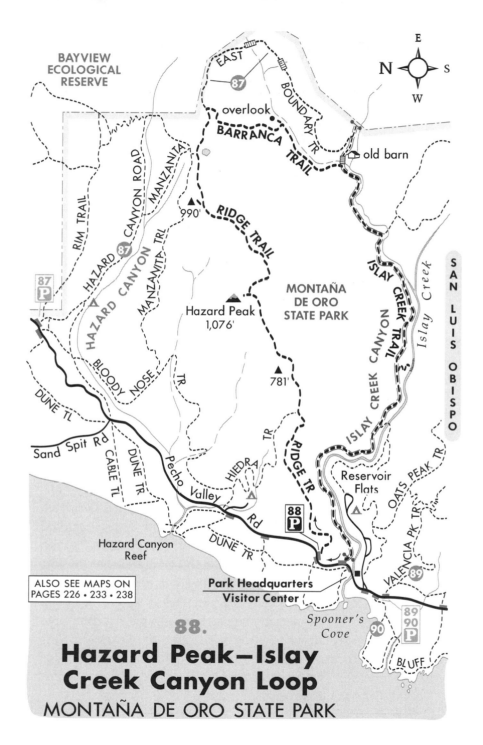

BAYVIEW
ECOLOGICAL
RESERVE

EAST

87

BOUNDARY TR

overlook

BARRANCA TRAIL

old barn

N E W S

RIM TRAIL

HAZARD CANYON ROAD

MANZANITA

87

MANZANITA TRL

HAZARD CANYON

990'

RIDGE TRAIL

MONTAÑA
DE ORO
STATE PARK

ISLAY CREEK TRAIL

ISLAY CREEK CANYON

Islay Creek

S A N   L U I S   O B I S P O

87
P

Hazard Peak
1,076'

781'

BLOODY NOSE

TR

TR

DUNE TL

Sand Spit Rd

CABLE TL

DUNE TR

Pecho Valley

HIEDRA

RIDGE TR

Reservoir
Flats

OATS PEAK TR

Rd

88
P

VALENCIA PK TR

Hazard Canyon
Reef

DUNE TR

89

ALSO SEE MAPS ON
PAGES 226 • 233 • 238

Park Headquarters
Visitor Center

Spooner's
Cove

90

89
90
P

BLUFF

88.

Hazard Peak–Islay
Creek Canyon Loop
MONTAÑA DE ORO STATE PARK

uphill grade. Weave through coastal scrub with views of Spooner's Cove, Valencia Peak, Oats Peak, and the campground. Continue the ascent to the west base of a rounded 781-foot hill. Curve right, circling around the hill, and traverse the south-facing slope above Islay Creek Canyon. Climb to the ridge overlooking Morro Bay and the estuary by a 4-foot cairn. Follow the ridge and cross a saddle between two steep canyons. Ascend the west slope to 1,076-foot Hazard Peak.

After savoring the views, continue on the narrow spine. Sweep downhill to the left, and cross two more saddles to a trail split. The left fork detours 100 yards to a 990-foot overlook of Hazard Canyon and the coastline to the Santa Lucia Range. From the junction, descend and pass a seasonal pond on the right to the end of the Ridge Trail at a junction with the East Boundary Trail at 3.2 miles. Bear right and stroll through the rolling valley surrounded by hills to a posted junction with the Barranca Trail. Go to the right (south), weaving through coastal scrub and pockets of oak trees on the east side of Hazard Peak. Top the upper north slope of Islay Creek Canyon past a junction on the left that leads to a coastal overlook with a picnic table. Stay right and descend for a mile to the canyon floor, 200 yards downstream from the old Spooner Ranch barn. The tin-roofed barn is now abandoned.

Bear right on the Islay Creek Trail, an old ranch road. The road once connected the Spooner Ranch house (now the visitor center) to the barn in the mountainous interior. Follow the old ranch road downstream along the north edge of the creek. Pass the South Fork Islay Trail on the left (a small loop trail), staying on the main road. At 6.5 miles is a narrow, unsigned trail on the left (creekside). This footpath leads down a steep cliff to the waterfall. (The scramble is difficult; the waterfall is visible from the main trail just downstream of the junction with the footpath.) At 6.8 miles is a signed junction on the left to the Reservoir Flats Trail. Continue down the main Islay Creek Trail another 1.0 miles to the park road. The visitor center is across the creek to the left (south). Go right, following the road 0.1 mile back to the trailhead.■

89. Valencia Peak Trail
MONTAÑA DE ORO STATE PARK

Hiking distance: 4 miles round trip
Hiking time: 2 hours
Elevation gain: 1,150 feet
Maps: U.S.G.S. Morro Bay South
       Montaña De Oro State Park map
Location: Los Osos

map
page 238

Summary of hike: Valencia Peak, rising over the coast at 1,347 feet, has spectacular 360-degree views of Montaña De Oro State Park; Morro Bay; Los Osos Valley; and the rugged coastline, from Point Sal to Piedras Blancas. The chain of morros leading from Morro Rock to San Luis Obispo are in view. The trail begins by Spooner's Cove, crosses grasslands, and straddles a ridge between two canyons before climbing directly up to the peak.

Driving directions: LOS OSOS. From the intersection of Los Osos Valley Road and South Bay Drive in Los Osos, drive 2.5 miles southwest on Los Osos Valley Road to the Montaña De Oro State Park entrance sign. (En route, Los Osos Valley Road becomes Pecho Valley Road.) From the entrance sign, continue 2.6 miles to the visitor center on the left. Drive another 100 yards past the visitor center on Pecho Valley Road to the trailhead parking area on the left.

Hiking directions: Hike east across the broad chaparral-covered marine terrace on the signed Valencia Peak Trail. Head toward the base of the mountain, passing the Rattlesnake Flats Trail on the right. As the trail begins to climb, views emerge of the scenic coastal plain. Switchbacks lead up to the first ridge above Spooner's Cove and the bluffs. Cross the grassy flat, in full view of Valencia Peak, to a junction with the Badger Trail at the base of the cone-shaped mountain. The left fork leads to the Oats Peak Trail. The right fork descends to Rattlesnake Flats. Stay on the Valencia Peak Trail, climbing the edge of the mountain to a narrow ridge. Follow the ridge east up two steep sections with loose shale. At the base of the final ascent is another connector trail to the Oaks Peak Trail—stay to the right. Continue uphill, reaching the summit at two miles. After resting and savoring the views, return along the same route. ■

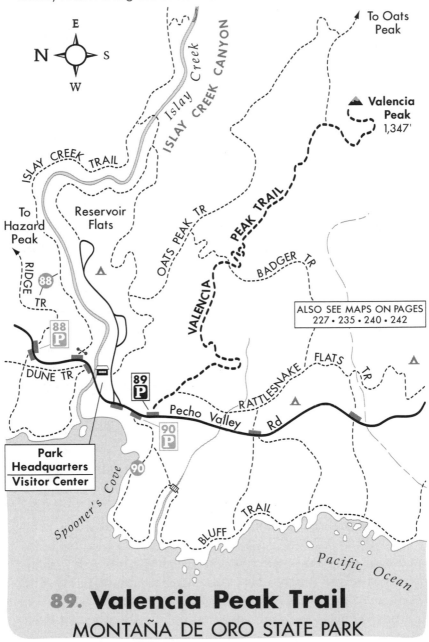

89. Valencia Peak Trail
MONTAÑA DE ORO STATE PARK

90. Bluff Trail
MONTAÑA DE ORO STATE PARK

Hiking distance: 3.4 miles round trip
Hiking time: 1.5 hours
Elevation gain: Level
Maps: U.S.G.S. Morro Bay South
Montaña De Oro State Park map
Location: Los Osos

*map
page 240*

Summary of hike: The Bluff Trail is an easy, level hike along one of the premier coastline locations in Central California. The popular trail snakes along the contours of a rugged network of eroding sandstone cliffs on a grassy, 40-foot marine terrace. Land extensions jut out into the ocean like fingers. There are hidden coves, sea caves, arches, sandy beaches, reefs, offshore outcroppings, clear tidepools, crashing surf, basking seals, and otters.

Driving directions: LOS OSOS. From the intersection of Los Osos Valley Road and South Bay Drive in Los Osos, drive 2.5 miles southwest on Los Osos Valley Road to the Montaña De Oro State Park entrance sign. (En route, Los Osos Valley Road becomes Pecho Valley Road.) From the entrance sign, continue 2.6 miles to the visitor center on the left. Drive another 80 yards past the visitor center on Pecho Valley Road to the trailhead parking area on the right.

Hiking directions: Head west on the wide trail, and cross a wooden bridge over an arroyo to a trail fork. Take the right branch, following the cliff's edge along Spooner's Cove. Spur trails intersect the main trail throughout the hike, leading back to the road. The main path generally follows the cliff's edge, passing coves and rocky reefs. At Corallina Cove—a sandy beach—curve inland. Cross a footbridge over a narrow ravine, and return to the oceanfront cliffs. Continue south past dramatic fingers of water-carved land to Quarry Cove, another sandy beach with tidepools. At 1.7 miles is Grotto Rock, a prominent castle-shaped rock with caves. Near the PG&E fenceline is the mouth of Coon

Creek. This is the turn-around spot. The trail leaves the coastline here and heads east to Pecho Valley Road and the Coon Creek Trail (Hike 91). To return, retrace your steps along the Bluff Trail.■

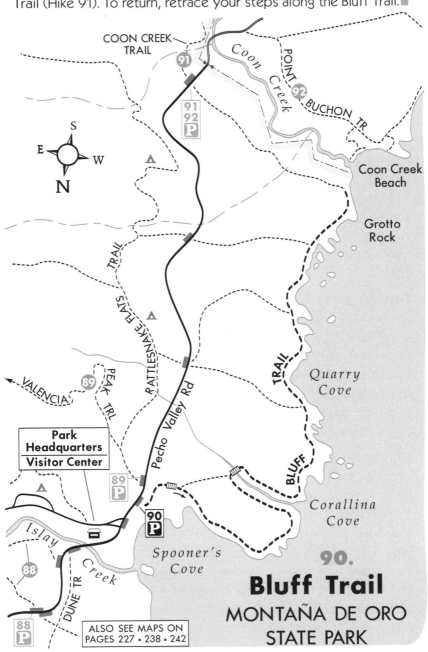

COON CREEK TRAIL

91

Coon Creek

POINT

92

BUCHON TR

Coon Creek Beach

Grotto Rock

91 92 P

S

E ⊙ W

N

TRAIL

RATTLESNAKE FLATS

TRAIL

Quarry Cove

VALENCIA

89

PEAK TRL

89 P

Park Headquarters Visitor Center

Pecho Valley Rd

BLUFF

TRAIL

Corallina Cove

90 P

Islay Creek

88

Spooner's Cove

DUNE TR

88 P

ALSO SEE MAPS ON PAGES 227 · 238 · 242

90.

Bluff Trail

MONTAÑA DE ORO STATE PARK

91. Coon Creek Trail
MONTAÑA DE ORO STATE PARK

Hiking distance: 5 miles round trip
Hiking time: 2.5 hours
Elevation gain: 250 feet
Maps: U.S.G.S. Morro Bay South and Port San Luis
Montaña De Oro State Park map
Location: Los Osos

map
page 242

Summary of hike: The Coon Creek Trail, at the south boundary of Montaña De Oro State Park, heads up Coon Creek Canyon alongside the winding watercourse of the perennial stream. The trail crosses six bridges over the creek through the shade of a lush riparian corridor. Willows, maples, cottonwoods, coast live oaks, cedars, and cypress grow in the canyon. Lace lichen hangs from the branches.

Driving directions: LOS OSOS. From the intersection of Los Osos Valley Road and South Bay Drive in Los Osos, drive 2.5 miles southwest on Los Osos Valley Road to the Montaña De Oro State Park entrance sign. (En route, Los Osos Valley Road becomes Pecho Valley Road.) From the entrance sign, continue 3.9 miles to the trailhead parking area on the left at the end of the road. It is 1.2 miles past the visitor center.

Hiking directions: Hike east past the trail sign and over a small ridge to a ravine. Bear right down wide steps, and follow the path along the fenced park boundary to Coon Creek at 0.3 miles. Head up the canyon through the forest along the north side of the creek. Cross the first two of six bridges over the willow-lined creek past beautiful rock outcroppings. At 1.2 miles, the trail rises to an overlook of Coon Creek Canyon at a signed trail junction with the Rattlesnake Flats Trail on the left. Continue straight ahead up the shady canyon, and cross four more bridges. At 2.4 miles is a junction on the left with the Oats Peak Trail. Continue a short distance ahead to the trail's end in a grove of cypress trees and large, twisted oaks at an old homestead cabin site from the 1920s. Return by retracing your steps. ∎

SAN LUIS OBISPO

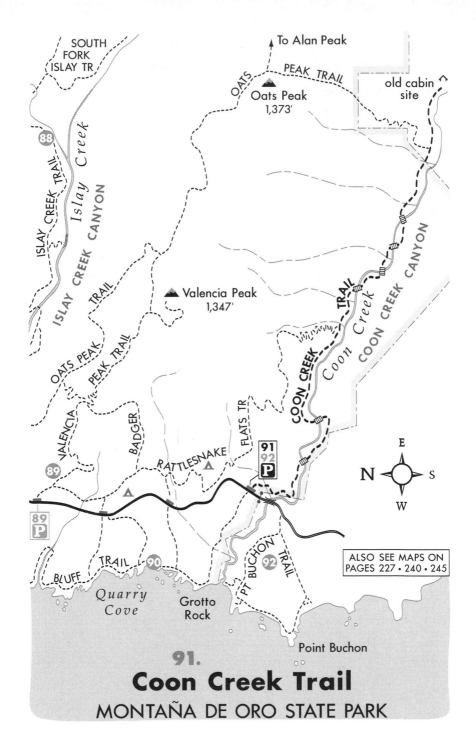

SOUTH FORK ISLAY TR

To Alan Peak

OATS PEAK TRAIL

Oats Peak
1,373'

old cabin site

ISLAY CREEK TRAIL

Islay Creek

ISLAY CREEK CANYON

88

TRAIL

COON CREEK TRAIL

COON CREEK CANYON

Coon Creek

Valencia Peak
1,347'

OATS PEAK

PEAK TRAIL

VALENCIA

BADGER

RATTLESNAKE

FLATS TR

COON CREEK

91 92 P

89

89 P

E
N ✦ S
W

TRAIL

90

BLUFF

PT BUCHON TRAIL

92

ALSO SEE MAPS ON PAGES 227 • 240 • 245

Quarry Cove

Grotto Rock

Point Buchon

91.
Coon Creek Trail
MONTAÑA DE ORO STATE PARK

92. Point Buchon Trail

Open 8 a.m. to 5 p.m. Fridays, Saturdays and Sundays

Hiking distance: 1.8 mile loop
Hiking time: 1 hour
Elevation gain: 150 feet
Maps: U.S.G.S. Morro Bay South
Pacific Gas and Electric Company Point Buchon Trail map
Location: Los Osos

map page 245

Summary of hike: Point Buchon is located just south of Montaña De Oro State Park and north of Diablo Canyon. The land, owned by the Pacific Gas and Electric Company, has been part of a security buffer zone around the Diablo Canyon Nuclear Plant. This stretch of spectacular coastline has been free of human impact for decades and remains relatively unspoiled.

Opened to the public in 2007, access to the Point Buchon Trail is from the south end of Montaña De Oro State Park at the end of Pecho Valley Road. The loop trail leads to U-shaped Coon Creek Beach, where Coon Creek empties into the ocean, and to Observation Hill, on a windswept promontory overlooking Point Buchon and the scalloped coastline. En route, the trail follows the coastal bluffs and meadows while passing sea stacks, beach coves with sea otters, and a sinkhole formed by the 1998 winter storms of El Nino. The rough surf during the storms cut an underground chamber and the roof collapsed. Although the Point Buchon beaches are visible from the trail, they are outside of the permitted hiking area.

Future plans are to extend the oceanfront path for three miles to Crowbar Canyon near Lion Rock, a prominent offshore rock.

Driving directions: LOS OSOS. From the intersection of Los Osos Valley Road and South Bay Drive in Los Osos, drive 2.5 miles southwest on Los Osos Valley Road to the Montaña De Oro State Park entrance sign. (En route, Los Osos Valley Road becomes Pecho Valley Road.) From the entrance sign, continue 3.9 miles to the trailhead parking area on the left at the end of the road. It is 1.2 miles past the visitor center.

Hiking directions: Walk down the road to the gated south boundary of Montaña De Oro State Park. Pass through the left side of the gate and enter the Pacific Gas and Electric land. Cross the Coon Creek bridge to the check-in station. After signing in and getting a trail map, take the right fork. Follow the dirt road/trail to a signed Y-fork.

Begin the loop to the right along the Coon Creek Bluffs on the south side of Coon Creek. The views extend across the south end of Montaña De Oro State Park. Valencia Peak rises 1,300 feet in the northeast. Descend to the oceanfront terrace to a junction overlooking Coon Creek Beach and the offshore rocks. Detour to the right, dropping down to the U-shaped sandy beach at the mouth of Coon Creek. After exploring the beach and the cave-carved cliffs, return to the Point Buchon Trail. Continue a short distance to a large, circular sinkhole. Loop around the sinkhole to the bluffs while overlooking Coon Creek Cove.

Continue on the main trail, heading south along the coastline. Follow the bluffs past magnificent offshore rocks to the exposed headland of Point Buchon. Unfortunately, the protected Point Buchon beaches below are off-limits. Skirt past the point to a posted fork. Veer right to Observation Hill. The sweeping vistas include Point Buchon, Montaña De Oro, Cayucos, and offshore beaches, coves, and rocks. Leave the overlook and head inland through open meadows, directly toward Valencia Peak. Complete the loop and return via the check-in station.■

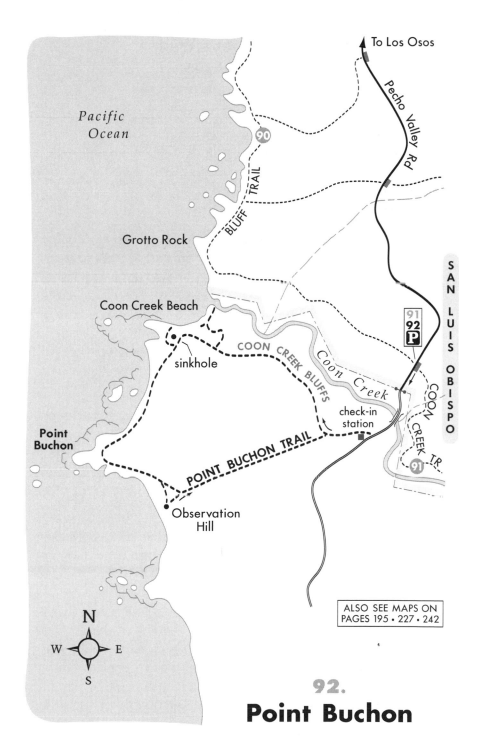

Pacific
Ocean

To Los Osos

Pecho Valley Rd

BLUFF TRAIL

90

Grotto Rock

SAN LUIS OBISPO

Coon Creek Beach

91
92
P

sinkhole

COON CREEK BLUFFS

Coon Creek

check-in
station

COON CREEK TR.

Point
Buchon

POINT BUCHON TRAIL

91

Observation
Hill

ALSO SEE MAPS ON
PAGES 195 • 227 • 242

N
W · E
S

92.
Point Buchon

93. Pecho Coast Trail
POINT SAN LUIS

Free docent-led hike on PG&E land
Reservations required: (805) 541-8735

Hiking distance: 3.5—7.4 miles round trip
Hiking time: 4 hours—7 hours
Elevation gain: 440 feet
Maps: U.S.G.S. Port San Luis
Location: Avila Beach

Summary of hike: The Pecho Coast Trail curves around the western point of San Luis Obispo Bay from Port San Luis towards Montaña De Oro State Park. Access is from two docent-led hikes across the privately owned PG&E land. Both hikes follow the steep cliffs to Point San Luis and the Port San Luis Lighthouse, a two-story Victorian redwood structure built in 1890. It is a great spot for watching the annual migration of the gray whales. The longer hike continues across the coastal bluffs and pastureland to an oak grove in Rattlesnake Canyon.

Driving directions: PISMO BEACH. From Highway 101 in Pismo Beach, take the Avila Beach Drive exit. Head 4.2 miles west on Avila Beach Drive, passing the town of Avila Beach, to the PG&E Diablo Canyon Power Plant entrance on the right at Port San Luis Harbor. Park in the wide area on the left, across the road from the PG&E entrance gate.

Hiking directions: Naturalists will lead the hike, providing geological, botanical, and historical details. Begin by walking up the steps past a locked gate west of the PG&E station. Ascend the hillside overlooking the bay and three piers. Bear left on the lighthouse road to the Pecho Coast Trail, and take the footpath left. Descend the hillside towards the ocean. Follow the contour of the mountains on a cliffside trail 200 feet above the ocean. The trail passes Smith Island and Whaler's Island. Continue around the point, rejoining the paved road to the lighthouse.

The longer hike continues past the lighthouse, crossing the

coastal terrace and grasslands to an oak woodland in Rattlesnake Canyon for lunch. Return by retracing your steps. ■

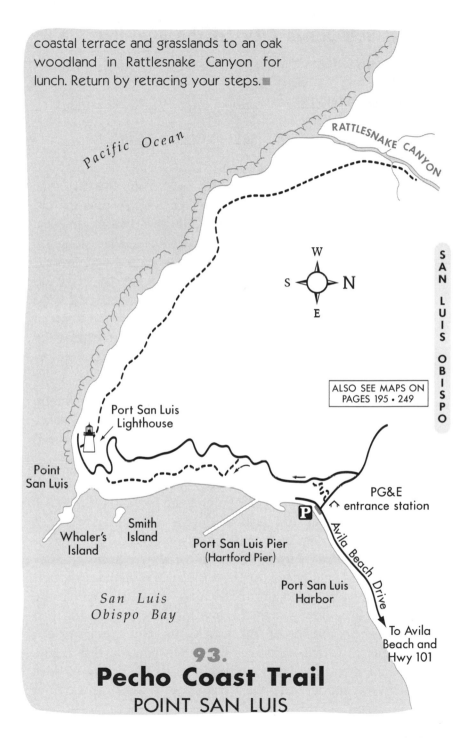

Pacific Ocean

RATTLESNAKE CANYON

W
S ◯ N
E

SAN LUIS OBISPO

ALSO SEE MAPS ON
PAGES 195 • 249

Port San Luis
Lighthouse

Point
San Luis

PG&E
entrance station

Whaler's
Island

Smith
Island

Port San Luis Pier
(Hartford Pier)

San Luis
Obispo Bay

Port San Luis
Harbor

Avila Beach Drive

To Avila
Beach and
Hwy 101

93.
Pecho Coast Trail
POINT SAN LUIS

94. Bob Jones City to the Sea Bike Trail

Hiking distance: 5.6 miles round trip
Hiking time: 2.5 hour
Elevation gain: 150 feet
Maps: U.S.G.S. Pismo Beach
The Thomas Guide—San Luis Obispo County
Location: Avila Beach

Summary of hike: The Bob Jones City to the Sea Bike Trail (originally known as the Avila Valley Bike Trail) follows the old Pacific Coast Railroad right-of-way. The paved hiking, jogging, and biking route winds through forested Avila Valley alongside San Luis Obispo Creek. The walk ends at Avila Beach, a quaint seaside town tucked between the rolling Irish Hills and San Luis Obispo Bay. From the trail are views of bridges spanning the wide creek, the Avila Beach Golf Course, a tidal estuary, the town of Avila Beach, and the Pacific Ocean. Future plans are to expand the paved path to San Luis Obispo.

Driving directions: PISMO BEACH. From Highway 101 in Pismo Beach, exit on Avila Beach Drive. Head west 0.3 miles to Ontario Road at Avila Hot Springs Spa. Turn right and continue 0.3 miles, crossing the bridge over San Luis Obispo Creek, to the trailhead parking lot on the right.

Hiking directions: Cross Ontario Road and pick up the signed trail heading west. Immediately enter a lush forest parallel to San Luis Obispo Creek. Although the creek is nearby, the dense foliage makes access to it nearly impossible. At 0.7 miles, cross a bridge over See Canyon Creek, and then cross San Luis Bay Drive at one mile. Continue past Avila Bay Club on the right, parallel to the creek on the left, to the trail's end at Blue Heron Drive. Bear left on the private road, staying close to the creek. The road curves around the hillside overlooking the creek, bridges, and golf course. A trail junction is located where the first bridge spans the creek. The left fork heads across the bridge to Avila Beach Drive and leads to the Front Street walkway and pier at

Avila Beach. The right fork continues to the golf course entrance by Mulligans Restaurant. To return, take the same trail back.■

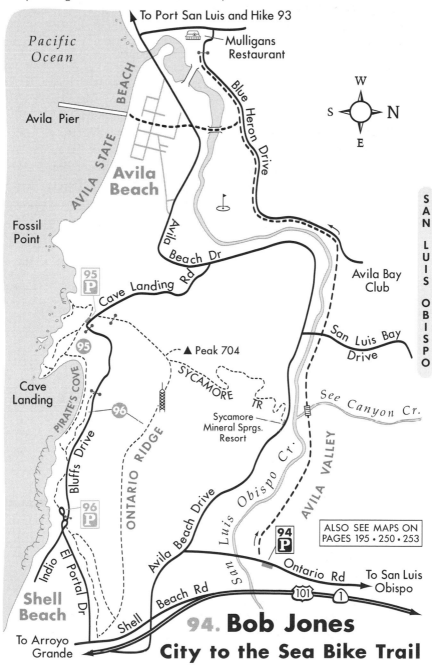

To Port San Luis and Hike 93

Pacific Ocean

Mulligans Restaurant

Avila Pier

BEACH

AVILA STATE

Avila Beach

Blue Heron Drive

W
S — N
E

Fossil Point

Avila Beach Dr

95 P

Cave Landing Rd

Avila Bay Club

San Luis Bay Drive

▲ Peak 704

95

Cave Landing

PIRATE'S COVE

SYCAMORE

San Luis Obispo Cr.

See Canyon Cr.

96

TR

Sycamore Mineral Sprgs. Resort

Bluffs Drive

ONTARIO RIDGE

AVILA VALLEY

96 P

ALSO SEE MAPS ON
PAGES 195 • 250 • 253

Avila Beach Drive

San Luis Obispo Cr.

94 P

Indio

El Portal Dr

Ontario Rd

To San Luis Obispo

Shell Beach

Beach Rd

101 1

Shell

To Arroyo Grande

S A N   L U I S   O B I S P O

94. **Bob Jones**
City to the Sea Bike Trail

95. Cave Landing and Pirate's Cove

Hiking distance: 2 miles round trip
Hiking time: 1 hour
Elevation gain: 120 feet
Maps: U.S.G.S. Pismo Beach
　　　The Thomas Guide—San Luis Obispo County
Location: Avila Beach / Shell Beach

Summary of hike: Cave Landing is a spectacular rocky promontory that juts out 150 feet into San Luis Obispo Bay. It forms a natural pier and a division between Avila Beach and Shell Beach. Cave Landing, originally called Mallagh Landing, was named for David Mallagh, who purchased the land in the 1870s. During the Prohibition Era of the 1920s, the point was used by boot-leggers to supply the local area with beverages. It then became known as Smuggler's Cove. The picturesque formation has wind-

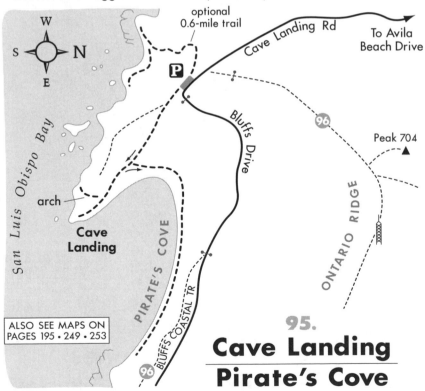

optional
0.6-mile trail

Cave Landing Rd

To Avila
Beach Drive

P

Bluffs Drive

96

Peak 704

ONTARIO RIDGE

arch

Cave
Landing

PIRATE'S COVE

San Luis Obispo Bay

BLUFFS COASTAL TR

96

ALSO SEE MAPS ON
PAGES 195 • 249 • 253

95.
Cave Landing
Pirate's Cove

swept caves and coves, including an arch chiseled through the cliffs near the end of the headland. From the dramatic point are great views of the steep, serrated cliffs along the rugged coastline. Pirate's Cove, a crescent-shaped, unsanctioned clothing-optional beach, sits at the base of the hundred-foot cliffs.

Driving directions: PISMO BEACH. From Highway 101 in Pismo Beach, exit on Avila Beach Drive. Head 2 miles west to Cave Landing Road and turn left. Continue 0.5 miles to the trailhead parking lot on the right at the end of the road.

Hiking directions: The trail heads southeast towards the rocky point overlooking the Shell Beach and Pismo Beach coastline. At 20 yards is a junction. Bear left to a trail split 0.2 miles ahead. The left fork descends to Pirate's Cove. Before descending, take the right fork to another trail split. To the right is a natural arch cave leading to an overlook on Cave Landing. To the left is an overlook at the edge of the cliffs. Return to the junction and bear right, curving gently down the cliffs to Pirate's Cove. Continue along the sandy beach beneath the cliffs. Return along the same path.

To walk an additional 0.6 miles, take the wide path heading west at the opposite end of the trailhead parking area. The trail leads down to a flat, grassy plateau. From the plateau, a path follows the cliff's edge to the left. Caves can be seen along the base of the cliffs. Return along the same route.■

96. Ontario Ridge
Shell Beach Bluffs Coastal Trail

Hiking distance: 2.8 mile loop
Hiking time: 1.5 hours
Elevation gain: 650 feet
Maps: U.S.G.S. Pismo Beach
Location: Shell Beach

map
page 253

Summary of hike: Ontario Ridge lies between Avila Valley and San Luis Obispo Bay. The 735-foot hill separates Avila Beach from Shell Beach. This hike follows Ontario Ridge while overlooking the ocean, with sweeping vistas of the Irish Hills, Avila Beach, Port San Luis, Whaler's Island, and the Shell Beach–Pismo Beach coastline. The views extend all the way to Point Sal in the south. The hike crosses the seaside ridge to Cave Landing by Avila Beach (Hike 95), then returns on the coastal trail along the scalloped cliffs, 100 feet above Pirate's Cove. Sea otters and sea lions are frequently seen along the shoreline.

Driving directions: From Highway 101 in Pismo Beach, exit on Avila Beach Drive. Head west to the first street—Shell Beach Road—and turn left. Continue 0.3 miles to El Portal Drive and turn right. Drive 0.6 miles, bearing right on Indio Drive. The trailhead is on the right, just before The Bluffs gated homes. Park in the lot below the gates at the end of the road.

Hiking directions: Walk back up to Indio Drive at the roundabout, and take the well-defined path across the road. Follow the base of the hillside 25 yards to an unsigned path on the left. Take the path up to an old rutted road and bear right, traversing the slope. At 0.6 miles, the trail reaches the ridge at a junction 200 feet above Highway 101. (For a shorter hike, the right fork leads up to an overlook, then descends a steep grade to the path at the base of the hillside.)

At the junction, head west up the ridge along an old fenceline. The trail climbs with intermittent level areas, straddling the ridge between the chaparral and gnarly oak groves. Parallel the ocean high above Pirate's Cove to the 735-foot summit near a radio tower. Descend on the two-track road. At the south foot of Peak 704, the Sycamore Trail descends the north-facing slope to Sycamore Mineral Springs Resort in Avila Valley. Stay atop the ridge and curve left. Quickly drop down to Cave Landing Road, cross a vehicle gate, and bear left on the road to a fork. The right fork leads to Cave Landing and Pirate's Cove (Hike 95). Curve left on the unpaved road, descending to the Shell Beach Bluffs Coastal Trail. Take the paved walkway above the rugged coastline along the cliffs overlooking the ocean. The trail joins Bluffs Drive for 100 yards, a private road that passes a few luxury homes. Continue on the cliffside trail back to the parking area.■

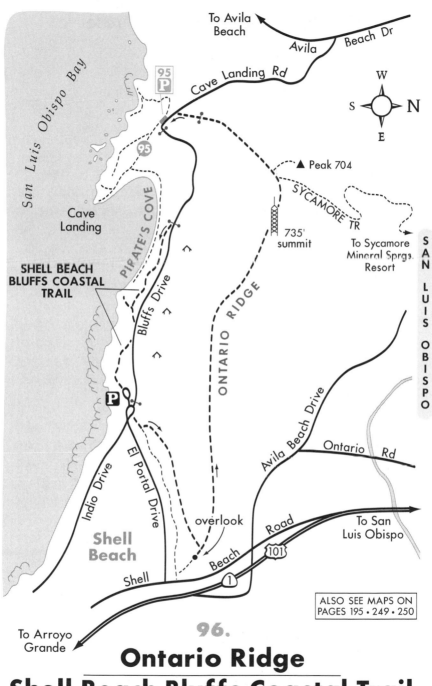

To Avila Beach

Avila Beach Dr

Cave Landing Rd

San Luis Obispo Bay

95 P

95

Cave Landing

PIRATE'S COVE

SHELL BEACH BLUFFS COASTAL TRAIL

Bluffs Drive

▲ Peak 704

SYCAMORE TR

735' summit

To Sycamore Mineral Sprgs. Resort

S A N   L U I S   O B I S P O

ONTARIO RIDGE

P

Indio Drive

El Portal Drive

Avila Beach Drive

Ontario Rd

overlook

Road

To San Luis Obispo

Shell Beach

Shell

Beach

101

1

ALSO SEE MAPS ON PAGES 195 • 249 • 250

To Arroyo Grande

W N S E

96.

Ontario Ridge
Shell Beach Bluffs Coastal Trail

97. Oceano Dunes Natural Preserve

Hiking distance: 2 or more miles round trip
Hiking time: 1 hour
Elevation gain: 100 feet
Maps: U.S.G.S. Oceano
　　　　Pismo State Beach map
Location: Pismo Beach

Summary of hike: The Oceano Dunes Natural Preserve (formerly the Pismo Dunes) is a 570-acre parcel of land at the southern boundary of Pismo State Beach. The preserve stretches 1.5 miles south of Arroyo Grande Creek. It is adjacent to the 3,600-acre Oceano Dunes Vehicular Recreation Area, the only beach in California that allows vehicles. The hike begins from this busy vehicle-filled, hard-packed sand beach. The trail soon crosses Arroyo Grande Creek and enters the quiet, undisturbed solitude of the most extensive coastal dunes in California. A ridge of wave-shaped dunes shields the preserve from the sound of the busy beachfront. The route meanders through the quiet and fragile natural preserve, crossing scrub-covered dunes sculpted by the wind.

Driving directions: PISMO BEACH. From Highway 101 in Pismo Beach, take the Pismo Beach/Highway 1 South exit. Take Highway 1 through the town of Pismo Beach (Dolliver Street, which becomes Pacific Boulevard) for 3 miles to Pier Avenue. Turn right and drive 0.4 miles to the Pismo State Beach parking lot at the beachfront.

ARROYO GRANDE. From Highway 101 in Arroyo Grande, take the Grand Avenue exit and head 2.5 miles west to Highway 1/Pacific Boulevard. Turn left and drive 1.1 miles to Pier Avenue. Turn right and drive 0.4 miles to the Pismo State Beach parking lot at the beachfront.

Hiking directions: Head south across the hard-packed sand between the ocean and the dunes. Hike 0.3 miles to Arroyo Grande Creek, passing beachfront homes along the way. After crossing the creek, curve left, entering the scrub-covered dunes at one of the many access trails. Meander south across the dunes, following the various interconnecting trails. Choose your own turn-around spot. On the return, continue north until reaching Arroyo Grande Creek. Follow the creek west, returning to the beach near the trailhead. ■

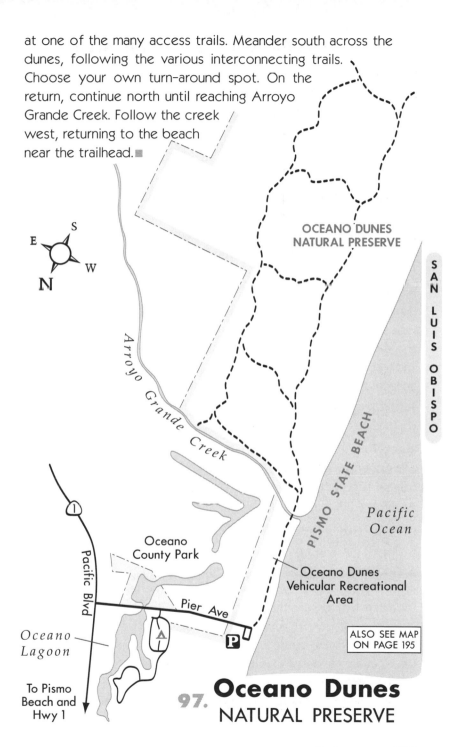

OCEANO DUNES
NATURAL PRESERVE

SAN LUIS OBISPO

Arroyo Grande Creek

Pacific
Ocean

PISMO STATE BEACH

Oceano
County Park

Pacific Blvd

Oceano Dunes
Vehicular Recreational
Area

Pier Ave

Oceano
Lagoon

ALSO SEE MAP
ON PAGE 195

To Pismo
Beach and
Hwy 1

97. **Oceano Dunes**
NATURAL PRESERVE

98. Oso Flaco Lake Natural Area

Hiking distance: 2.2 miles round trip
Hiking time: 1 hour
Elevation gain: Level
Maps: U.S.G.S. Oceano
      Oso Flaco Lake Natural Area map
Location: 10 miles west of Nipomo

Summary of hike: The Oso Flaco Lake Natural Area is located east of Nipomo in the heart of the Nipomo Dunes. Oso Flaco Lake, Oso Flaco Creek, and the surrounding wetlands are among the central coast's largest refuges for migrating and resident birds, with more than 300 species. The 75-acre freshwater lake is surrounded by a variety of habitats, including dry, wind-swept dunes with low-growing shrubs; riparian forest with arroyo willow and wax myrtle trees; and marshland with sedges, tules, and cattails. It is a great place for observing birds and wildlife. The trail crosses a footbridge over the lake and follows a wooden boardwalk through the rolling dunes to the ocean.

Driving directions: NIPOMO. From Highway 101 in Nipomo, take the Tefft Street exit, and head 0.8 miles west to Orchard Road. Turn left and drive 0.7 miles to Division Street. Turn right and continue 3.2 miles to Oso Flaco Lake Road. Bear right and go 5.3 miles to the Oso Flaco Lake parking lot at the end of the road. A parking fee is required.

Hiking directions: Head west on the paved road past the trailhead gate and through the shady cottonwood forest to the north shore of Oso Flaco Lake. Bear left on the long footbridge spanning the lake. From the west end of the lake, continue on a wooden boardwalk that ambles across the fragile, vegetated coastal dunes. Most of the trail follows the boardwalk except for a short, well-marked sandy stretch. The boardwalk ends at the ocean on a long and wide stretch of beach at 1.1 miles. To the south, the trail crosses the mouth of Oso Flaco Creek to the Mobil Coastal Preserve and Coreopsis Hill, a prominent dune at

2.3 miles. To the north is the Oceano Dunes Natural Preserve (Hike 97). Explore at your own pace along the coastline, and return on the boardwalk. ■

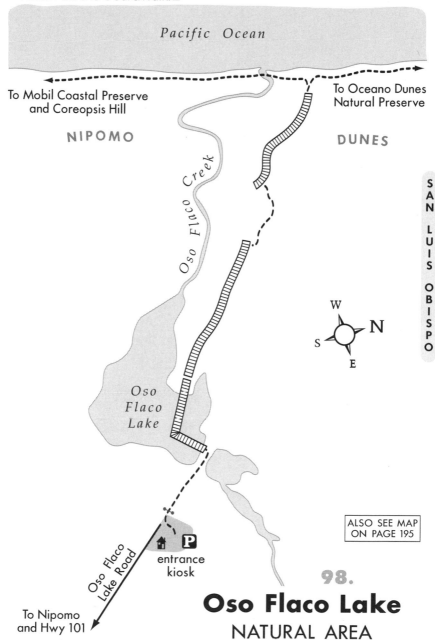

Pacific Ocean

To Mobil Coastal Preserve
and Coreopsis Hill

To Oceano Dunes
Natural Preserve

NIPOMO

DUNES

Oso Flaco Creek

W

S · N

E

Oso
Flaco
Lake

ALSO SEE MAP
ON PAGE 195

Oso Flaco
Lake Road

entrance
kiosk

98.

Oso Flaco Lake

To Nipomo
and Hwy 101

NATURAL AREA

Santa Barbara County

The Santa Barbara area is known for its calendar-like scenery of the crashing surf and rolling green mountains. The city of Santa Barbara is a captivating, inviting community located in a beautiful, natural setting along the coast. The temperate climate and refreshing ocean breezes, very similar to the Mediterranean, have distinguished this area as "the jewel of the American Riviera."

The landscape around Santa Barbara includes mountainous terrain, preserved forests and wilderness areas, and stretches of undeveloped coast. To the north of the coast, the Santa Ynez Mountains rise 3,000 feet, serving as a backdrop to Santa Barbara and the nearby coastal communities. These mountains separate the coastal plain from the rolling farmlands and mountainous interior of Santa Barbara County. The cities of San Luis Obispo (100 miles northwest) and Los Angeles (90 miles south) are a comfortable drive away.

Quiet, inviting trails explore coastal wildlife habitats, wetlands, marine terraces, rocky beach coves, and the largest coastal dune system in the country. Several pastoral paths meander through oceanfront communities.

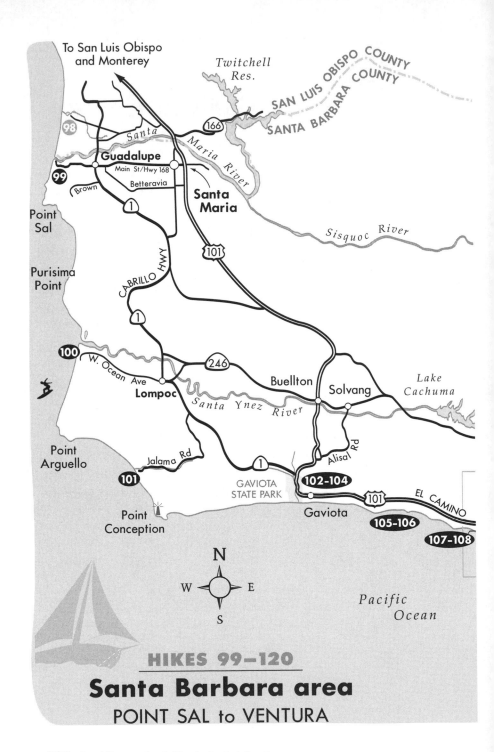

To San Luis Obispo
and Monterey

*Twitchell
Res.*

SAN LUIS OBISPO COUNTY

SANTA BARBARA COUNTY

98

166

Santa

Maria River

99

Guadalupe

Main St/Hwy 168

Brown

Betteravia

1

**Santa
Maria**

Sisquoc River

Point
Sal

101

Purisima
Point

CABRILLO HWY

1

100

W. Ocean Ave

Lompoc

246

Santa Ynez River

Buellton

Solvang

*Lake
Cachuma*

Point
Arguello

Jalama Rd

101

1

Alisal Rd

GAVIOTA
STATE PARK

102-104

Point
Conception

Gaviota

101

EL CAMINO

105-106

107-108

N
W · E
S

*Pacific
Ocean*

HIKES 99–120

Santa Barbara area
POINT SAL to VENTURA

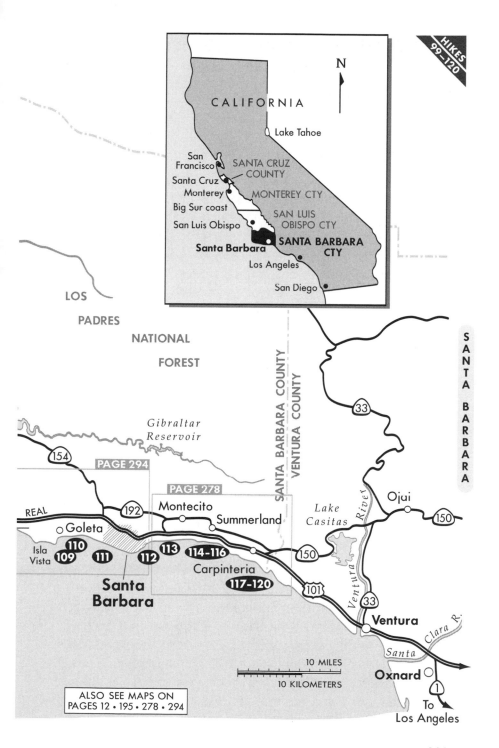

N

CALIFORNIA

Lake Tahoe

San Francisco

SANTA CRUZ COUNTY

Santa Cruz
Monterey

MONTEREY CTY

Big Sur coast

SAN LUIS OBISPO CTY

San Luis Obispo

Santa Barbara

SANTA BARBARA CTY

Los Angeles

San Diego

LOS

PADRES

NATIONAL

FOREST

S A N T A   B A R B A R A

Gibraltar
Reservoir

154

PAGE 294

PAGE 278

REAL

192

Montecito

Summerland

Lake
Casitas

Ojai

150

Goleta

Isla
Vista

110
109

111

112

113

114-116

150

33

Carpinteria

117-120

101

Santa
Barbara

Ventura

33

Oxnard

1

To
Los Angeles

SANTA BARBARA COUNTY
VENTURA COUNTY

River

Ventura

Santa

Clara R.

10 MILES

10 KILOMETERS

ALSO SEE MAPS ON
PAGES 12 • 195 • 278 • 294

99. Guadalupe—Nipomo Dunes Preserve to Mussel Rock

Hiking distance: 6 miles round trip
Hiking time: 3 hours
Elevation gain: Level
Maps: U.S.G.S. Point Sal
Location: 12 miles west of Guadalupe

Summary of hike: The Guadalupe—Nipomo—Oceano dunes complex composes the largest remaining coastal dune system in the nation. The windswept dunes stretch for 18 miles, from Pismo Beach to Vandenberg Air Force Base by Point Sal. The Guadalupe-Nipomo Dunes Preserve encompasses over 3,400 acres at the county's southern coast, west of Santa Maria. The preserve sits among a range of towering, rolling sand mountains that was once inhabited by the Chumash Indians. This hike follows the isolated shoreline along the sandy beach, parallel to the highest sand dunes on the west coast (which reach a height of 500 feet). The north end of the preserve is bordered by the Santa Maria River and the county line. At the mouth of the river is a wetland area, providing a habitat for migrating shorebirds and native waterfowl. The south end of the dune complex is bordered by Mussel Rock, a towering 450-foot promontory jutting out into the sea.

Driving directions: SANTA MARIA/HIGHWAY 101. From Highway 101 in Santa Maria, take the Main Street/Highway 166 exit, and head west towards Guadalupe. Drive 11.7 miles, passing Guadalupe, to the Guadalupe—Nipomo Dunes Preserve entrance. Continue 2 miles to the parking area on the oceanfront.

Hiking directions: Walk to the shoreline. First head north a half mile to the mouth of the Santa Maria River. The river widens out, forming a lagoon at the base of scrub-covered dunes. At low tide, a sandbar separates the river estuary from the ocean, allowing easy access from the north along the Nipomo Dunes.

Return to the south, meandering along the beach. Various side paths lead inland and up into the dunes. Follow the coastline towards the immense dunes at Mussel Rock. At 3 miles, reach the cliffs of Mussel Rock at the foot of the dunes. The enormous, jagged formation extends out into the ocean. For great coastal views to Point Sal, head a short distance up Mussel Rock to a sandy path that contours around to the south side of the formation. Return back along the beach to the parking area.■

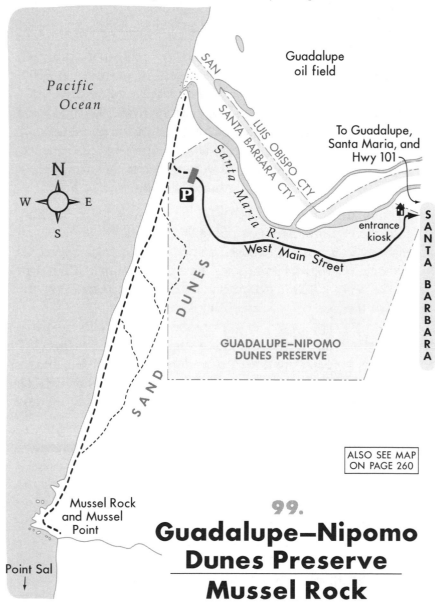

Pacific Ocean

Guadalupe oil field

To Guadalupe, Santa Maria, and Hwy 101

SAN LUIS OBISPO CTY

SANTA BARBARA CTY

Santa Maria R.

West Main Street

entrance kiosk

SANTA BARBARA

N
W   E
S

DUNES

SAND

GUADALUPE–NIPOMO DUNES PRESERVE

ALSO SEE MAP ON PAGE 260

Mussel Rock and Mussel Point

Point Sal

99.

Guadalupe–Nipomo Dunes Preserve
Mussel Rock

100. Ocean Beach County Park

Hiking distance: 7 miles round trip
Hiking time: 3 hours
Elevation gain: Level
Maps: U.S.G.S. Surf
Location: 26 miles west of Buellton; 10 miles west of Lompoc

Summary of hike: Ocean Beach is a 36-acre park between Purisima Point and Point Arguello west of Lompoc in Santa Barbara County. The park borders the Santa Ynez River by a 400-acre lagoon and marsh at the mouth of the river. The estuary is a resting and foraging habitat for migrating birds and waterfowl. This hike parallels the ocean along expansive sand dunes. Vandenberg Air Force Base, which surrounds the park, allows beach access for 1.5 miles north and 3.5 miles south.

Driving directions: BUELLTON. From Highway 101 in Buellton, take the Highway 246/Lompoc exit. Drive 25.7 miles west on Highway 246, passing through Lompoc, to Ocean Park Road. (In Lompoc, Highway 246 becomes West Ocean Avenue.) Turn right on Ocean Park Road, and go one mile to the parking lot at the end of the road by the Santa Ynez River.

GAVIOTA/HIGHWAY 1 EXIT. From the Highway 1/Lompoc exit off Highway 101 by Gaviota State Park, turn left and drive 17.7 miles to the Highway 246/Ocean Avenue junction in Lompoc. Turn left and continue 9.5 miles to Ocean Park Road. Turn right on Ocean Park Road, and go one mile to the parking lot at the end of the road.

Hiking directions: To the north, a path with interpretive nature panels borders the lagoon. After enjoying the estuary, take the quarter-mile paved path along the south bank of the Santa Ynez River. Cross under the railroad trestle to the wide sandy beach. (Or take the footpath over the hill and cross the tracks.) Walk past the dunes to the shoreline, where the river empties into the Pacific. At times, a sandbar separates the ocean from the river, allowing access up the coast. This hike heads south along the coastline. At just over a half mile, the railroad tracks curve away from the water as the dunes grow higher, rising 120 feet. The wide beach narrows to a strip at one mile. Vandenberg Air Force Base sits atop the cliffs. At just over 3 miles, pass the mouth of Bear Valley, an extensive wetland. The beach soon ends as the cliffs meet the reef. Point Pedernales can be seen ahead, extending out to sea. Return along the same route.■

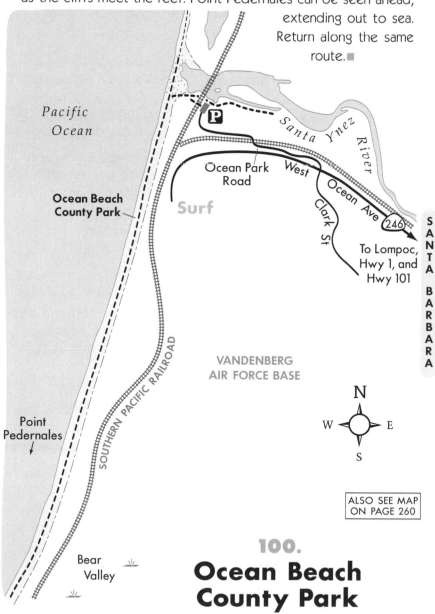

Pacific
Ocean

Ocean Beach
County Park

Surf

Ocean Park
Road

West

Santa Ynez River

Ocean Ave

Clark St

(246)

To Lompoc,
Hwy 1, and
Hwy 101

SANTA BARBARA

SOUTHERN PACIFIC RAILROAD

VANDENBERG
AIR FORCE BASE

Point
Pedernales

N
W ← → E
S

Bear
Valley

ALSO SEE MAP
ON PAGE 260

100.
Ocean Beach
County Park

101. Jalama Beach County Park

Hiking distance: 2 miles round trip
Hiking time: 1 hour
Elevation gain: Level
Maps: U.S.G.S. Lompoc Hills, Tranquillon Mountain, and Point
Conception
Location: 27 miles southwest of Lompoc

Summary of hike: Jalama Beach County Park is a picturesque 28-acre park south of Lompoc in Santa Barbara County. The park surrounds the mouth of Jalama Creek between Point Arguello and Point Conception. The beautiful area includes a year-round campground with a half mile of shoreline, shallow dunes, a small wetland habitat, a picnic area, and a general store. This isolated stretch of coastline at the west end of the Santa Ynez Mountains is backed by cliffs and lush, rolling hills. For centuries it was a Chumash Indian settlement. (*Jalama* is the Chumash name for *blowing sand*.) It is now bordered by Vandenberg Air Force Base.

Driving directions: BUELLTON/HIGHWAY 101. From Highway 101 in Buellton, take the Highway 246/Lompoc exit. Drive 16.2 miles west to Highway 1 in Lompoc. Turn left and continue 4.2 miles to Jalama Road. Turn right and continue 14 miles, weaving up and over the Santa Ynez Mountains, to the campground and parking lot. A parking fee is required.

GAVIOTA/HIGHWAY 1 EXIT. From the Highway 1/Lompoc exit off Highway 101 by Gaviota State Park, turn left and drive 13.5 miles to Jalama Road. Turn left and continue 14 miles to the oceanfront campground and parking lot.

Hiking directions: Follow the shoreline north for a short distance to the park boundary near a small estuary along Jalama Creek. The 30-foot bluffs above the creek are fenced. At low tide you may beachcomb northwest for a mile beyond the creek to the Vandenberg Air Force Base boundary. Along the way, cross narrow, rocky beaches with sheer cliff walls.

Heading south, the sandy beach with cobbled stones begins to narrow and ends along the seawall cliffs. At low tide, the shoreline can be followed along the rock formations and tidepools for one mile to a view of the lighthouse at Point Conception.■

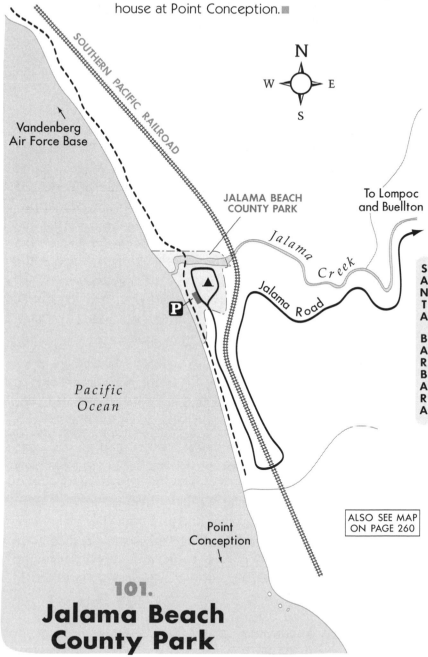

N
W ← → E
S

Vandenberg
Air Force Base

SOUTHERN PACIFIC RAILROAD

JALAMA BEACH
COUNTY PARK

To Lompoc
and Buellton

Jalama Creek

Jalama Road

P

S
A
N
T
A

B
A
R
B
A
R
A

*Pacific
Ocean*

ALSO SEE MAP
ON PAGE 260

Point
Conception

101.
Jalama Beach
County Park

102. Gaviota Peak
from GAVIOTA STATE PARK

Hiking distance: 6 miles round trip
Hiking time: 4 hours
Elevation gain: 1,900 feet
Maps: U.S.G.S. Solvang and Gaviota
Gaviota State Park map
Location: 35 miles west of Santa Barbara

*map
page 271*

Summary of hike: Gaviota Peak towers over the Santa Barbara Coastline in the southern branch of the Santa Ynez Mountains. The isolated peak, located in the Los Padres National Forest, is accessed from Gaviota State Park on the inland side of Highway 101. The hike to Gaviota Peak is a substantial workout. Atop the 2,458-foot summit are magnificent 360-degree vistas of the Santa Ynez Mountains, Las Cruces Hills, Lompoc Valley, the Gaviota coast, and the Channel Islands. The trail weaves through sycamore and oak woodlands, grasslands, and chaparral. En route, the hike passes Gaviota Hot Springs, a series of luke-warm primitive pools fed by sulphurous springs.

Driving directions: SANTA BARBARA. From Santa Barbara, drive 35 miles northbound on Highway 101 to the Highway 1/Lompoc exit. Turn sharply to the right onto the frontage road, and continue 0.3 miles to the Gaviota State Park parking lot at road's end.

Hiking directions: Hike east past the trailhead on the wide, unpaved road under the shade of oak and sycamore trees. Stay on the main trail past a junction with the Trespass Trail (Hike 103). Cross a stream to a junction at 0.4 miles. The right fork is a short side trip to Gaviota Hot Springs.

After enjoying the springs, return to the junction and continue on the main trail, following the old road as it curves around the grassy hillside. The views include the rolling hills and ranches of the Lompoc Valley. Long, gradual switchbacks lead up to the national forest boundary at 1.5 miles. At two miles, the trail reaches a saddle with more great views. The grade of the trail is never steep, but it rarely levels out. Near the top, pass a metal gate to a junction. The left fork follows the ridge east. The path straight ahead descends into San Onofre Canyon. Take the right fork for the final ascent to Gaviota Peak and the spectacular views. Return along the same trail.■

103. Tunnel View—Trespass Trail Loop
GAVIOTA STATE PARK

Hiking distance: 2.5-mile loop
Hiking time: 1.5 hours
Elevation gain: 600 feet
Maps: U.S.G.S. Solvang and Gaviota
      Gaviota State Park map
Location: 35 miles west of Santa Barbara

map
page 271

Summary of hike: The Tunnel View and Trespass Trails sit at the western base of Gaviota Peak on the inland side of Gaviota State Park. The hike follows the forested paths on the east side of Highway 101, which bisects the 2,776-acre park. The trail winds through shaded groves of gnarled oaks, sycamores, open grasslands, and native chaparral. Throughout the loop hike are panoramic views of the tunnels along Highway 101, the Pacific Ocean, the Gaviota coastline, the Channel Islands, and the rolling hills of the inland valley.

SANTA BARBARA

Driving directions: SANTA BARBARA. From Santa Barbara, drive 35 miles northbound on Highway 101 to the Highway 1/Lompoc exit. Turn sharply to the right onto the frontage road, and continue 0.3 miles to the Gaviota State Park parking lot at road's end.

Hiking directions: Head east past the trailhead sign on the wide, unpaved road under the shade of oak and sycamore trees. At 0.2 miles is a signed junction. The left fork leads to Gaviota Peak (Hike 102). Bear right on the Trespass Trail past large oak trees to a signed junction. Leave the old road and begin the loop to the right on the Tunnel View Trail. Cross over two seasonal drainages, and traverse the lower grassy foothills of Gaviota Peak. Cross Corral Springs on a lush stream-fed knoll. Curve east, heading up the hillside through a grove of stately oaks. At 0.7 miles, the path reaches an overlook on the ridge descending from Gaviota Peak. From the ridge are views of the Highway 101 tunnels and the Pacific Ocean. Bear left around the hillside up the stream-fed side canyon. Pass sedimentary rock outcroppings to a ridge at a T-junction with the Trespass Trail, the old ranch road. The right fork climbs steeply to Gaviota Peak (Hike 102). Instead, bear left and descend on the wide path through chaparral and grass meadows, completing the loop. Take the right fork and return along the same trail.■

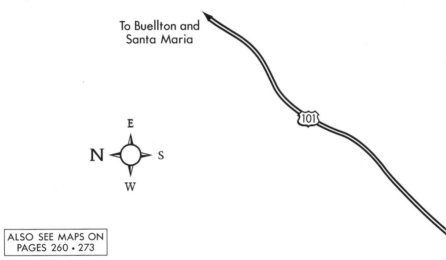

To Buellton and
Santa Maria

ALSO SEE MAPS ON
PAGES 260 • 273

HIKE 102
Gaviota Peak
HIKE 103
Tunnel View—
Trespass Trail Loop
GAVIOTA STATE PARK

To
Lompoc

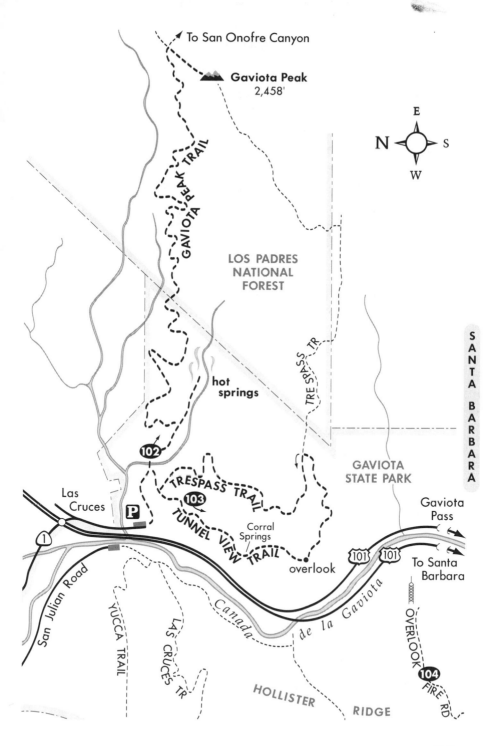

To San Onofre Canyon

Gaviota Peak
2,458'

N E S W (compass)

LOS PADRES
NATIONAL
FOREST

GAVIOTA PEAK TRAIL

TRESPASS TR

hot
springs

102

Las
Cruces

P

TRESPASS TRAIL

103

TUNNEL VIEW TRAIL

Corral
Springs

overlook

1

San Julian Road

YUCCA TRAIL

LAS CRUCES TR

Cañada de la Gaviota

HOLLISTER RIDGE

GAVIOTA
STATE PARK

Gaviota
Pass

101 101

To Santa
Barbara

OVERLOOK FIRE RD

104

SANTA BARBARA

104. Beach to Backcountry Trail
GAVIOTA STATE PARK

Hiking distance: 3 miles round trip
Hiking time: 1.5 hours
Elevation gain: 750 feet
Maps: U.S.G.S. Gaviota
  Gaviota State Park map
Location: 33 miles west of Santa Barbara

Summary of hike: In the mountainous backcountry of Gaviota State Park, a network of trails lead to scenic overlooks, sandstone outcroppings, intriguing caves, and oak-studded rolling hills. This hike begins on the bluffs overlooking Gaviota Pier and the undeveloped coastline. The trail crosses the rolling terrain in the Santa Ynez Mountains to a vista point high above Gaviota Pass. There are great views of Gaviota Peak, the Gaviota tunnel, the Pacific Ocean, and the Channel Islands.

Driving directions: SANTA BARBARA. From Santa Barbara, drive 33 miles northbound on Highway 101 to the Gaviota State Park turnoff on the left. Turn left and drive 0.4 miles, bearing right near the entrance kiosk. Drive to the trailhead parking area on the right.

Hiking directions: Head north past the locked gate on the paved road. The half-mile road leads through dense scrub brush. A hundred yards before the end of the road is a signed multi-purpose trail on the left—the Beach to Backcountry Trail. Take this footpath up the south-facing hillside of the canyon. Views open to the Pacific Ocean and Gaviota Peak during the ascent. Steadily zigzag up to a ridge. At one mile the trail levels out near large, sculpted sandstone outcroppings and caves. Begin a second ascent to the largest formation, and curve around to the backside of the outcropping. Cross a ravine and continue uphill to the top and a junction with the Overlook Fire Road. The left fork heads north along Hollister Ridge into the mountainous interior of Gaviota State Park. Take the right fork for a half mile, contouring up and down the rolling ridge. The panoramic overlook is located by the radio tower at the edge of the ridge, where it drops off sharply on all three sides. After enjoying the views, return by retracing your steps.■

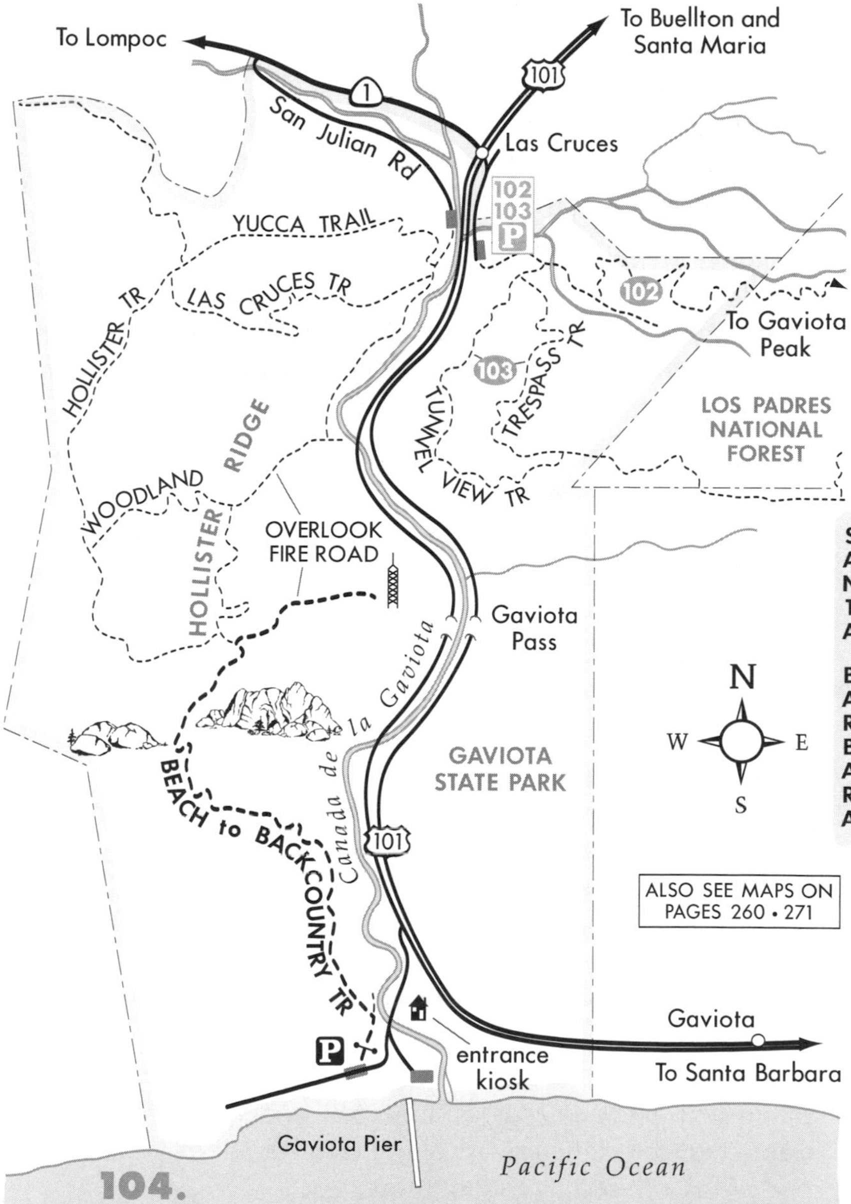

To Lompoc

To Buellton and
Santa Maria

101

San Julian Rd

1

Las Cruces

102
103
P

YUCCA TRAIL

102

HOLLISTER TR

LAS CRUCES TR

To Gaviota
Peak

103

TRESPASS TR

LOS PADRES
NATIONAL
FOREST

WOODLAND

HOLLISTER RIDGE

TUNNEL VIEW TR

OVERLOOK
FIRE ROAD

Gaviota
Pass

Cañada de la Gaviota

GAVIOTA
STATE PARK

N
W   E
S

S A N T A   B A R B A R A

BEACH to BACKCOUNTRY TR

101

ALSO SEE MAPS ON
PAGES 260 • 271

P

entrance
kiosk

Gaviota

To Santa Barbara

Gaviota Pier

Pacific Ocean

104.
Beach to Backcountry Trail
GAVIOTA STATE PARK

105. El Capitan State Beach

Hiking distance: 1.5 miles round trip
Hiking time: 1 hour
Elevation gain: Level
Maps: U.S.G.S. Tajiguas
     El Capitan and Refugio State Beach—Park Service Map
Location: 20 miles west of Santa Barbara

Summary of hike: El Capitan State Beach, located along the coastline west of Santa Barbara, has a beautiful sandy beach with rocky tidepools. El Capitan Creek flows through a forested canyon to the tidepools at El Capitan Point. Nature trails weave through stands of sycamore and oak trees alongside the creek.

Driving directions: SANTA BARBARA. From Santa Barbara, drive 20 miles northbound on Highway 101 to the El Capitan State Beach exit. It is located 0.8 miles past the El Capitan Ranch Road exit. Turn left (south) and drive 0.3 miles to the state park entrance. Park in the day-use lot straight ahead.

Hiking directions: For a short walk, take the paved path down the hillside from the general store to the oceanfront. The quarter-mile paved trail follows the sandy shoreline a short distance to the east before looping back to the parking lot.

For a longer hike, continue along the shore on the unpaved path past a picnic area to El Capitan Creek at the point. Near the mouth of the creek are the tidepools. Take the nature trail foot-path, heading inland through the woods while following El Capitan Creek upstream. Pass several intersecting trails that loop back to the park entrance station and parking lot. Near the entrance station, pick up the trail on the west side of the road. Parallel the western edge of El Capitan Creek through the forested canyon. The trail ends at a railroad bridge where the trail meets the road. Return by reversing your route or by exploring one of the intersecting nature trails.

For a longer walk, the Aniso Trail (Hike 106) continues along the shoreline to Refugio State Beach, 2.5 miles west. ∎

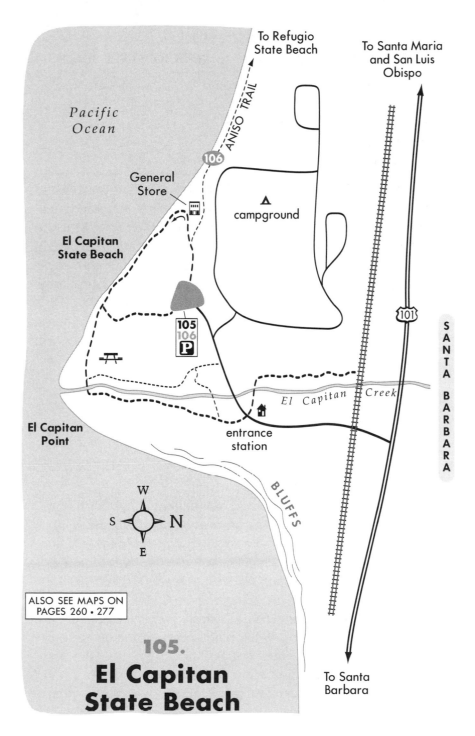

To Refugio
State Beach

To Santa Maria
and San Luis
Obispo

Pacific
Ocean

ANISO TRAIL

106

General
Store

campground

El Capitan
State Beach

105
106
P

El Capitan Creek

El Capitan
Point

entrance
station

BLUFFS

101

SANTA BARBARA

W

S · N

E

ALSO SEE MAPS ON
PAGES 260 · 277

To Santa
Barbara

105.

El Capitan
State Beach

106. Aniso Trail

EL CAPITAN STATE BEACH to REFUGIO STATE BEACH

Hiking distance: 5 miles round trip
Hiking time: 2.5 hours
Elevation gain: Near level
Maps: U.S.G.S. Tajiguas
Location: 20 miles west of Santa Barbara

Summary of hike: The Aniso Trail (Chumash for *seagull*) is a paved hiking and biking trail along the sea cliffs and marine terraces on the Gaviota coast, connecting El Capitan State Beach to Refugio State Beach. The trail, an ancient Chumash trade route, follows the sandstone bluffs past weathered rock formations and secluded coves, offering constant views of the coastline. El Capitan State Beach sits at the mouth of El Capitan Creek in a extensive riparian woodland of coastal oaks and sycamores. Refugio State Beach lies at the mouth of Refugio Canyon, where there is a palm-lined sandy beach cove and rocky shoreline with tidepools. Refugio Creek meanders through the park.

Driving directions: <u>SANTA BARBARA</u>. From Santa Barbara, drive 20 miles northbound on Highway 101 to the El Capitan State Beach exit. It is located 0.8 miles past the El Capitan Ranch Road exit. Turn left (south) and drive 0.3 miles to the state park entrance. Park in the day-use lot straight ahead.

Hiking directions: The paved trail begins on the north (right) side of the general store. (See the map on page 275.) Head west, skirting around the edge of the campground, and follow the contours of the cliffs past a lifeguard station. Two side paths descend to the beach and marine terraces. Descend from the bluffs to the beach at the south end of Corral Canyon. A side path curves left to Corral Beach, a small pocket beach. Continue straight ahead, returning to the bluffs past weathered rock formations. At 2.5 miles, enter Refugio State Beach near the palm-lined bay. Refugio Creek forms a tropical-looking freshwater lagoon near the ocean. Refugio Point, a low bluff, extends

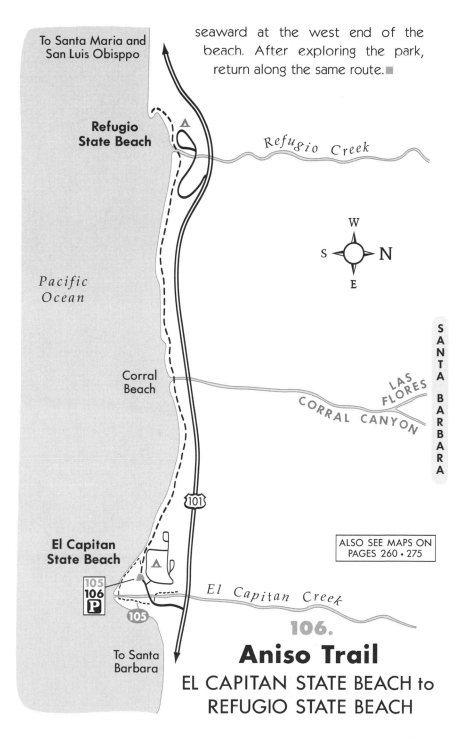

seaward at the west end of the beach. After exploring the park, return along the same route. ■

To Santa Maria and San Luis Obisppo

Refugio State Beach

Refugio Creek

W

S N

E

Pacific Ocean

Corral Beach

LAS FLORES

CORRAL CANYON

SANTA BARBARA

101

ALSO SEE MAPS ON PAGES 260 • 275

El Capitan State Beach

105
106
P

105

El Capitan Creek

To Santa Barbara

106.
Aniso Trail
EL CAPITAN STATE BEACH to REFUGIO STATE BEACH

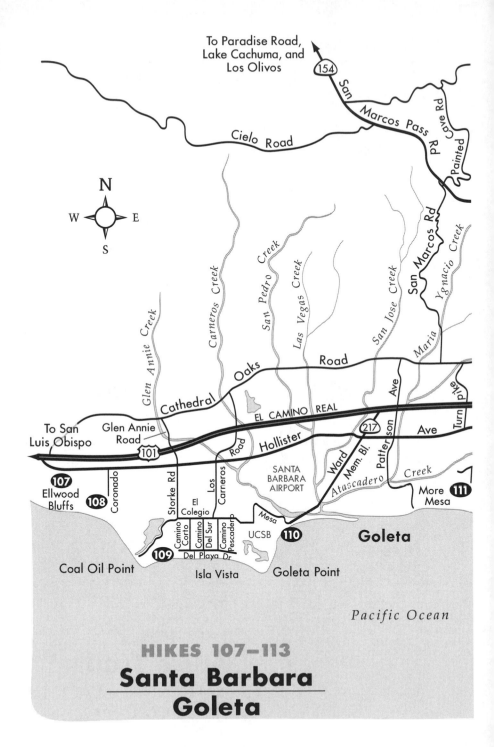

To Paradise Road,
Lake Cachuma, and
Los Olivos

154

San

Marcos Pass Rd

Cielo Road

Cave Rd

Painted

N
W · E
S

Carneros Creek

San Pedro Creek

Las Vegas Creek

San Jose Creek

San Marcos Rd

Ygnacio Creek

Glen Annie Creek

Oaks

Road

Maria

Cathedral

EL CAMINO REAL

Ave

Turnpike

To San
Luis Obispo

Glen Annie
Road

101

217

Hollister

Ave

Patterson

Ward

Mem. Bl.

Atascadero

Creek

107

Ellwood
Bluffs

108

Coronado

Storke Rd

Carneros

Los

El
Colegio

Road

SANTA
BARBARA
AIRPORT

More
Mesa

111

Mesa

109

Camino
Corto

Camino
Del Sur

Camino
Pescadero

UCSB

110

Goleta

Del Playa Dr

Coal Oil Point

Isla Vista

Goleta Point

Pacific Ocean

HIKES 107–113

Santa Barbara
Goleta

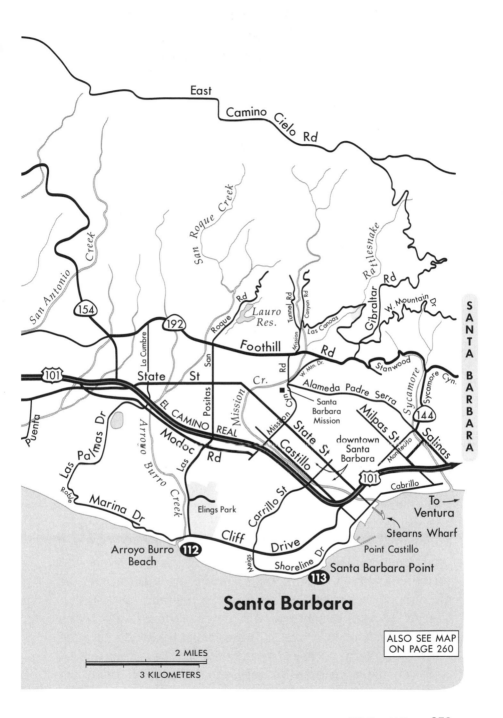

East Camino Cielo Rd

San Roque Creek

San Antonio Creek

Rattlesnake

154

192

La Cumbre

San Roque

Lauro Res.

Roque Rd

Tunnel Rd

Mission Canyon Rd

Las Canoas

Gibraltar Rd

W. Mountain Dr.

Foothill Rd

Stanwood

W. Mtn. Dr.

101

State St

Cr. Rd

Alameda Padre Serra

Sycamore

Sycamore Cyn.

144

S A N T A   B A R B A R A

Positas

San

Mission

Santa Barbara Mission

Mission Cyn.

Milpas St

Salinas

Puente

Arroyo Burro Creek

EL CAMINO REAL

Modoc Rd

Las

State St

Castillo

downtown Santa Barbara

Montecito

101

Las Palmas Dr

Roble

Marina Dr

Elings Park

Carrillo St

Cabrillo

To → Ventura

Cliff Drive

Stearns Wharf

Point Castillo

Arroyo Burro Beach

112

Meigs

Shoreline Dr

Santa Barbara Point

113

Santa Barbara Point

Santa Barbara

ALSO SEE MAP ON PAGE 260

2 MILES

3 KILOMETERS

107. Ellwood Bluffs

SANTA BARBARA SHORES COUNTY PARK
and SPERLING PRESERVE at ELLWOOD MESA

Hiking distance: 3.5 miles round trip
Hiking time: 1.5 hours
Elevation gain: Level
Maps: U.S.G.S. Dos Pueblos Canyon
　　　　Santa Barbara County Recreational Map Series #8
Location: Goleta

Summary of hike: Santa Barbara Shores County Park has a network of interconnecting trails across 200 acres of flat grasslands with eucalyptus groves, vernal pools, and spectacular ocean views. The Ellwood Bluffs Trail parallels 80-foot cliffs along the ocean's edge. The eucalyptus groves in the area are home to monarch butterflies during the winter months.

Driving directions: SANTA BARBARA. From Santa Barbara, drive northbound on Highway 101 to the Glen Annie Road/Storke Road exit in Goleta. Turn left on Storke Road, and drive a quarter mile to Hollister Avenue, the first intersection. Turn right on Hollister Avenue, and continue 1.5 miles to the Santa Barbara County Park parking lot on the left, directly across from Ellwood School.

Hiking directions: The right fork follows the west edge of the parkland, skirting a walled subdivision. Take the trail straight ahead. Walk south along the edge of the eucalyptus grove to seasonal Devereaux Creek. Cross the creek to the open grasslands and veer to the right. Follow the path as it curves left and heads south to the bluffs, overlooking the ocean. Follow the trail to the left along the cliff's edge. Several trails cut across the open space to the left, returning to the trailhead for a shorter hike. At 0.5 miles is a junction with a beach access trail heading down to the mile-long beach. Farther along the bluffs, take the trail inland, heading north along a row of eucalyptus trees. As you approach the eucalyptus groves, return along the prominent

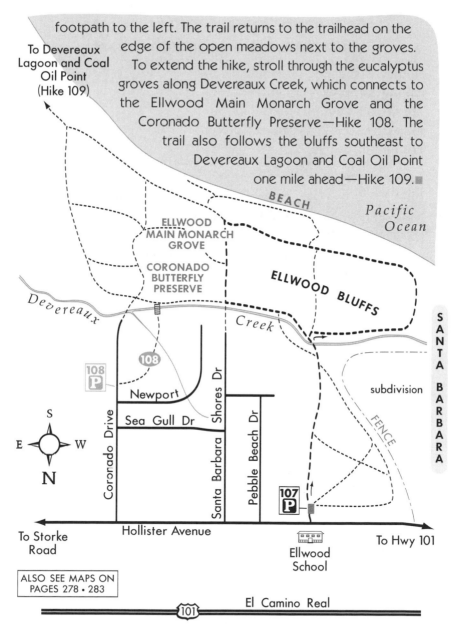

footpath to the left. The trail returns to the trailhead on the edge of the open meadows next to the groves. To extend the hike, stroll through the eucalyptus groves along Devereaux Creek, which connects to the Ellwood Main Monarch Grove and the Coronado Butterfly Preserve—Hike 108. The trail also follows the bluffs southeast to Devereaux Lagoon and Coal Oil Point one mile ahead—Hike 109.■

To Devereaux Lagoon and Coal Oil Point (Hike 109)

Pacific Ocean

BEACH

ELLWOOD MAIN MONARCH GROVE

CORONADO BUTTERFLY PRESERVE

Devereaux

Creek

ELLWOOD BLUFFS

SANTA BARBARA

108

108 P

Newport

Sea Gull Dr

Coronado Drive

Santa Barbara Shores Dr

Pebble Beach Dr

subdivision

FENCE

S
E ⊕ W
N

107 P

Hollister Avenue

To Storke Road

Ellwood School

To Hwy 101

ALSO SEE MAPS ON PAGES 278 · 283

El Camino Real

101

107. Ellwood Bluffs

SANTA BARBARA SHORES COUNTY PARK
SPERLING PRESERVE at ELLWOOD MESA

108. Coronado Butterfly Preserve and Ellwood Main Monarch Grove

Hiking distance: 1 mile round trip
Hiking time: 30 minutes
Elevation gain: 40 feet
Maps: U.S.G.S. Dos Pueblos Canyon
Location: Goleta

Summary of hike: The Coronado Butterfly Preserve was established as a nature preserve by the Land Trust for Santa Barbara in 1998. The 9.3-acre preserve and the Ellwood Main Monarch Grove are among the largest monarch butterfly wintering sites in southern California. Thousands of monarch butterflies hang from the eucalyptus trees in thick clusters and fly wildly around. The peak season for the migrating butterfly runs from December through February. Within the small preserve are woodlands, native coastal sage scrub, meadows, and a creek. Interconnecting trails link the preserves with the Ellwood Bluffs and beach to the west (Hike 107) and Coal Oil Point to the east (Hike 109).

Driving directions: SANTA BARBARA. From Santa Barbara, drive northbound on Highway 101 to the Glen Annie Road/Storke Road exit in Goleta. Turn left on Storke Road, and drive a quarter mile to Hollister Avenue, the first intersection. Turn right on Hollister Avenue, and continue 1.1 mile to Coronado Drive. Turn left and go 0.3 miles to the posted butterfly preserve on the right. Park alongside the street.

Hiking directions: Follow the wide path up the hill to the monarch butterfly information station. Gently descend into the large eucalyptus grove in the heart of the Coronado Butterfly Preserve. Cross a footbridge over seasonal Devereaux Creek to a T-junction. The right fork meanders through the grove to the west, connecting with the trails along Ellwood Bluffs (Hike 107). Bear left and head deeper into the grove to another junction. The left fork returns to the south end of Coronado Drive. Take the right fork, meandering through the Ellwood Main Monarch Grove.

Climb up the hill through the towering eucalyptus trees to an expansive open meadow. A network of interconnecting trails weaves across the bluffs. At the south edge of the 80-foot ocean bluffs, the left fork leads to Devereaux Lagoon and Coal Oil Point (Hike 109). The right fork heads west, connecting with Ellwood Bluffs.■

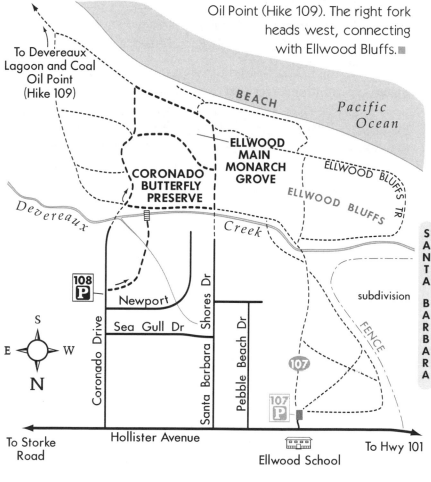

ALSO SEE MAPS ON PAGES 278 • 281 • 285

108.
Coronado Butterfly Preserve
Ellwood Main Monarch Grove

109. Coal Oil Point Reserve

Hiking distance: 3 miles round trip
Hiking time: 1.5 hours
Elevation gain: Near level
Maps: U.S.G.S. Goleta and Dos Pueblos Canyon
　　　　The Thomas Guide—Santa Barbara and Vicinity
Location: Goleta

Summary of hike: Coal Oil Point, located in the Isla Vista section of Goleta, is named for its numerous natural oil seeps near the coast. At the point is a rocky reef and a great tidepool area. Coal Oil Point Reserve has several coastal wildlife habitats set aside for research, education, and preservation. The 117-acre ecological study enclave, managed by UCSB, has undisturbed coastal dunes, eucalyptus groves, grasslands, a salt marsh, and a 45-acre lagoon. The trail parallels the eroding bluffs from the western edge of Isla Vista to the reserve. Devereaux Lagoon, in the heart of the reserve, is a seasonally flooded tidal lagoon where a mix of freshwater and saltwater provides several coastal lagoon habitats. The slough is a bird-watcher's paradise, home to a wide variety of native and migratory species.

Driving directions: SANTA BARBARA. From Santa Barbara, drive northbound on Highway 101 to the Glen Annie Road/Storke Road exit in Goleta. Turn left on Storke Road, and drive 1.3 miles to El Colegio Road. Turn left and drive 0.2 miles to Camino Corto. Turn right and continue 0.5 miles to Del Playa Drive. Turn right and park in the parking area at the end of the block.

Hiking directions: Take the well-defined path to the ocean bluffs and a T-junction. To the left, a stairway descends to the beach, and the blufftop path continues 0.2 miles east to Del Playa Park and Isla Vista County Beach. Take the right fork, parallel to the edge of the cliffs, and pass through a eucalyptus grove. Several surfing paths lead down the cliffs to the sandy beach and tidepools. The main trail leads to the Coal Oil Point Reserve. Pass through the habitat gate to Sands Beach. Several paths meander across the dunes to Devereaux Lagoon. The Pond Trail circles the lagoon, returning on the paved Slough Road along the east side of the lagoon. You may also follow the beach for another mile northwest to the Ellwood Bluffs and the Coronado Butterfly Preserve (Hikes 107 and 108).■

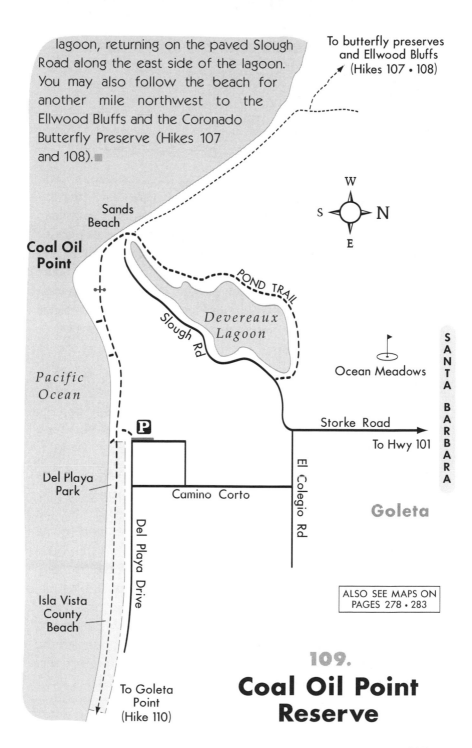

To butterfly preserves and Ellwood Bluffs (Hikes 107 • 108)

Sands Beach

Coal Oil Point

Pacific Ocean

Slough Rd

Devereaux Lagoon

POND TRAIL

Ocean Meadows

SANTA BARBARA

Storke Road

To Hwy 101

P

Del Playa Park

Camino Corto

El Colegio Rd

Del Playa Drive

Goleta

Isla Vista County Beach

ALSO SEE MAPS ON PAGES 278 • 283

To Goleta Point (Hike 110)

109.
Coal Oil Point Reserve

110. Goleta Beach and the UCSB Lagoon

Hiking distance: 4 miles round trip
Hiking time: 2 hours
Elevation gain: 50 feet
Maps: U.S.G.S. Goleta
The Thomas Guide—Santa Barbara and Vicinity
Location: Goleta

Summary of hike: Goleta Beach County Park, sheltered by Goleta Point, is a long, narrow peninsula sandwiched between Goleta Slough and the ocean. This hike begins on the park's grassy lawn backed by the white sand beach, west of Goleta Pier, and follows the coastal cliffs into the University of California—Santa Barbara. The trail circles the brackish waters of the UCSB Lagoon to Goleta Point (also called Campus Point). The ocean surrounds the point on three sides, where there are tidepools and a beautiful coastline.

Driving directions: GOLETA. From Highway 101 in Goleta, exit onto Ward Memorial Boulevard/Highway 217. Continue 2 miles to the Sandspit Road exit, and turn left at the stop sign, heading towards Goleta Beach Park. Drive 0.3 miles to the beach parking lot turnoff. Turn right and cross the lagoon into the parking lot.

Hiking directions: Head west along the park lawn to the bluffs overlooking the ocean. Continue past the natural bridge, and walk parallel to the cliff edge into the university. At the marine laboratory, take the right fork, crossing the road to the UCSB Lagoon on Goleta Point. Take the path to the right around the northeast side of the lagoon. At the north end, the trail joins a walking path in the university. At the west end of the lagoon, the trail heads south on the return section of the loop. Once back at the ocean, climb up the bluff to the left. Continue around the lagoon, and descend the steps between the lagoon and the ocean. Complete the loop back at the marine laboratory and bluffs. Head east, back to Goleta Beach County Park. ■

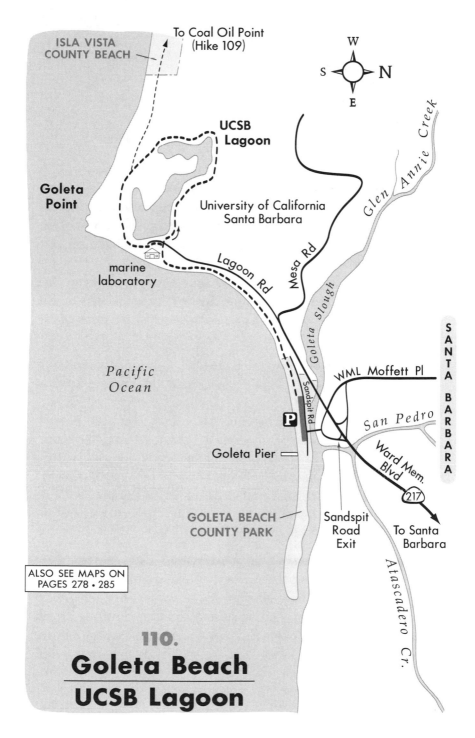

ISLA VISTA
COUNTY BEACH

To Coal Oil Point
(Hike 109)

W
S ✦ N
E

UCSB
Lagoon

Goleta
Point

University of California
Santa Barbara

Glen Annie Creek

marine
laboratory

Lagoon Rd

Mesa Rd

Goleta Slough

Pacific
Ocean

Sandspit Rd

WML Moffett Pl

San Pedro

Ward Mem. Blvd

217

P

Goleta Pier

GOLETA BEACH
COUNTY PARK

Sandspit
Road
Exit

To Santa
Barbara

S A N T A   B A R B A R A

Atascadero Cr.

ALSO SEE MAPS ON
PAGES 278 · 285

110.
Goleta Beach
UCSB Lagoon

111. More Mesa

Hiking distance: 2.6 miles round trip
Hiking time: 1.5 hours
Elevation gain: Near level
Maps: U.S.G.S. Goleta
    The Thomas Guide—Santa Barbara and Vicinity
Location: Goleta

Summary of hike: More Mesa is an undeveloped 300-acre oceanfront expanse in Goleta. The blufftop mesa includes oak woodlands, riparian habitats, and wetlands that connect to Atascadero Creek. The gently sloping grassland is marbled with hiking, biking, and equestrian trails. The main trail follows the edge of the sandstone bluffs 120 feet above the ocean. The panoramic views extend from the Santa Ynez Mountains to the Channel Islands. The secluded, mile-long beach at the base of the mesa is clothing optional.

Driving directions: SANTA BARBARA. From Santa Barbara, drive northbound on Highway 101, and exit on Turnpike Road in Goleta. Turn left (south) and drive 0.4 miles to Hollister Avenue. Turn left (east) and go 0.3 miles to the first signal at Puente Drive. Turn right and continue 0.7 miles to Mockingbird Lane. (En route, Puente Drive becomes Vieja Drive.) Parking is not allowed on Mockingbird Lane, so park on Vieja Drive by Mockingbird Lane.

To access More Mesa from the west end, take Highway 101 to Patterson Avenue. Drive south 1.6 miles to the trailhead by the Orchid Drive Sign at the right bend in the road.

Hiking directions: Walk up Mockingbird Lane to the hiking path at the end of the street. Pass the metal trailhead gate, and cross the wide, sloping marine terrace towards the ocean. At 0.6 miles, the path reaches a grove of mature eucalyptus trees lining the edge of the cliffs 120 feet above the ocean. A steep, narrow path descends down the cliffs to the secluded sandy beach. The left fork leads a short distance to a fenced residential area. Take the right fork, following the edge of the bluffs to the west. At 1.3 miles, the trail ends by oceanfront homes. Various interconnecting trails crisscross the open space.

From the west end trailhead (Shoreline Drive), walk through the lush riparian corridor on the south side of Atascadero Creek. Pass under an oak canopy and emerge at a T-junction at 0.3 miles. Both paths gently climb out of the arroyo to the network of informal paths that marble More Mesa.■

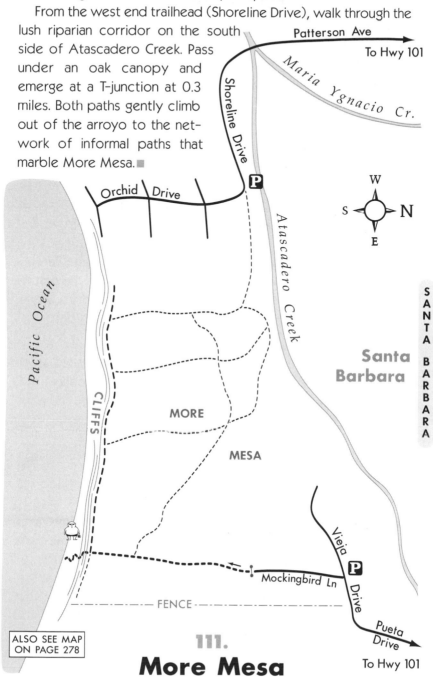

ALSO SEE MAP
ON PAGE 278

111.
More Mesa

To Hwy 101

112. Douglas Family Preserve

Hiking distance: 1.5 miles round trip
Hiking time: 1 hour
Elevation gain: 150 feet
Maps: U.S.G.S. Santa Barbara
        The Thomas Guide—Santa Barbara and Vicinity
Location: Santa Barbara

Summary of hike: The Douglas Family Preserve is a 70-acre grassy mesa with over 2,200 feet of rare, undeveloped ocean frontage. The dog-friendly preserve is covered with mature coast live oak, eucalyptus trees, and cypress woodlands. Migrating monarch butterflies cluster in the eucaluptus grove. The trail loops around the flat, 150-foot mesa along the edge of the cliffs. From the bluffs are expansive views of the Santa Barbara coast, from Point Mugu to Gaviota. Below the cliffs is the picturesque Arroyo Burro Beach, locally known as Hendry's Beach. There are picnic areas and a paved biking and walking path.

Driving directions: SANTA BARBARA. From Highway 101 in Santa Barbara, exit on Las Positas Road. Head 1.8 miles south (towards the ocean) to Cliff Drive and turn right. Continue 0.2 miles to the Arroyo Burro Beach parking lot on the left and park.

Hiking directions: From the parking lot, walk east on Cliff Drive to Las Positas Road. From here, the Oak Grove Trail, a narrow road, heads south past a chained gate into the forest. The trail curves left through the shady canopy and up the hill to the mesa, where the trail levels out. Continue south along the eastern edge of the open space. Along the way, several paths intersect from the right and several access trails merge from the left. At the bluffs overlooking the ocean, head west along the cliffs. At the west end of the cliffs is an overlook of Arroyo Burro Beach. The trail curves to the right and loops back to a junction at the top of the hill. Head left, retracing your steps down the hill and back to the parking lot.■

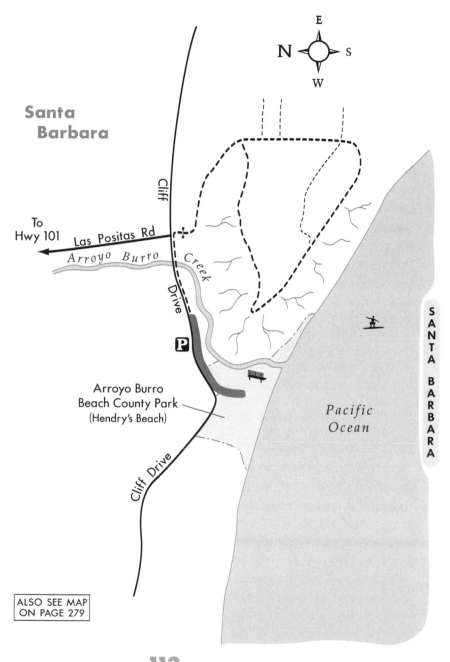

Santa Barbara

E
N ◇ S
W

To Hwy 101

Cliff

Las Positas Rd

Arroyo Burro Creek

Drive

⟵

P

Arroyo Burro
Beach County Park
(Hendry's Beach)

Cliff Drive

Pacific
Ocean

S A N T A   B A R B A R A

ALSO SEE MAP
ON PAGE 279

112.
Douglas Family Preserve

113. Shoreline Park

Hiking distance: 1—2 miles round trip
Hiking time: 30 minutes—1 hour
Elevation gain: Level
Maps: U.S.G.S. Santa Barbara
　　　　 The Thomas Guide—Santa Barbara and Vicinity
Location: Santa Barbara

Summary of hike: Shoreline Park is a long and narrow 15-acre park along La Mesa Bluff. From the landscaped bluffs are panoramic vistas of Leadbetter Beach, the Santa Barbara Harbor, Stearns Wharf, the Channel Islands, and the Santa Ynez Mountains. The grassy park hugs the ocean bluffs on the west side of Santa Barbara Point. This paved, level path is an easy stroll along the marine terrace. A stairway leads down to the shore for a sandy beach stroll at the base of the cliffs.

Driving directions: SANTA BARBARA. From Stearns Wharf at the south end of State Street in Santa Barbara, drive 1.4 miles west on Cabrillo Boulevard (which becomes Shoreline Drive) to the first Shoreline Park parking lot on the left.

Hiking directions: The paved path heads west along the oceanfront bluffs between the cliff's edge and Shoreline Drive. At 0.3 miles, a stairway leads down to the sandy beach and shoreline. Along the way are benches and information stations about the Chumash Indians, the Channel Islands, grey whales, and dolphins. A half mile ahead, at the west end of the park, is a picnic area and another parking lot. From the east end of the park, a steep path descends through cypress trees to Leadbetter Beach and tidepools.

　　　To continue hiking along the shoreline, return to the stairway and descend to the beach. Stroll along the sand beneath the cliffs.■

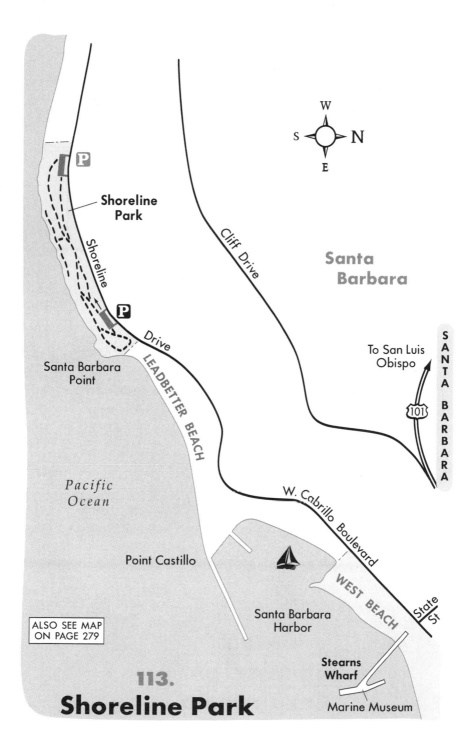

P

Shoreline Park

Shoreline

P

Santa Barbara
Point

Drive

LEADBETTER BEACH

*Pacific
Ocean*

Point Castillo

ALSO SEE MAP
ON PAGE 279

Cliff Drive

**Santa
Barbara**

W
S ◇ N
E

To San Luis
Obispo

S A N T A   B A R B A R A

101

W. Cabrillo Boulevard

WEST BEACH

Santa Barbara
Harbor

State St

**Stearns
Wharf**

Marine Museum

113.
Shoreline Park

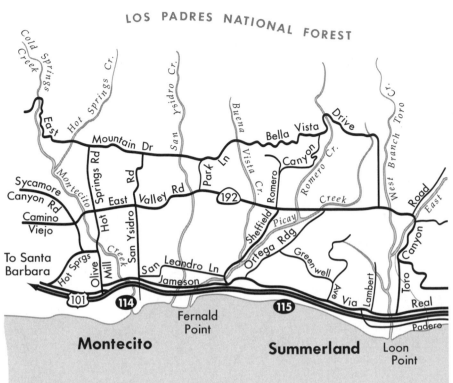

LOS PADRES NATIONAL FOREST

Montecito

Summerland

Fernald
Point

Loon
Point

N
W — E
S

Montecito
Summerland
Carpinteria

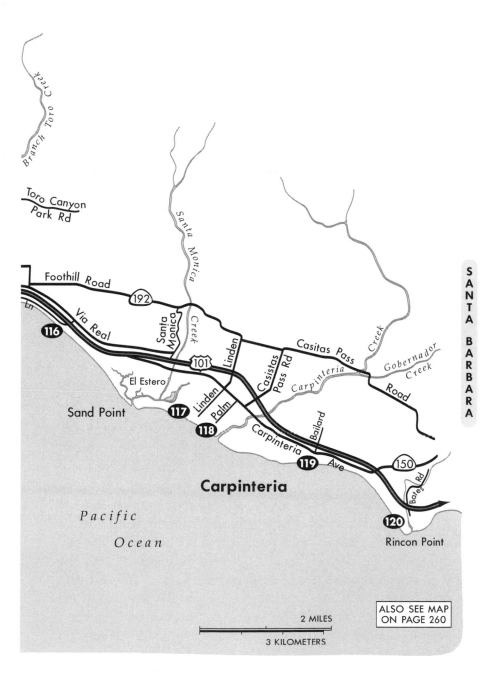

Branch Toro Creek

Toro Canyon
Park Rd

Foothill Road

SANTA BARBARA

192

Via Real

Ln

116

Santa Monica Creek

Santa Monica

101

Linden

El Estero

Sand Point

117

Linden

Palm

118

Casistas Pass Rd

Casitas Pass

Carpinteria

Gobernador Creek

Road

Carpinteria Ave

Bailard

119

150

Carpinteria

Bates Rd

120

Rincon Point

Pacific

Ocean

2 MILES

3 KILOMETERS

ALSO SEE MAP
ON PAGE 260

114. Hammonds Meadow Trail

Hiking distance: 2 miles round trip
Hiking time: 1 hour
Elevation gain: Level
Maps: U.S.G.S. Santa Barbara
      The Thomas Guide—Santa Barbara and Vicinity
Location: Montecito

Summary of hike: The Hammonds Meadow Trail strolls through a forest of palm and eucalyptus trees with high hedges and flowering bougainvillea bushes in the town of Montecito. Hammonds Beach sits near the foot of Eucalyptus Lane at the trailhead. The pastoral path connects Miramar Beach, Hammonds Beach, and Butterfly Beach, linking the old Miramar Hotel to the Biltmore Hotel. The walking path passes beautiful homes to a bridge crossing over Montecito Creek. Trails on both sides of the creek provide access to the beachfront.

Driving directions: SANTA BARBARA. From Santa Barbara, drive southbound on Highway 101 to Montecito, and exit on San Ysidro Road south. Turn right on Eucalyptus Lane, and drive south 0.1 mile (towards the ocean) to a small parking lot at the end of the road, just past Bonnymede Drive. If the lot is full, additional parking is located on Humphrey Road, the first street north.

Hiking directions: A short detour straight ahead to the south leads down a few steps to coastal access at Miramar Beach. Return to the trailhead and take the signed Hammonds Meadow Trail to the west. The path traverses through a beautiful forested lane surrounded by every color of flowering bougainvillea. At 0.2 miles, a bridge crosses Montecito Creek. Along both sides of the creek are coastal access paths. Cross the bridge and parallel the west side of the creek to Hammonds Beach. Follow the shoreline to the west for a quarter mile, reaching the Biltmore Hotel at the east end of Butterfly Beach. Continue along the coastline west on Butterfly Beach below the bluff terrace. Several staircases lead up to Channel Drive, the turn-around point. After beach combing, return along the same path. ■

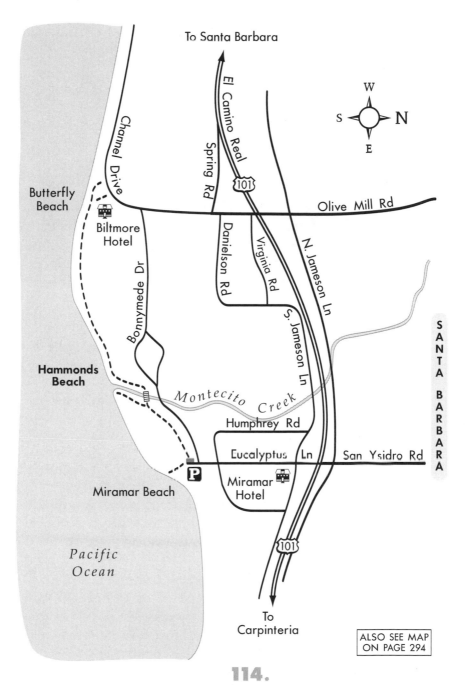

114.
Hammonds Meadow Trail

115. Summerland Beach from Lookout Park

Hiking distance: 1-mile loop
Hiking time: 30 minutes
Elevation gain: 50 feet
Maps: U.S.G.S. Carpinteria
       The Thomas Guide—Santa Barbara and Vicinity
Location: Summerland

Summary of hike: Lookout Park is a beautiful grassy flat along the oceanfront cliffs in Summerland. From the 4-acre park perched above the sea, paved walkways and natural forested trails lead down to a sandy beach, creating a one-mile loop. There are tidepools and coves a short distance up the coast from the beach.

Driving directions: SANTA BARBARA. From Santa Barbara, drive southbound on Highway 101 and take the Summerland exit. Turn right (south), crossing the railroad tracks in one block, and park in the Lookout Park parking lot.

From the south, heading northbound on Highway 101, take the Evans Avenue exit and turn left. Cross Highway 101 and the railroad tracks to Lookout Park.

Hiking directions: From the parking lot, head left (east) through the grassy flat along the cliff's edge to an open gate. A path leads through a shady eucalyptus forest. Cross a wooden bridge and head to the sandy shoreline. At the shore, bear to the right, leading to the paved walkways that return up to Lookout Park.

To extend the walk, continue along the coastline to the west. At low tide, the long stretch of beach leads to coves, rocky points, and tidepools. The beach continues west past charming beachfront homes, reaching Eucalyptus Lane and the Hammonds Meadow Trailhead (Hike 114) at 2 miles. From Lookout Park, the beach heads 1.5 miles east to Loon Point (Hike 116).■

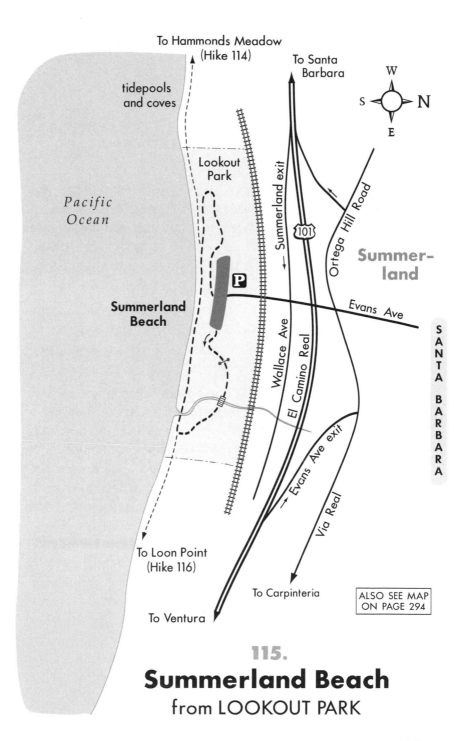

To Hammonds Meadow
(Hike 114)

To Santa
Barbara

tidepools
and coves

Lookout
Park

*Pacific
Ocean*

**Summerland
Beach**

P

Summerland exit

Ortega Hill Road

101

**Summer-
land**

Evans Ave

Wallace Ave

El Camino Real

S A N T A   B A R B A R A

Evans Ave exit

Via Real

To Loon Point
(Hike 116)

To Carpinteria

ALSO SEE MAP
ON PAGE 294

To Ventura

115.

Summerland Beach
from LOOKOUT PARK

116. Loon Point

Hiking distance: 3 miles round trip
Hiking time: 1.5 hours
Elevation gain: Near level
Maps: U.S.G.S. Carpinteria
       The Thomas Guide—Santa Barbara and Vicinity
Location: Summerland

Summary of hike: Loon Point sits between Summerland and Carpinteria at the mouth of Toro Canyon Creek. Dense stands of sycamores, coastal oaks, Monterey cypress, and eucalyptus trees line the creek. The path to Loon Point follows an isolated stretch of coastline along the base of steep 40-foot sandstone cliffs.

Driving directions: SANTA BARBARA. From Santa Barbara, drive southbound on Highway 101 to Summerland, and exit on Padero Lane south. Turn right and drive 0.2 miles to the signed Loon Point Beach parking lot on the left.

Hiking directions: Take the signed Loon Beach access trail parallel to the railroad tracks. Curve to the left, under the Padero Lane bridge, past a grove of eucalyptus trees. The path descends through a narrow drainage between the jagged, weathered cliffs to the shoreline. Bear to the right on the sandy beach along the base of the sandstone cliffs. Loon Point can be seen jutting out to sea. Follow the shoreline, reaching large boulders at Loon Point in 1.5 miles. At high tide, the water level may be too high to reach the point. At a lower tide, the beach walk can be extended from Loon Point to Lookout Park (Hike 115), an additional 1.5 miles west.■

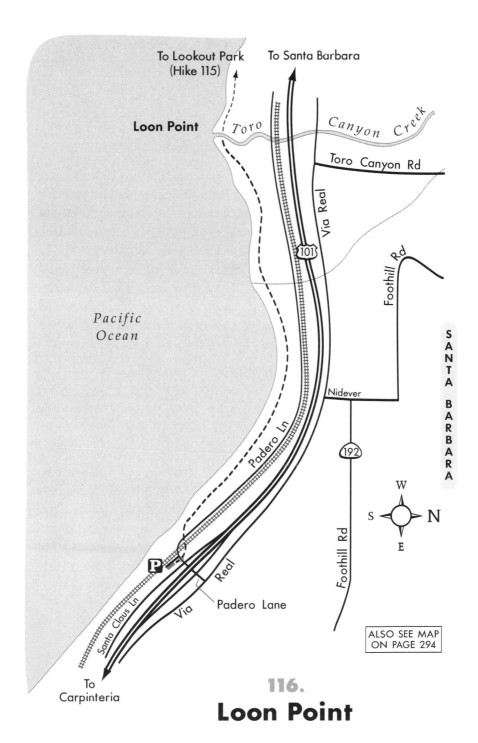

To Lookout Park
(Hike 115)

To Santa Barbara

Loon Point

Toro

Canyon Creek

Toro Canyon Rd

Via Real

101

Foothill Rd

Pacific
Ocean

Nidever

192

S A N T A   B A R B A R A

W
S ◈ N
E

Padero Ln

Foothill Rd

P

Real

Via

Padero Lane

Santa Claus Ln

To
Carpinteria

ALSO SEE MAP
ON PAGE 294

116.
Loon Point

117. Carpinteria Salt Marsh Nature Park

Hiking distance: 1 mile round trip
Hiking time: 30 minutes
Elevation gain: Level
Maps: U.S.G.S. Carpinteria
　　　　　The Thomas Guide—Santa Barbara and Vicinity
Location: Carpinteria

Summary of hike: The Carpinteria Salt Marsh, historically known as El Estero (the estuary), is one of California's last remaining wetlands. The area was once inhabited by Chumash Indians. The 230-acre estuary is fed by Franklin Creek and Santa Monica Creek. The reserve is a busy, healthy ecosystem with an abundance of sea and plant life. It is a nesting ground for thousands of migratory waterfowl and shorebirds. The Carpinteria Salt Marsh Nature Park sits along the east end of the salt marsh with a trail system, interpretive panels, and several observation decks.

Driving directions: CARPINTERIA. From Highway 101 in Carpinteria, exit on Linden Avenue. Turn right and drive 0.6 miles south to Sandyland Road, the last corner before reaching the ocean. Turn right and continue 0.2 miles to Ash Avenue. Park alongside the road by the signed park.

Hiking directions: From the nature trail sign, walk 20 yards to the west, reaching an observation deck. A boardwalk to the left leads to the ocean. Take the wide, meandering path to the right, parallel to Ash Avenue and the salt marsh. At the north end of the park, curve left to another overlook of the wetland. At the T-junction, the left fork leads a short distance to another observation deck. The right fork follows a pole fence along Franklin Creek to the trail's end. Return along the same path.■

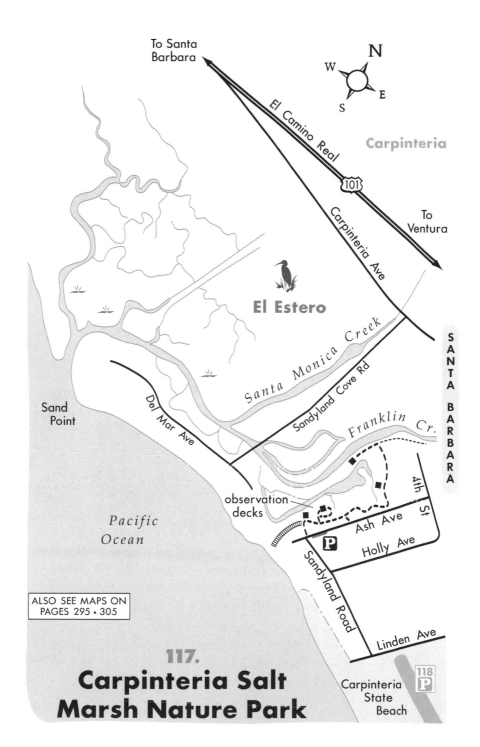

To Santa
Barbara

N
W   E
S

El Camino Real

Carpinteria

101

To
Ventura

Carpinteria Ave

El Estero

Santa Monica Creek

Sandyland Cove Rd

S
A
N
T
A

B
A
R
B
A
R
A

Franklin Cr.

Sand
Point

Del Mar Ave

4th St

observation
decks

Ash Ave

P

Holly Ave

Pacific
Ocean

Sandyland Road

ALSO SEE MAPS ON
PAGES 295 • 305

Linden Ave

117.
Carpinteria Salt
Marsh Nature Park

Carpinteria
State
Beach

118
P

118. Tarpits Park
CARPINTERIA STATE BEACH

Hiking distance: 1.5 miles round trip
Hiking time: 1 hour
Elevation gain: 50 feet
Maps: U.S.G.S. Carpinteria
Location: Carpinteria

Summary of hike: Tarpits Park is an 9-acre blufftop park at the east end of Carpinteria State Beach. The park was once the site of a Chumash Indian village. It is named for the natural tar (tarry asphaltum) that seeps up from beneath the soil. The Chumash used the tar for caulking canoes (called *tomols*) and sealing cooking vessels. Interconnecting trails cross the bluffs overlooking the steep, jagged coastline. Along Carpinteria Creek are riparian willow and sycamore woodlands. Benches are placed along the edge of the bluffs.

Driving directions: CARPINTERIA. From Highway 101 in Carpinteria, exit on Linden Avenue. Turn right and drive 0.5 miles south to 6th Street. Turn left and go 0.2 miles to Palm Avenue. Turn right and drive one block to the Carpinteria State Beach parking lot on the right. A parking fee is required.

Hiking directions: Two routes lead to Tarpits Park: follow the sandy beach east, or walk along the campground road east, crossing over Carpinteria Creek. At a half mile, the campground road ends on the grassy bluffs. From the beach, a footpath ascends the bluffs to the campground road. Several interconnecting paths cross the clifftop terrace. The meandering trails pass groves of eucalyptus trees and Monterey pines. A stairway leads down to the shoreline. As you near the Chevron Oil Pier, the bluffs narrow. This is a good turn-around spot.

To hike farther, cross the ravine and continue past the pier along the edge of the cliffs. The Carpinteria Bluffs and Seal Sanctuary (Hike 119) is a half mile ahead.■

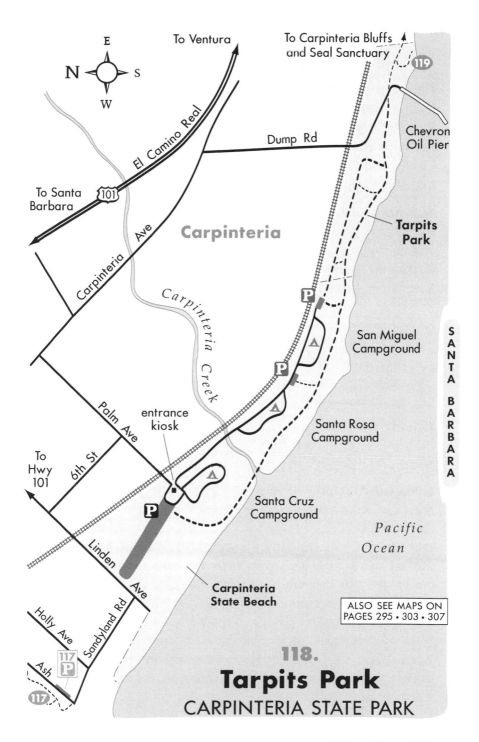

N E S W

To Ventura

To Carpinteria Bluffs and Seal Sanctuary

119

El Camino Real

Dump Rd

Chevron Oil Pier

To Santa Barbara

101

Carpinteria

Carpinteria Ave

Carpinteria Creek

Tarpits Park

P

San Miguel Campground

P

Palm Ave

entrance kiosk

Santa Rosa Campground

To Hwy 101

6th St

P

Santa Cruz Campground

Pacific Ocean

Linden Ave

Carpinteria State Beach

ALSO SEE MAPS ON PAGES 295 • 303 • 307

SANTA BARBARA

Holly Ave

Sandyland Rd

117 **P**

Ash

117

118.
Tarpits Park
CARPINTERIA STATE PARK

119. Carpinteria Bluffs
Nature Preserve and Seal Sanctuary

Hiking distance: 2 miles round trip
Hiking time: 1 hour
Elevation gain: Level
Maps: U.S.G.S. White Ledge Peak and Carpinteria
The Thomas Guide—Santa Barbara and Vicinity
Location: Carpinteria

Summary of hike: The Carpinteria Bluffs and Seal Sanctuary encompass 52 oceansfront acres with grasslands, coastal sage, and eucalyptus groves. The area has panoramic views from the Santa Ynez Mountains to the islands of Anacapa, Santa Cruz, and Santa Rosa. At the cliff's edge, 100 feet above the ocean, is an overlook of the seal sanctuary. A community of harbor seals often plays in the water below, lounging and sunbathing on the rocks and shoreline. The sanctuary is a protected birthing habitat for harbor seals during the winter and spring from December 1 through May 31. Beach access is prohibited during these months, but the seals may be observed from the blufftop.

Driving directions: CARPINTERIA. From Highway 101 in Carpinteria, exit on Bailard Avenue. Drive one block south towards the ocean, and park at the road's end.

Hiking directions: From the end of the road, hike south on the well-worn path across the open meadow towards the ocean. As you near the ocean cliffs, take the pathway to the right, parallel to a row of stately eucalyptus trees. At the west end of the eucalyptus grove, bear left and cross the railroad tracks. The trail resumes across the tracks. For an optional side trip, take the beach access trail on the left down to the base of the cliffs.

Back on the main trail, continue west along the edge of the ocean bluffs to a bamboo fence—the seal sanctuary overlook. After enjoying the seals and views, return along the same path or explore the open space.■

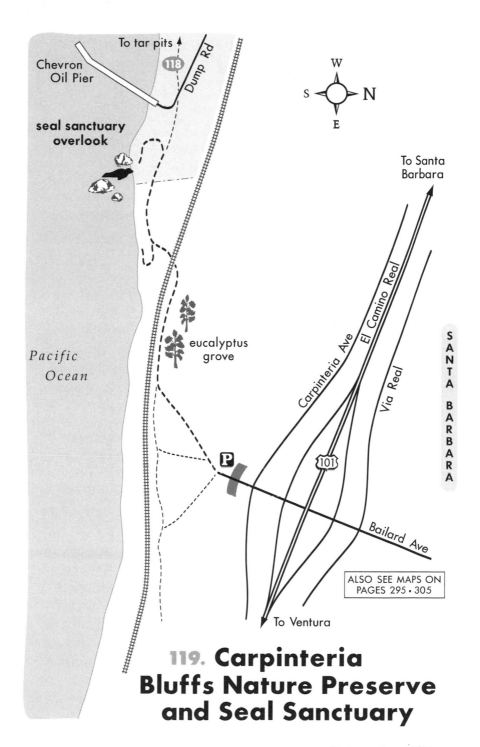

To tar pits

Chevron
Oil Pier

Dump Rd

118

W
S — N
E

seal sanctuary
overlook

To Santa
Barbara

Pacific
Ocean

eucalyptus
grove

Carpinteria Ave

El Camino Real

Via Real

S
A
N
T
A

B
A
R
B
A
R
A

P

101

Bailard Ave

ALSO SEE MAPS ON
PAGES 295 • 305

To Ventura

119. Carpinteria Bluffs Nature Preserve and Seal Sanctuary

120. Rincon Point and Rincon Beach Park

Hiking distance: 2 miles round trip
Hiking time: 1 hour
Elevation gain: 100 feet
Maps: U.S.G.S. White Ledge Peak
      The Thomas Guide—Santa Barbara and Vicinity
Location: 3 miles southeast of Carpinteria

Summary of hike: Rincon Point is a popular surfing location that straddles the Santa Barbara/Ventura County line. The point is bisected by Rincon Creek. The creek flows out of the mountains and carries rocks to the shoreline, forming a cobblestone beach with tidepools. Rincon Beach Park lies on the west side of the point on a steep, forested bluff with eucalyptus trees and Monterey pines. There is a large picnic area, great views of the coastline, and a stairway to 1,200 feet of beach frontage.

Driving directions: SANTA BARBARA/CARPINTERIA. From Santa Barbara, drive southbound on Highway 101 for 3 miles past Carpinteria. Take the Bates Road exit to the stop sign. Park in either of the lots for Rincon Point or Rincon Park.

Hiking directions: Begin from the Rincon Park parking lot on the right (west). From the edge of the cliffs, a long staircase and a paved service road both lead down the cliff face, providing access to the sandy shoreline and tidepools. Walk north along the beach, strolling past a series of tidepools along the base of the sandstone cliffs. After beachcombing, return to the parking lot.

From the west end of the parking lot, a well-defined trail heads west past the metal gate. The path is a wide shelf cut on the steep cliffs high above the ocean. At 0.3 miles, the trail reaches the railroad tracks. The path parallels the railroad right-of-way west to Carpinteria. Choose your own turn-around spot.

From the Rincon Point parking lot on the east, take the wide beach access path. Descend through a shady, forested grove to the beach. Bear right on the rocky path to a small bay near the tree-lined point. This is an excellent area to explore the tide-pools and watch the surfers. Return along the same route. ■

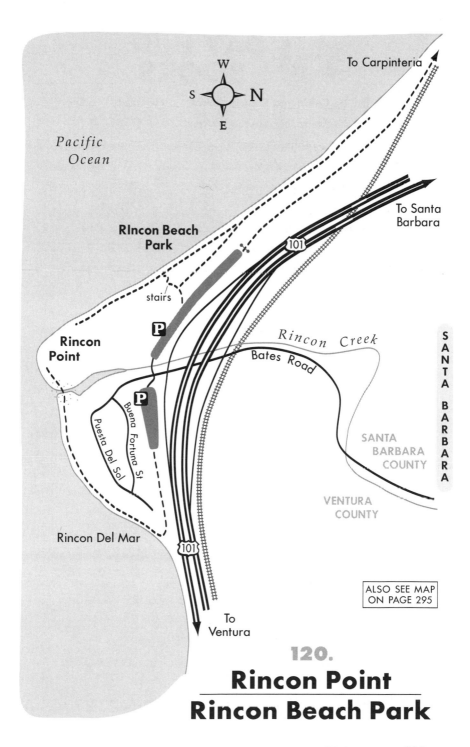

W

S — N

E

To Carpinteria

Pacific
Ocean

RIncon Beach
Park

stairs

P

Rincon
Point

Rincon Creek

Bates Road

To Santa
Barbara

101

SANTA BARBARA

P

Buena Fortuna St

Puesta Del Sol

SANTA
BARBARA
COUNTY

VENTURA
COUNTY

Rincon Del Mar

101

ALSO SEE MAP
ON PAGE 295

To
Ventura

120.

Rincon Point
Rincon Beach Park

DAY HIKE
BOOKS

Day Hikes On the California Central Coast ....978-1-57342-058-7 ....17.95

Day Hikes On the California Southern Coast ....978-1-57342-045-7 ......14.95

Day Hikes Around Sonoma County ....978-1-57342-053-2 ......16.95

Day Hikes Around Napa Valley ....978-1-57342-057-0 ....16.95

Day Hikes Around Monterey and Carmel ....978-1-57342-036-5 ....14.95

Day Hikes Around Big Sur ....978-1-57342-041-9 ....14.95

Day Hikes Around San Luis Obispo ....978-1-57342-051-8 ....16.95

Day Hikes Around Santa Barbara ....978-1-57342-042-6 ......14.95

Day Hikes Around Ventura County ....978-1-57342-043-3 ......14.95

Day Hikes Around Los Angeles ....978-1-57342-044-0 ......14.95

Day Hikes Around Orange County ....978-1-57342-047-1 ....15.95

Day Hikes In Yosemite National Park ....978-1-57342-059-4 ....13.95

Day Hikes In Sequoia and Kings Canyon N.P. ....978-1-57342-030-3 ....12.95

Day Hikes Around Sedona, Arizona ....978-1-57342-049-5 ....14.95

Day Hikes On Oahu ....978-1-57342-038-9 ....11.95

Day Hikes On Maui ....978-1-57342-039-6 ....11.95

Day Hikes On Kauai ....978-1-57342-040-2 ....11.95

Day Hikes In Hawaii ....978-1-57342-050-1 ....16.95

Day Hikes In Yellowstone National Park ....978-1-57342-048-8 ....12.95

Day Hikes In Grand Teton National Park ....978-1-57342-046-4 ....11.95

Day Hikes In the Beartooth Mountains
Billings to Red Lodge to Yellowstone N.P. ....978-1-57342-052-5 ....13.95

Day Hikes Around Bozeman, Montana ....978-1-57342-054-9 ....13.95

Day Hikes Around Missoula, Montana ....978-1-57342-032-7 ....13.95

These books may be purchased at your local bookstore or
outdoor shop. Or, order them direct from the distributor:

The Globe Pequot Press

246 Goose Lane • P.O. Box 480 • Guilford, CT 06437-0480
on the web: www.globe-pequot.com

800-243-0495 DIRECT   **800-820-2329** FAX

Day Hikes Around Monterey and Carmel

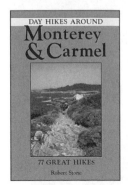

Monterey County in California is home to a hundred miles of picture-perfect coastline, from Monterey Bay to the rugged Big Sur oceanfront. Mountains backdrop the coast, separating the coastline from the rich agricultural land. Carmel and other quaint communities dot a landscape abundant with green valleys, woodlands, beaches, parks, natural preserves, and calm bays along the scalloped coastline.

Day Hikes Around Monterey and Carmel includes 75 great hikes throughout this area. Highlights include numerous waterfalls, canyons, huge stands of redwoods, tidepools, isolated beaches, rugged peninsulas, long-spanning bridges, walking paths that weave through the county's towns, and incredible views from the coast to the inland valleys.

176 pages • 75 hikes • 1st Edition 2002 • ISBN 978-1-57342-036-5

Day Hikes Around Big Sur

Big Sur is an awesome stretch of spectacular coastline in central California where the Santa Lucia Mountains rise over 5,000 feet from the ocean. The area is characterized by craggy coastal headlands backed by mountains and carved canyons. The area's topography, as well as its wilderness and national forest designations, have kept Big Sur unspoiled.

Day Hikes Around Big Sur includes a cross-section of 80 excellent hikes lying along the coastline and throughout the interior mountains. Hikes range from beach strolls to elevated climbs with far-reaching views. Undoubtedly, the trails reveal some of the best scenery in Big Sur and California.

184 pages • 80 hikes • 1st Edition 2003 • ISBN 978-1-57342-041-9

Day Hikes Around San Luis Obispo

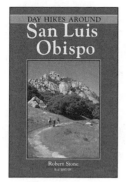

San Luis Obispo County is located where the white sand beaches of central California merge with the dramatic Big Sur coastline. Inland from the Pacific Ocean are oak-studded hills, verdant farmland, mountain lakes, and the Santa Lucia Range of the Los Padres National Forest.

Day Hikes Around San Luis Obispo includes 128 day hikes throughout the California central coast country. These trails take the hiker along the Pacific coast to secluded coves and tidepools, to rocky promontories along the chain of volcanic morros, through wetland sanctuaries, and up cool interior valleys. Many hikes are found in or near the college community; most are located in undeveloped tracts of land, state and county parks, and national forest which are home to an extensive network of hiking trails.

288 pages • 128 hikes • 2nd Edition 2006 • ISBN 978-1-57342-051-8

Day Hikes Around Santa Barbara

Santa Barbara is a captivating, inviting community that is located in a beautiful setting along the Pacific coast. The temperate climate and refreshing ocean breezes, very similar to the Mediterranean, have distinguished this area as "the jewel of the American Riviera."

Day Hikes Around Santa Barbara is a comprehensive guide to 82 day hikes with a 50-mile radius of the city. The landscape around Santa Barbara includes mountainous terrain, preserved forests and wilderness areas, and stretches of undeveloped coast, allowing this scenic area to have miles of quiet, secluded hiking trails.

184 pages • 82 hikes • 2nd Edition 2003 • ISBN 978-1-57342-042-6

Day Hikes On the California Southern Coast

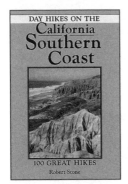

This 224-page guide is a collection of 100 great day hikes along 238 miles of southern California coastline, from Ventura County to the U.S.—Mexico border. The area has some of the most diverse geography in the state...a blend of verdant canyons, arid bluffs, and sandy coastline.

Discover hundreds of miles of trails in scenic and undeveloped land, despite the expansive urban areas. Highlights include wide sand beaches, marine terraces, rocky headlands, tidal estuaries that are ideal for exploring, bay-side coves and caves, sandstone cliffs, lighthouses, great locations for viewing wildlife, expansive dunes, forested canyons, waterfalls, thousands of acres of undeveloped public lands, and panoramic ocean-front overlooks.

224 pages • 100 hikes • 1st Edition 2004 • ISBN 978-1-57342-045-7

INDEX

A

Allan Memorial Grove, 118
Andrew Molera State Park, 135, 138, 140, 144
Aniso Trail, 274, 276
Año Nuevo Island, 20
Año Nuevo State Reserve, 18, 20
Aptos, 59, 60, 64
Aptos Rancho Trail, 60
arches, 44,125,156,178,198, 239, 251
Arroyo Burro Beach, 290
Asilomar Conference Grounds, 94
Asilomar State Beach, 94, 96, 98
Atkinson Bluff Trail, 18
Avila Beach, 248, 250, 251
Avila Valley Bike Trail, 248

B

Bay Nature Walk, 96, 98
Beach to Backcountry Trail, 272
Berry Creek Falls, 24, 27
Big Basin Redwoods State Park, 24, 26
Big Sur, 111, 112
Big Sur Ranger Station, 152
Big Sur River, 138, 141, 144, 146
Bird Island, 123, 125
Bird Rock, 100, 102
bird watching, 31, 37, 42, 72, 74, 80, 82, 83, 106, 108, 125, 212, 214, 224, 256, 262, 264, 284, 302
Bixby Bridge, 134, 135
Black Hill, 218
Black Swift Falls, 196
blowholes, 156
Bluff Trail, 239
Bluffs Trail, 140
Bob Jones City to the Sea Bike Trail, 248
Bonny Doon Beach and Bluffs, 34
Bonny Doon Ecological Reserve, 36
bougainvillea, 296
Buckeye Trail, 185
Butterfly Beach, 296

C

Cambria, 204, 206
Cannery Point, 118
Canyon Falls, 168
Capitola, 57
Carmel, 67, 68, 88, 104, 106, 108
Carmel Beach, 104
Carmel Meadows, 108
Carmel Point, 104
Carmel River Lagoon and Wetlands, 106
Carmel River State Beach, 106, 108
Carpinteria, 294, 302, 304, 306
Carpinteria Bluffs and Seal Santuary, 304, 306
Carpinteria Salt Marsh, 302
Carpinteria State Beach, 304
Cascade Beach, 18
Cascade Creek Trail, 19
Castle Rock State Park, 26
Cave Landing, 250, 252
China Beach, 57
China Cove, 125
Cloisters Wetland, 212
Coal Oil Point, 281, 284
Coast Ridge Trail, 152, 153
Coast Road. See Old Coast Road
Cone Peak, 174
Coon Creek Beach, 243
Coon Creek Canyon, 241
Cooper Cabin, 138
Corallina Cove, 239
Coreopsis Hill, 256
Coronado Butterfly Preserve, 281, 282, 284
Cove Beach, 20
Creamery Meadow, 140, 141, 144
Cruickshank Trail, 184
Cypress Cove, 116, 120
Cypress Grove Trail, 118

D

Dani Ridge, 136

Davenport Beach and Bluffs, 31, 35
Del Playa Park, 284
DeLaveaga Park, 54
Devereaux Lagoon, 281, 284
Devil's Cauldron, 122
Diablo Canyon, 243
docent-led hikes, 246
Doud Peak, 130
Douglas Family Preserve, 290
dunes, 76, 77, 80, 86, 94, 96, 102,
    104, 178, 229, 254, 259, 262, 264,
    284

E
East West Ranch, 206
El Capitan Point, 274
El Capitan State Beach, 274, 276
El Estero, 302
Elfin Forest Natural Area, 222
Elkhorn Slough, 72, 74, 82, 83, 84
Ellwood Bluffs, 280, 282, 284
Estero Bay, 229
Estero Bluffs State Park, 208
Ewoldsen Trail, 168

F
Fairbank Point, 214
Fern Grotto, 39
Fire Road Trail, 162, 163
Fiscalini Bluff Trail, 206
Five Fingers Loop, 82
Forest of Nisene Marks State Park, 60
Four Mile Beach, 37, 39
Franklin Point, 18
Franklin Point Trail, 19

G
Garrapata Beach, 132
Garrapata State Park, 126, 128, 132
Gaviota Hot Springs, 268
Gaviota Peak, 268, 269
Gaviota State Park, 268, 269, 272
Gazos Creek Trail, 19
Gibson Beach, 125
Goleta, 278, 280, 282, 284, 286, 288
Goleta Beach County Park, 286

Goleta Point, 286
Greyhound Rock, 30
Grotto Rock, 239
Guadalupe—Nipomo Dunes Preserve,
    262
Guillemot Island, 116

H
Hammonds Beach/Meadow, 296, 298
hang gliding launch sites, 86
Hare Creek, 173, 174
Hazard Canyon, 230
Hazard Peak, 234
Headland Cove, 120
Hearst State Beach. See William R.
    Hearst State Beach
Hendry's Beach, 290
Henry Cowell Redwoods State Park,
    36, 50, 52
Heron Rookery Natural Preserve, 214
Hidden Beach, 123
Hidden Trail, 144
homestead cabin, 149

I
Isla Vista County Beach, 284

J
Jacks Peak County Park, 90
Jetty Beach. See Moss Landing State
    Beach
Julia Pfeiffer Burns State Park, 158,
    160, 162, 163, 168

K
Kirk Creek Trail. See Vicente Flat

I
Indian Village, 102
The Inn at Spanish Bay, 96, 98
Islay Creek Canyon, 230, 234

J
Jalama Beach County Park, 266

L
La Mesa Bluff, 292
Laguna Creek Beach and Bluffs, 36
Leadbetter Beach, 292

Lighthouse Field State Beach, 47
Lighthouse Point. See Point Santa Cruz
Lighthouse Trail, 47
lighthouses, 18, 20, 47, 198, 246
Limekiln Falls, 172
Limekiln State Park, 170
The Limekilns, 170
The Links at Spanish Bay, 96
The Links Nature Walk, 96, 98
Lion Rock, 243
Little Sur River, 134, 135
Loma Prieta earthquake, 62
Lookout Park, 298, 300
Loon Point, 298, 300

M

Mallagh Landing. See Cave Landing
Manresa State Beach, 64
Marina, 77
Marina Dunes Open Space, 86
Marina State Beach, 86
McWay Canyon, 166, 168
McWay Falls, 166
Middle Beach, 108
Miramar Beach, 296
Mobile Coastal Preserve, 256
Molera Beach, 138
Molera Point, 138
Molera Ridge. See Pfeiffer Ridge
monarch butterflies, 44, 57, 67, 224, 280, 282
Monastery Beach, 108
Montaña De Oro State Park, 226, 228, 229, 230, 234, 237, 239, 241, 243
Montecito, 294, 296
Monterey, 67, 68, 88
Monterey Bay, 67, 68
Monterey Bay Aquarium, 92
Monterey Bay Coastal Trail, 92
Monterey Bay National Marine Sanctuary, 67
Monterey County, 67
Monterey cypress, 111, 116, 118
Monterey Peninsula, 67, 88, 90, 92, 94, 96, 100, 102, 112

Monterey pines, 206
Moonstone Beach, 204
Moore Creek Preserve, 42
More Mesa, 288
Morro Bay, 210, 214, 224, 229
Morro Bay Estuary, 220
Morro Bay State Park, 214, 218, 220
Morro Dunes Natural Preserve, 229
Morro Dunes Sand Spit, 229
Morro Estuary Natural Preserve, 214
Morro Rock, 212, 229
Morro Strand State Beach, 212
morros, 193, 218, 237
Moss Landing, 57, 67, 74, 76
Moss Landing State Beach, 70, 72
Moss Landing State Wildlife Area, 74
Mount Manuel, 148
Mount McAbee Overlook, 27
Museum of Natural History, 214
Mussel Rock/Point, 262

N

Natural Bridges State Beach, 42, 44, 47
Needle Rock Point, 40
New Brighton State Beach, 57, 60
Nipomo Dunes, 256, 262
Nisene Marks State Park, 60
North Moss Beach. See Asilomar State Beach
North Shore Trail, 116

O

Oats Peak, 237, 241
Observation Hill, 243
Ocean Beach County Park, 264
Oceano Dunes Natural Preserve, 254
Oceano Dunes Vehicular Recreation Area, 254
Ohlone Bluff Trail, 38, 40
Old Coast Road, 134, 135
Old Cove Landing, 39
Old Salinas River, 76, 77
Old Veteran, 116
Ontario Ridge, 251
Oso Flaco Lake Natural Area, 256

P

Pacific Gas & Electric land, 243, 246
Pacific Grove, 67, 88, 92, 94
Pacific Grove Marine Gardens Fish Refuge, 92
Pacific Valley Flats, 178, 180
Pacific Valley Ranger Station, 178
Palo Alto, 59
Panorama Trail, 140
Parson's Slough, 82
Partington Canyon, 160, 162, 163
Partington Cove and Landing, 160
Pebble Beach, 67, 88, 96, 98, 100, 102
Pecho Coast, 246
Pelican Point, 125
Pfeiffer Beach/Point, 156
Pfeiffer Big Sur State Park, 146, 148, 152
Pfeiffer Falls, 146
Pfeiffer Ridge, 141, 144, 149
Pico Blanco, 137
Piedras Blancas Lighthouse, 198
Pigeon Point Lighthouse, 18
Pine Ridge Trail, 152, 153
The Pinnacle, 120
Pinnacle Cove, 120
Pirate's Cove, 251, 252
Pismo Dunes, 254
Pismo State Beach, 254
Plaskett Rock, 178, 180
Pogonip Clubhouse, 50
Pogonip Park, 48, 52
Point Año Nuevo, 20
Point Arena, 21
Point Buchon, 243
Point Joe, 100
Point Lobos State Reserve, 111, 114, 116, 118, 120, 123, 125
Point Pinos, 92
Point San Luis, 246
Point San Luis Lighthouse, 246
Point Santa Cruz, 47
Portola Point, 220
Portola-Crespi Cross, 106, 108
pygmy oaks, 222

Q

Quarry Cove, 239

R

Ragged Point Inn, 196
Ragged Point Trails, 196
Rancho del Oso, 24, 28
Rattlesnake Canyon, 246
Rattlesnake Flats, 237
redwoods (old growth), 26, 52, 60, 128, 135, 175, 184
Refugio State Beach, 274, 276
Reservoir Flats, 234
Ridge Trail, 234
Rincon Beach Park, 308
Rincon Point, 308
Rio del Mar Beach, 59, 60
Rocky Ridge, 130

S

Salinas River National Wildlife Refuge, 80
Salinas River State Beach, 76, 77
Salinas River Wildlife Area, 76
Salmon Creek Falls, 188, 190
Salmon Creek Trail, 188, 190
San Jose Creek Beach. See Monastery Beach.
San Luis Obispo Bay, 246, 248, 250, 251
San Luis Obispo County, 193, 194
San Simeon Beach State Park, 202
San Simeon Point/Bay, 200
San Simeon Trail, 202
Sand Dollar Beach, 180
sand dunes. See dunes
Sand Hill Bluff, 36
Sand Hill Cove, 123
Sand Plant Beach, 39
Santa Barbara, 259, 260, 278
Santa Barbara Point, 292
Santa Barbara Shores County Park, 280, 292
Santa Cruz, 15, 47, 48, 54
Santa Cruz County, 15, 16
Santa Ynez River, 264

Saratoga Gap, 26
Scenic Bluff Pathway, 104
Sea Lion Point/Cove, 120, 123
Sea Lion Rocks, 122
Seacliff Pier, 59
Seacliff State Beach, 57, 59
Seal Rock, 48, 102
Seventeen Mile Drive, 96, 98, 100, 102
Shell Beach, 248, 250, 251
Shell Beach Bluffs Coastal Trail, 251
shipwrecks, 21, 59
Shoreline Park, 292
Silver Peak Wilderness, 183, 184, 185,
   188, 190
sinkholes, 243
Skyline-to-the-Sea Trail, 24, 26
Skyline Trail, 90
The Slot, 123
Smuggler's Cove, 250
Soberanes Canyon, 128
Soberanes Point, 126
Soquel Cove, 57, 59
South Coast Ridge Road, 188, 190
South Marsh Loop, 83
South Moss Beach, 98, 100
South Point, 120
South Shore Trail, 123
Spanish Bay, 96, 98, 100
Spooner Ranch, 230, 236
Spooner's Cove, 234, 237
Strawberry Beach, 40
Summerland, 294, 298, 300
surfing locations, 34, 64, 72, 308
surfing museum, 47
Sweet Springs Nature Preserve, 224
Sykes Camp, 152

T

Table Rock, 18
Tanbark Trail, 162
Tarpits Park, 304
Terrace Creek, 152, 153
Three Mile Beach, 37, 40

tidepools, 30, 34, 44, 47, 67, 92, 94,
   96, 98, 100, 104, 108, 111, 123, 198,
   200, 204, 206, 208, 228, 239,
   286, 298, 308
Tin House, 162, 163
Top of the World, 54
Trespass Trail, 269
Tunnel View Trail, 269

U

University of California—Santa
   Barbara, 286

V

Valencia Peak, 237
Vandenberg Air Force Base, 264, 266
Ventana Inn, 153
Ventana Wilderness, 149, 152, 153,
   170, 173
Vicente Flat, 173, 174
Villa Creek, 184
Vista Point, 153

W

Waddell Beach, 24, 26
waterfalls, 24, 26, 166, 168, 172, 188,
   190, 196, 234
Weston Beach, 123
Whale Peak, 126
Whalers Cabin, 116
Whalers Knoll, 116
Whitaker Flats, 202
White Point, 214
Whitehouse Beach, 18
Whitehouse Creek Trail, 19
Wilder Beach, 39
Wilder Ranch Cultural Preserve, 39
Wilder Ranch State Park, 37, 39
wildlife observation, 20, 39, 74, 82,
   100, 102, 116, 122, 126, 198, 204,
   206, 239, 243, 246, 252, 256,
   284, 292, 306
William R. Hearst State Beach, 200

Z

Zmudowski State Beach, 70, 72

About the Author

Since 1991, Robert Stone has been writer, photographer, and publisher of *Day Hike Books*. He is a Los Angeles Times Best Selling Author and an award-winning author of Rocky Mountain Outdoor Writers and Photographers, the Outdoor Writers Association of California, and the Northwest Outdoor Writers Association.

Robert has hiked every trail in the *Day Hike Book* series. With 23 hiking guides in the series, many in their third and fourth editions, he has hiked thousands of miles of trails throughout the western United States and Hawaii. When Robert is not hiking, he researches, writes, and maps the hikes before returning to the trails. He spends summers in the Rocky Mountains of Montana and winters on the California Central Coast.